Professors in the Gig Economy

PROFESSORS IN THE GIG ECONOMY

Unionizing Adjunct Faculty in America

EDITED BY KIM TOLLEY

Johns Hopkins University Press
Baltimore

© 2018 Johns Hopkins University Press
All rights reserved. Published 2018
Printed in the United States of America on acid-free paper

2   4   6   8   9   7   5   3   1

Johns Hopkins University Press
2715 North Charles Street
Baltimore, Maryland 21218-4363
www.press.jhu.edu

Library of Congress Cataloging-in-Publication Data
Names: Tolley, Kimberley, editor.
Title: Professors in the gig economy : unionizing adjunct faculty in America /
edited by Kim Tolley.
Description: Baltimore : Johns Hopkins University Press, 2018. | Includes
bibliographical references and index.
Identifiers: LCCN 2017038117| ISBN 9781421425337 (paperback : alk. paper) |
ISBN 9781421425344 (electronic) | ISBN 1421425335 (paperback : alk. paper) |
ISBN 1421425343 (electronic)
Subjects: LCSH: College teachers, Part-time—Labor unions—United States. |
Universities and colleges—Faculty—Employment—United States. | BISAC:
EDUCATION / Higher. | BUSINESS & ECONOMICS / Education. | BUSINESS &
ECONOMICS / Labor. | LAW / Labor & Employment.
Classification: LCC LB2331.72 .P78 2018 | DDC 378.1/2—dc23
LC record available at https://lccn.loc.gov/2017038117

A catalog record for this book is available from the British Library.

*Special discounts are available for bulk purchases of this book. For more information,
please contact Special Sales at 410-516-6936 or specialsales@press.jhu.edu.*

Johns Hopkins University Press uses environmentally friendly book materials,
including recycled text paper that is composed of at least 30 percent post-consumer
waste, whenever possible.

contents

In 2012 Kathleen Colligan, who taught for more than 30 years as a part-time instructor at San Jose City College in California, died of cancer. Her obituary noted, "She was the original freeway flyer, charging between several schools to teach English classes, where she enjoyed the broad range of students she encountered." Colligan had worked since the 1970s as an adjunct faculty member at the college, where she was highly regarded as a talented teacher. After her death, her colleagues remembered her dedication. She would frequently stay until late at night to grade papers. "I'm talking about 9 p.m. on the last day of finals," said English instructor Alice Gosak. "She gave and gave." Nevertheless, despite all her years of hard work and service, when Kathleen Colligan came down with cancer in her mid-sixties, she had no health benefits and no retirement savings.[1]

Similar stories have emerged about the underpaid part-time faculty who teach in colleges and universities across the country. Colligan was relatively fortunate: a sister in Texas took her in and cared for her during her final days. Others have fared less well. Dave Heller, an adjunct philosophy instructor at Seattle University, was living in a dilapidated boardinghouse when he died in 2015 from an untreated thyroid condition at age 61. He had been teaching part-time for only $18,000 a year.[2] Margaret Mary Vojtko, who had taught part-time at Duquesne University for 25 years, was destitute and nearly homeless in Pittsburgh when she died in 2013 after a heart attack at age 83.[3] Such cases are not unusual: a 2011 study reported that adjunct faculty comprised 76 percent of US faculty in colleges and universities. In 2015, researchers at the University of California at Berkeley found that 25 percent of the nation's part-time faculty members were living in poverty and eligible for public assistance programs like Medicaid, food stamps, or welfare.[4]

Since the 1990s, adjunct faculty members have begun to fight back, turn-

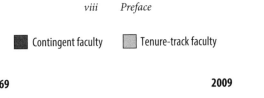

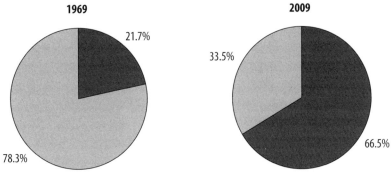

Figure P.1. Changing Faculty Demographics in US Higher Education, 1969 and 2009. Source: Adapted from Adrianna Kezar and Daniel Maxey, "The Changing Academic Workforce," *Trusteeship* 21 (2013), http://agb.org/trusteeship/2013/5 /changing-academic-workforce.

ing to labor unions to improve their working conditions through collective bargaining. "Adjuncts," a term that includes graduate student employees and part-time and full-time contingent faculty who are hired off the tenure track, are not just demanding a living wage. They are also publicizing higher education's increasing reliance on contingent labor.[5] In 1969, 78.3 percent of the instructional staff in American colleges and universities were tenured or in tenure-track positions, and adjunct faculty filled the remaining 21.7 percent. By 2009, the numbers had flipped: the proportion of tenured or tenure-track faculty had fallen to just over a third, and the proportion of adjunct faculty had risen to 66.5 percent (see figure P.1).

When graduate student instructors are added to these figures, the proportion of contingent instructional staff is even higher: 76 percent nationally in 2011.[6] Some claim that this is simply a reflection of the law of supply and demand; universities continue to churn out too many PhDs for an increasingly limited number of tenure-track positions in higher education. Others argue that this is part of a larger structural shift related to the privatization and corporatization of the university, a development that harms not only the academic professions and students' learning but also society as a whole.[7]

During the last few decades, many professional organizations, including the American Association of University Professors (AAUP), have criticized the growing reliance on contingent and part-time faculty in higher education.

Some professional organizations, including the American Historical Association, the American Philological Association, the American Studies Association, the Modern Language Association, and the National Council of Teachers of English, have tried to raise the profile of contingent faculty by issuing special rewards to scholars off the tenure track. Efforts to improve working conditions have included recommendations for long-term and renewable contracts, some form of teaching tenure, and increased access to professional development opportunities. Nevertheless, as scholars have noted, improvements to working conditions for contingent faculty have been few and far between, prompting faculty on many campuses to consider unionizing.[8]

After more than 50 years of declining memberships, some of the nation's largest labor unions, including the American Federation of Teachers, the National Education Association, the United Auto Workers (UAW), the Service Employees International Union (SEIU), and the United Steelworkers, have reached out to help adjunct faculty organize. The UAW helped graduate student instructors at Columbia University wage a campaign to affiliate with the union. After the National Labor Relations Board ruled on August 23, 2016, that graduate students who work as research assistants and teachers at private universities can join or form unions, unions such as the United Electrical Workers, the Communications Workers of America, and the Hotel Employees and Restaurant Employees Union began providing support to students in around 40 institutions engaged in collective bargaining or legal challenges.[9] The shift toward organizing in higher education has helped traditional unions staunch a long decline in memberships. National population survey data show that in 2014 and 2015, the number of union members stabilized compared to previous years, with some of the highest unionization rates in education, training, and library occupations. The SEIU has run one of the most aggressive campaigns to unionize adjunct faculty to date; three years after SEIU's launch of the national Faculty Forward campaign in 2013, contingent faculty at more than 40 colleges and universities had voted to affiliate with the union, often despite fierce opposition from employers.[10]

This book explores the history, context, processes, and outcomes of unionization among adjunct faculty. The chapters in this volume address the following questions: Why have colleges and universities come to rely so heavily on contingent faculty, and what have been the results? How have federal and state laws influenced efforts to unionize adjunct faculty? What happens *after* unionization: How has collective bargaining affected faculty working conditions and participation in shared governance? How have relations among part-time and full-time faculty helped or hindered collective bargaining in specific institutions? To what extent has collective bargaining strengthened adjunct faculty's participation in shared governance and resulted in more full-time and tenure-line teaching positions? The overall goal of this volume is to offer new insights and evidence for considering the causes, processes, and outcomes of unionization among contingent faculty in American higher education.

Scholars have only begun to analyze the changing academic workforce. Since the 1990s, a growing list of books has drawn attention to the rising numbers and poor working conditions of adjunct faculty on college campuses. Most of these studies include recommendations to improve these working conditions, such as providing professional development options, implementing multiyear contracts, developing orientation programs, and providing access to office space and other resources. Despite the increased attention, however, adjunct instructors remain largely invisible on many campuses. In 2009, based on a survey of the teaching workforce at Berkeley, Cornell, Duke, Illinois, Michigan, MIT, Northwestern, Virginia, Washington, and Washington University (Missouri), John G. Cross and Edie N. Goldenberg concluded that most college administrators were unaware of the tenure-track versus contingent composition of their own faculties and the hiring trends at their own institutions.[11]

Although the unionization of adjunct faculty is increasing across the United States, relatively few books have focused specifically on this topic. What's missing is a book that asks a group of experts to write about adjunct unionization from a range of perspectives and is addressed to a broad audience of faculty members, policy makers, and general readers.[12]

This volume meets this need by bringing together scholars from education, labor history, economics, religious studies, and the law who have been involved with unionization and other efforts to improve the working conditions of adjunct faculty. Their chapters contribute to previous work on the changing professoriat by providing historical and contemporary perspectives on the changing demographics of higher education faculty in the United States and analyses of the laws that apply to unionization in public, private, and religious colleges and universities. The detailed case studies in this volume examine the unionization processes and outcomes at specific institutions, including adjunct faculty's organization and the first contract negotiations at the University of Illinois, Urbana-Champaign (UIUC), and Georgetown University; the wall-to-wall bargaining units in the City University of New York

(CUNY); the near-strike and contract agreement reached in 2016 by part-time and full-time faculty collaborating at California State University, East Bay; the impact of unionization on shared governance in Historically Black Colleges and Universities (HBCUs), such as Howard and Florida A&M; and the unionization of Notre Dame de Namur University in California, which in 2016 became the first private religious school to unionize the entire faculty, both adjunct and tenure-track, since the US Supreme Court decision in *NLRB v. Yeshiva University* (1980).

Many of this book's authors pay attention to the issue of shared governance. A policy of shared governance can ensure a practice of shared decision-making, allowing faculty a voice in decisions that affect their students and programs. According to the AAUP, collective bargaining can increase shared governance, but on some campuses where the faculty have begun unionizing, administrators have threatened to withdraw shared governance once a union is in place. As a result, administrators and faculty members on some campuses are now wondering what happens after the faculty unionizes: Can union members serve and vote on university committees? Can they vote in the faculty assembly or senate? Several chapters investigate the impact of unionization on shared governance practices in a number of colleges that have recently unionized and explore the way some faculty unions have negotiated for stronger and more effective models of shared decision-making.[13]

This book is distinctive in its attention to the relationship between adjunct and tenure-track faculty during and after unionization. The unionization of adjunct faculty never takes place in a vacuum; it is ignored, opposed, or supported by tenure-track faculty. Some scholars have found that the priorities and interests of tenure-track faculty are sometimes at odds with those of part-time instructors. Nevertheless, the poor working conditions of adjunct faculty affect those on the tenure track as well. The increasing reliance on low-paid, part-time instructors has eroded the availability of tenure-track positions at many institutions. Moreover, the same desire for cost savings that has motivated colleges and universities to rely heavily on adjunct faculty has led, in many institutions, to worsening working conditions for tenure-track faculty in the form of growing teaching loads, a lack of administrative support, and diminishing funds for research. Given these developments, it is possible that adjunct and tenure-track faculty may come together more often to unionize in the future, as happened at Notre Dame de Namur University. Whether this occurs or not, on every campus where adjunct faculty choose a union, all faculty must then work effectively together to provide an excellent education to students. How the entire faculty functions together after the establishment of a union on campus is addressed in several of this volume's chapters and case studies.[14]

The chapters in Part I, "The Changing Academic Workforce: Influences and Outcomes," investigate the rise of contingent faculty, the impact of this demographic shift on student learning and faculty working conditions, and the social conditions and laws that have facilitated or hindered the unionization of adjunct faculty. A. J. Angulo opens the volume with a chapter on the trajectory from the so-called golden age of midcentury academic life to the present state of universities in today's gig economy as ushered in by Uber and Airbnb. Adrianna Kezar and Tom DePaola follow with a review of research that illuminates the poor working conditions of adjunct faculty and the negative impact of those conditions on student learning. Timothy Reese Cain explores the history of contingent faculty activism and organizing with a focus on the origin of the University of Wisconsin–Madison's Teaching Assistants Association and the organization of the graduate assistants' union at the University of Michigan in 1975. Finally, Gregory M. Saltzman summarizes the labor law provisions that are particularly relevant to the unionization of part-time or non-tenure-track faculty and graduate student teaching assistants at public and private colleges and universities in the United States.

Part II, "Unionization in Private and Public Institutions," investigates unionization in specific institutions. The case studies in these chapters examine a range of public and private colleges and universities, from small liberal arts schools to large urban systems of higher education. Together, the contributors in this part highlight the processes of faculty activism, organization, and collective bargaining and also explore the extent to which unionized adjunct faculty have improved working conditions and gained access to shared governance at their institutions.

The first three case studies focus on unionization in private schools. Nicholas M. Wertsch and Joseph A. McCartin demonstrate how Georgetown University's existing Just Employment policy allowed adjunct faculty to unionize amicably on the campus in the context of a national debate among Catholic colleges over whether their religious heritage should exempt them from coverage by the National Labor Relations Act. Kim Tolley, Marianne Delaporte, and Lorenzo Giachetti examine the factors that enabled adjunct and tenure-line faculty to join forces and unionize at Notre Dame de Namur University. Elizabeth K. Davenport analyzes the potential impact of unionization on shared governance in HBCUs.

The last three case studies tackle issues of organization, collective bargaining, and contract outcomes in large public institutions. Shawn Gilmore analyzes the processes involved in the ratification of the first contract for adjunct faculty at UIUC. Luke Elliott-Negri explores the wall-to-wall negotiation strategies of full-time faculty, part-time faculty, and graduate student instructors in the CUNY system. And Kim Geron and Gretchen M. Reevy present a case study of how lecturers and tenure-line faculty worked together at California State University, East Bay, to address the needs and concerns of union members and nonmembers and to strengthen tenure-line faculty's and lecturers' rights, equity, and shared governance, both in the California Faculty Association and in the academic senate.

In the book's concluding chapter, Kim Tolley and Kristen Edwards explore the possibilities and limitations of collective bargaining by analyzing evidence from 35 contracts that adjunct faculty unions have ratified since 2010. They conclude that collective bargaining has improved the salaries and working conditions of contingent faculty in a wide range of institutions, but they also find that unionization has not stopped the nationwide trend toward a reliance on part-time gig labor in higher education. They argue that collaboration among full-time and part-time faculty is important throughout the unionization and collective bargaining process, not only to improve working conditions and reduce the gap in salary and benefits, but also to advocate and bargain collectively for increased full-time positions to which qualified part-time faculty could apply. More important, a united faculty affiliated with a strong union can advocate for legislative reforms that will fully fund public higher education systems and require institutions to ensure that students have access to a well-supported faculty.

NOTES

1. Steve Hill, "Longtime English Teacher Loses Her Fight with Cancer," *City College Times Online*, Mar. 7, 2012, https://sjcctimes.com/1705/news/longtime-english-teacher-loses-her-fight-with-cancer.

2. Danny Westneat, "Gifted Professor's 'Life of the Mind' Was Also Life of Near Destitution," *Seattle Times* (Sept. 25, 2015).

3. Claudio Sanchez, "The Sad Death of an Adjunct Professor Sparks a Labor Debate," National Public Radio, Sept. 22, 2013, www.npr.org/2013/09/22/224946206/adjunct-professor-dies-destitute-then-sparks-debate.

4. John Curtis, *The Employment Status of Instructional Staff Members in Higher Education, Fall 2011* (Washington, DC: American Association of University Professors, 2014); Ken Jacobs, Ian Perry, and Jenifer MacGillvary, "The High Public Cost of Low Wages: Low Wages Cost U.S.

Taxpayers $152.8 Billion Each Year in Public Support for Working Families," UC Berkeley Labor Center, Apr. 13, 2015, http://laborcenter.berkeley.edu/the-high-public-cost-of-low-wages.

5. The terms "adjunct," "non-tenure-track," and "contingent" refer to both full- and part-time faculty who are not eligible for tenure. Job titles, such as lecturers and instructors or term, research, or clinical faculty, vary by campus. For perspectives by adjunct faculty on working conditions and the need for unionization, see Joe Berry, *Reclaiming the Ivory Tower: Organizing Adjuncts to Change Higher Education* (New York: Monthly Review Press, 2005); Keith Hoeller, ed., *Equality for Contingent Faculty: Overcoming the Two-Tier System* (Nashville, TN: Vanderbilt University Press, 2014); Professor X, *In the Basement of the Ivory Tower: Confessions of an Accidental Academic* (New York: Viking, 2011).

6. See appendix table 2 in this volume.

7. National Center for Education Statistics, *Integrated Postsecondary Education Data System* (Washington, DC: National Center for Education Statistics, 2013); Jack H. Schuster and Martin J. Finkelstein, *The American Faculty: The Restructuring of Academic Work and Careers* (Baltimore, MD: Johns Hopkins University Press, 2006); Adrianna Kezar and Daniel Maxey, "The Changing Academic Workforce," *Trusteeship* 21 (2013), agb.org/trusteeship/2013/5/changing-academic-workforce; Paul D. Umbach and Matthew R. Wawrzynski, "Faculty Do Matter: The Role of College Faculty in Student Learning and Engagement," *Research in Higher Education* 46 (Mar. 2005): 153–84.

8. American Association of University Professors, "Contingent Appointments and the Academic Profession," 2003, www.aaup.org/file/Contingent%20Appointment.pdf. For professional associations that have provided recognitions for adjunct faculty and recommendations to improve their working conditions, see Sue Doe et al., "Discourse of the Firetenders: Considering Contingent Faculty through the Lens of Activity Theory," *College English* 73 (Mar. 2011): 428–49. Also see Eva R. Brumberger, "The Best of Times, the Worst of Times: One Version of the 'Humane' Lectureship," in *Moving a Mountain: Transforming the Role of Contingent Faculty in Composition Studies and Higher Education*, ed. Eileen Schell and Patricia Stock (Urbana, IL: National Council of Teachers of English, 2001), 91–106; Linda R. Robertson, Sharon Crowley, and Frank Lentricchia, "The Wyoming Conference Resolution Opposing Unfair Salaries and Working Conditions for Post-Secondary Teachers of Writing," *College English* 49 (Mar. 1987): 274–80; Berry, *Reclaiming the Ivory Tower*.

9. For statistics on the national decline in union membership in the late twentieth century, see Barry T. Hirsch, David A. Macpherson, and Wayne G. Vroman, "Estimates of Union Density by State," *Monthly Labor Review* 124 (July 2001): 51–55. For the NLRB's ruling on the unionization of graduate students in private institutions, see Catie Edmondson, "Columbia, GWC File Briefs in Graduate Student Unionization Case," *Columbia Spectator*, Mar. 2, 2016; American Association of University Professors, "Columbia University, NLRB Case No. 02-RC-143012," aaup.org (accessed July 6, 2016); Danielle Douglas-Gabriel, "NLRB Rules That Graduate Students Are Employees, Overturning Brown University Decision," *Washington Post*, Aug. 23, 2016, www.providencejournal.com/news/20160823/nlrb-rules-that-graduate-students-are-employees-overturning-brown-university-decision; Vimal Patel, "Graduate-Student Union Efforts Gain Momentum, Despite New Uncertainties," *Chronicle of Higher Education* (Dec. 13, 2016).

10. Colleen Flaherty, "Big Gains for Adjuncts," *Inside Higher Ed*, Jan. 15, 2016, www.insidehighered.com; Service Employees International Union Local 509, "About Faculty Forward," www.seiu509.org/category/higher-education (accessed May 4, 2016); Katy Murphy, "Saint Mary's College and Dominican University Untenured Profs Vote to Unionize," *East Bay Times*, Jan. 6, 2015, www.eastbaytimes.com; Bureau of Labor Statistics, "Union Members Summary—2016," www.bls.gov/news.release/union2.nro.htm. For statistics from the SEIU's Faculty Forward campaign, see "SEIU Contract Highlights: The Union Difference," www.seiufacultyforward

.org/seiu-contract-highlights-the-union-difference (accessed Jan. 29, 2017). Also see William A. Herbert, "The Winds of Changes Shift: An Analysis of Recent Growth in Bargaining Units and Representation Efforts in Higher Education," *Journal of Collective Bargaining in the Academy* 8 (Dec. 2016), http://thekeep.eiu.edu/jcba/vol8/iss1/1.

11. See Judith M. Gappa and David W. Leslie, *The Invisible Faculty: Improving the Status of Part-Timers in Higher Education* (San Francisco, CA: Jossey-Bass, 1993); Gary Rhoades, "The Changing Role of Faculty," in *Higher Education in Transition: The Challenges of the New Millennium*, ed. Joseph Losco and Brian L. Fife (Westport, CT: Greenwood, 2000), 29–50; Jenny J. Lee et al., "Professors as Knowledge Workers in the New, Global Economy," in *Higher Education Handbook of Theory and Research*, vol. 20, ed. John C. Smart (New York: Springer, 2006), 55–132; Roger G. Baldwin and Jay L. Chronister, *Teaching without Tenure: Policies and Practices for a New Era* (Baltimore, MD: Johns Hopkins University Press, 2001); Schell and Stock, *Moving a Mountain*; Hoeller, *Equality for Contingent Faculty*; Adrianna Kezar, *Embracing Non-Tenure-Track Faculty: Changing Campuses for the New Faculty Majority* (New York: Routledge, 2012); John G. Cross and Edie N. Goldenberg, *Off-Track Profs: Nontenured Teachers in Higher Education* (Cambridge, MA: MIT Press, 2009).

12. For studies that focus on unionization, see Berry, *Reclaiming the Ivory Tower*; Robert A. Rhoades and Gary Rhoades, "Graduate Employee Unionization as Symbol of and Challenge to the Corporatization of U.S. Research Universities," *Journal of Higher Education* 76, no. 3 (2005): 243–75. Also see Vincent Tirelli, "The Invisible Faculty Fight Back: Contingent Academic Labor and the Political Economy of the Corporate University," PhD diss., City University of New York, 2007. For books that include chapters on unionization, see Kezar, *Embracing Non-Tenure-Track Faculty*; and Hoeller, *Equality for Contingent Faculty*.

13. American Association of University Professors, "Statement on Collective Bargaining," www.aaup.org/report/statement-collective-bargaining (accessed Apr. 15, 2016).

14. For the different priorities of tenure-track and part-time faculty, see Arthur M. Cohen and Carrie B. Kisker, *The Shaping of American Higher Education: Emergence and Growth of the Contemporary System* (San Francisco, CA: Wiley, 2009), 490–91. For discussion of the ways tenure-track and part-time faculty can build community and work effectively together, see Richard Moser, "The AAUP Organizes Part-Time Faculty: An Experiment in Community Responsibility Suggests That Part- and Full-Time Faculty Can Enrich One Another's Professional Lives," in *Unionization in the Academy: Visions and Realities*, ed. Judith Wagner DeCew (New York: Rowman and Littlefield, 2003), 217–22. Also see Gary Rhoades, *Managed Professionals: Unionized Faculty and Restructuring Academic Labor* (Albany: State University of New York Press, 1998).

acknowledgments

In August 2014, part-time lecturer Lorenzo Giachetti stood up at a faculty senate retreat and gave a riveting presentation about the poor working conditions of adjunct faculty at my university, Notre Dame de Namur. That talk was like a pebble tossed into a still pond—the ripples expanded and moved outward, with consequences that would be realized two years afterward. I'm grateful to Lorenzo, Kristen Edwards, and the many other faculty members, adjunct, tenured, and tenure-track, who stepped forward to organize at my university. My experience on the organizing committee at NDNU triggered this project.

One of the great pleasures of working on this book has been the chance to discuss ideas with colleagues from a range of fields. I'm grateful to the contributors, who brought an enormous amount of experience and expertise to this project. I also thank David Hoskins of the Service Employees International Union, who kindly provided copies of several recent collective bargaining agreements. I was fortunate to receive supportive and critical feedback from the members of my writing group at NDNU—Pearl Chaozon Bauer, Marianne Delaporte, Therese Madden, and Pia Walawalkar. Bruce Tolley's encouragement and editorial comments were also extremely helpful. Finally, I thank Greg Britton for his assistance in bringing this project to Johns Hopkins University Press, Juliana McCarthy and Merryl A. Sloane for their impeccable editing, and Mary Lou Kenney for her assistance through the production process.

PART I

The Changing Academic Workforce

Influences and Outcomes

chapter 1

From Golden Era to Gig Economy

Changing Contexts for Academic Labor in America

A. J. ANGULO

There's a period in American history that scholars recognize as the golden era of higher education, and it began with a signature.[1]

When President Franklin Delano Roosevelt signed the Servicemen's Readjustment Act of 1944, known as the GI Bill, he unleashed an unprecedented boom period for colleges and universities. Millions of World War II veterans received benefits—in the form of tuition and stipend payments—to attend institutions of their choice. As a result, campuses faced intense pressure to expand. Existing facilities at the time had little chance of meeting the demand. With enrollments skyrocketing, new classrooms, laboratories, and residence halls sprang up. The GI Bill, in short, not only provided financial support for college-going veterans but also physically transformed the campuses they wanted to attend. Just as capital projects got under way, these institutions went on a hiring spree. Administrators looking to fill new classroom spaces began a massive search for professors. Finding those with the necessary skills, training, and expertise, however, wasn't easy. The surge in faculty openings created an urgency to fill vacancies and a frenzy of competition between campuses. The arms race that followed meant increasingly attractive faculty salaries, benefits, teaching loads, and research opportunities. A golden era was born, and the path ahead only looked brighter.[2]

Those who experienced or recall the golden era have reason to do so with wistful nostalgia. Those who learn about the period today, as they make their way through the so-called gig economy, might be excused for wondering if there's more myth than memory to the golden stories. Their skepticism is warranted. At no point before or after the postwar boom in higher education have observers witnessed such a rapid, across-the-board expansion of post-secondary education. By contrast, important indicators suggest that the current academic labor market continues to hit new lows. Colleges and universities appear more committed than ever to relying on adjunct faculty to replace tenure-track positions. Some institutions, like those in the for-profit sector, prefer using only temporary faculty. How did we reach this nadir? What's brought about such an extreme reversal in the fortunes of the American professoriat?[3]

Since the GI Bill era, the United States has undergone significant social, economic, and political upheavals that have destabilized what many considered to be pillars of the academic profession. The usual suspects when it comes to social developments include '60s era student protest movements that were later replaced with an increasing demand for advanced education and a consumer-oriented view of higher education. Student movements, rising doctoral-level graduation rates, and expanding consumer services generated new, competing demands for campus administrators. Faculty-hiring priorities followed these trends and began to change dramatically in the last quarter of the twentieth century.[4]

But social developments don't tell the whole story. Economic explanations for the professoriat's decline often identify the '70s petrodollar crisis as a leading culprit. Relationships between employers and employees underwent a wholesale transformation during this crisis period. Higher education leaders and consultants across America began entertaining the idea of using new market-based strategies for handling personnel decisions in light of decreasing state and private revenues. The change in context provided colleges and universities with the opportunity to rewrite the academic social contract.[5]

Joining these social and economic developments since the start of the twenty-first century has been a political turn that's made it difficult for beginning professors to even imagine a previous golden age. An oligarchy, as researchers have empirically demonstrated, has exercised its will in American politics. Its influence in the halls of power has displaced the needs and interests of the vast majority of the population, or what some call the 99 percent. With startling movements of wealth from the bottom upward, as economists have traced in recent decades, a tiny segment of the American population and business class has secured striking political privileges. Consider, for instance, the handling of the Trans-Pacific Partnership agreement in Congress, the extreme secrecy surrounding the agreement's text, and the way the nation's largest multinationals favored its speedy passage. In such an age, it's no surprise that politicians have shown a lack of willingness to pass new labor laws for what's euphemistically, almost cheerfully, described as an economy made of "gigs." The temporary work arrangements of this new economy offer no benefits or job security. Without legal and regulatory safeguards in place, the dominant forces of political economy in the early twenty-first century normalized contingent work. For many in higher education, this absence of protections has created two unfortunate trends: the displacement of aspiring academics and, at times, the exploitation of part-time instructors, graduate teaching assistants, and other contingent faculty.[6]

These broad social, economic, and political contexts have shaped policy changes in higher education in ways that merit a closer look. Rather than being mere abstractions, these developments have produced tangible consequences, particularly for those struggling to maintain a foothold in America's academic labor market. Taken together, the changing contexts—from golden era to gig economy—not only help explain the professoriat's eroding status, but also offer a starting point for understanding past and present unionization efforts among adjunct faculty in the United States.

Golden Era

It's now well known among scholars that academia's golden era produced favorable market conditions for professors. Returning World War II veterans ditched their military uniforms and came to campuses in droves, but it wasn't clear who would teach them all. In the years following the GI Bill, more than 2 million former soldiers lined up at the registrar's office. Another 5.5 million enrolled in job-skills programs at a variety of nonprofit and for-profit postsecondary institutions. Enrollments doubled across the country with veterans comprising as much as 49 percent of the overall US student body.[7]

The burst of new enrollments gave faculty leverage in the golden era. If employment numbers from that time are any indicator, the leverage was impressive. During the decade before the GI Bill, the number of newly created higher education positions aligned fairly closely with the number of graduating PhDs. At the start of the 1930s, there were approximately 80,000 professors in the country. By the end of the decade, the total number of faculty positions grew to just over 110,000. Rising to fill those new spots were 15,000 new PhDs. The pool of potential candidates to fill half of the 30,000 new openings was made of recent graduates. After the GI Bill, however, the gap widened substantially. Colleges advertised nearly 80,000 new openings during the 1940s, a decade that produced fewer than 25,000 new PhDs. The '50s

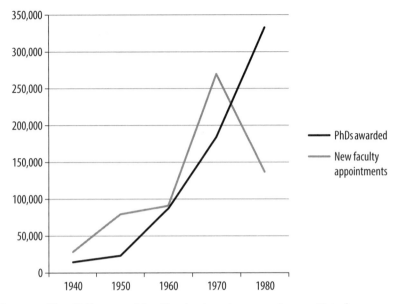

Figure 1.1. New PhDs versus New Faculty Appointments. Source: Data from Thomas D. Snyder, ed., *120 Years of American Education: A Statistical Portrait* (Washington, DC: US Department of Education, Office of Educational Research and Improvement, 1993), 75, 83–84; Howard R. Bowen and Jack H. Schuster, *American Professors: A National Resource Imperiled* (New York: Oxford University Press, 1986), 176.

proved better for campuses trying to recruit, but the breather was short-lived. During the 1960s, the gap appeared again. Despite the record PhD completion rates of that decade (i.e., 183,898 newly minted graduates), the pool of applicants filled only two-thirds of the new positions (see figure 1.1).[8]

The golden era, and the faculty leverage that came with it, peaked just as the '60s protest movements began influencing the purposes and practices of American higher education. Student unrest, marked by off-campus and on-campus demands, took center stage as campus administrators looked to satisfy competing budget priorities. Students rallied on domestic and international issues, pressing for free expression, civil rights, an end to the Vietnam War, and an end to the draft. Closer to home, they found sympathetic faculty who supported their fights against in loco parentis, the bureaucratization of campus life, traditional courses of study, and, at some institutions, classified military research. Students decried campuses for what they viewed as a turn toward the bureaucratic. Processes and rules had replaced relationships, and the shift came across as dehumanizing. That's partly what student leaders like Mario Savio meant when they spoke of universities as "the machine" that "makes you so sick at heart that you can't take part! You can't even passively take part! And you've got to put your bodies upon the gears and upon the wheels, upon the levers, upon all the apparatus—and you've got to make it stop!" Students demanded more say in college governance, more responsiveness to their needs, more relevance in their courses of study, and more services for student groups. University administrators listened, and they began reallocating institutional resources. Hundreds of universities established new specialized departments and programs, rewrote their student conduct policies, and hired increasing numbers of what we now call student affairs personnel.[9]

Out of the protest period also came a surge of '60s era graduate students wanting to join the ranks of university faculty. The number of those pursuing PhDs had shown a sharp upward trend since 1950. Key legislation kept the trend going. While the GI Bill had kicked off the golden era expansion, the National Defense Education Act of 1958 and the Higher Education Act (HEA) of 1965 accelerated the PhD enrollment growth. Reauthorizations of the HEA in the '70s, for instance, expanded access to grant and loan programs beyond those students demonstrating financial need. Professional, graduate, advanced, and doctoral programs all benefited from these midcentury developments. During the '60s and '70s alone, universities graduated more than a half million new PhDs.[10]

Student demands and doctorate attainment rates went a long way toward eroding the professoriat's place and authority in the '70s. Golden age faculty compensation packages began to disappear as universities changed the composition of their personnel. Noninstructional staff increased by more than 600 percent nationwide between the 1950s (fewer than 250,000) and the late 1980s (more than 1.5 million). Compared to total college personnel, the proportion rose from 54 percent to more than 60 percent, as shown in figure 1.2.

However critical for student development and compliance needs, the new full-time staff commitments competed against costly faculty expenditures. Just as significant as the new personnel was the rise of student consumerism. College-going students, worn out from a decade of protests and war, came into the 1970s and '80s preferring amenities to activism. The end of the draft, along with the Kent State and Jackson State shootings, marked a turn in student culture toward customer satisfaction. With increasing expectations came increasing demands. Students, parents, alumni, and others clamored for ex-

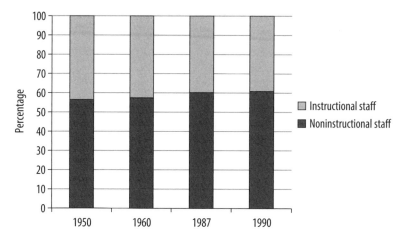

Figure 1.2. Expansion of Noninstructional Staff (% of Total College Personnel). Source: Data from Thomas D. Snyder, ed., *120 Years of American Education: A Statistical Portrait* (Washington, DC: US Department of Education, Office of Educational Research and Improvement, 1993), 75.

pensive athletic, recreational, and residential amenities. This gave rise to long-term capital campaigns and ongoing maintenance projects.[11]

As campus budgets faced the market crunch of the 1970s and state retrenchment in the decades that followed, university leaders sought less expensive alternatives to their single biggest budget expenditure: full-time, tenured professors. A surplus of PhDs created a pool of applicants willing to take decreasingly attractive, temporary faculty positions. Some did so in the hope of getting a foot in the door and making the move to a tenure-line position. Others did so because they had no intention of seeking a tenured, full-time commitment. Those balancing work and home demands found temporary positions attractive. Still others were already retired, and they wanted to supplement their income by teaching intermittently.[12]

Given the exceptionally high PhD completion rates that continued into the '70s, however, the expanding use of temporary, adjunct, and nontenured appointments telegraphed a worrisome trend for aspiring young faculty. The boom time of the golden era in academic employment hit a wall and dropped. Those already in the doctoral pipeline felt the pinch. Promises of improved employment prospects through faculty attrition failed to materialize as professors kept their positions for longer than anticipated. Demographics and the market—increasing numbers of PhD graduates, the sharp decline in new

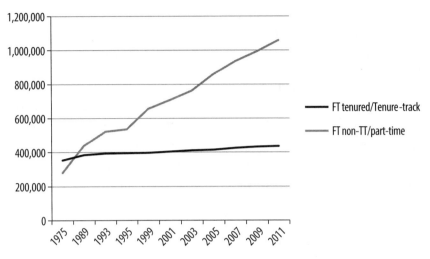

Figure 1.3. Increase in Number of Adjunct Faculty in Higher Education, 1975–2011. Source: Created by author from data in John Curtis, *The Employment Status of Instructional Staff Members in Higher Education, Fall 2011* (Washington, DC: American Association of University Professors, 2014), 2–3, 5–6.

faculty positions generally, the longevity of senior professors—collided at precisely the time when institutions looked to minimize their costs quickly and quietly. With increasing numbers of '70s era applicants lining up for scarce new openings, the seller's market for professors came to an end. The age of the adjunct was under way (see figure 1.3).[13]

Downsized America

The turn toward using adjunct faculty occurred at a time when fundamental changes to employer-employee relationships were taking hold in late twentieth-century corporate America. Inflation—or, more accurately, stagflation—jolted the economic system of the '70s, knocking previous employment practices off balance. The instability led to a wave of layoffs in the broader economy. But trends that started in the early '70s continued long after the stagflation crisis passed, and not all trends followed a clear path from macroeconomic developments. More important, basic assumptions in corporate life changed dramatically. New management styles were promoted by business schools, practiced by executives, and experienced by millions of employees across the country. Companies, large and small, consumed the new alphabet soup of abbreviations—HCT, PPBS, MBO, ZBB, TQM, CQI, BPR—which stood for one "breakthrough" business strategy after another. These workplace reforms almost always privileged efficiency and flexibility over employee stability and institutional loyalty. Human capital theory (HCT) encouraged viewing employees as resources, rather than as members of the "family" business. Planning, programming, and budgeting system (PPBS) rationalized cost-benefit decision-making in boardrooms that stood far removed from those on the ground floor. Management by objectives (MBO), zero-based budgeting (ZBB), total quality management (TQM), continuous quality improvement (CQI), and business process reengineering (BPR) all pointed in the same direction: increase productivity, decrease costs, minimize personnel expenditures. Corporate executives of the mid- to late twentieth century experimented with such strategies, and some dramatic layoffs followed.[14]

Downsizing, a term first used to describe trading large, inefficient cars for small ones after the oil crisis of the '70s, hit the corporate community with a blizzard of pink slips. Institutions formerly known for making long-term commitments to their employees cut personnel at an accelerating pace. Jack Welch, the CEO of General Electric, earned the nickname "Neutron Jack" for decimating his workforce while keeping the company's buildings and infrastructure intact. His downsizing blasts wiped out approximately 100,000 workers during the 1980s. Under CEO Louis Gerstner Jr., IBM erased a sterling reputation for employee-management relations by cutting its rank and file too. During the early '90s, Gerstner implemented one of the all-time biggest layoffs in American history: 60,000 employees within a four-month period. *Newsweek* called these kinds of executives "corporate killers" and the "hit men" of the US economy. According to the magazine, "It used to be a mark of shame to fire workers en masse. Today Wall Street loves it. But the layoffs have scared the pants off the public and stirred a political backlash." Between the mid-1970s and the mid-1990s, more than 40 million American jobs disappeared. Many went overseas. Some faded out entirely.[15]

College and university presidents came under pressure to follow corporate America's lead, adopt its strategies, and cut personnel costs through expanding the use of adjunct faculty. They faced trustees from the business world who saw no reason that the latest in management science couldn't also benefit higher education. Nearly a third of campuses in the United States gave PPBS a try in the early '70s. They did so despite internal opposition from faculty and senior campus administrators. Donald Thompson, vice president for administrative affairs at Slippery Rock University, called the management trend "economically optimal, yet potentially educationally unsound." When PPBS ultimately failed to deliver as college reformers had promised, MBO took its place at institutions like the University of Tennessee. There, as everywhere else, MBO took root, and measurement became the mantra: if it couldn't be measured, then it wouldn't factor in the decision-making process. This opened the door for administrators to measure the cost reduction benefits of contingent faculty while ignoring changes to such intangibles as the campus community and culture.[16]

In the early '80s, reformers and consultants moved on to ZBB. As with MBO, alternative instructional delivery methods (e.g., large lecture hall classes) became increasingly attractive to those conducting cost-benefit analyses. Campus consultants, not surprisingly, favored the use of the least costly methods delivered by the least costly instructors. By the mid- to late 1980s, TQM and CQI came to campuses across the country. The focus on quality, defined as customer satisfaction, brought student input into the decision-making equation. The TQM and CQI trends privileged replicability, standardization, and documented accountability when it came to teaching and learning processes. This made adjunct faculty who might be willing to comply with the new corporate-style mandates even more attractive to reformers than permanent faculty who preferred their autonomy. Adjunct instructors, for these reasons, had significant "value" and "quality" appeal when interpreted through the lens of the university's bottom line.[17]

Behind these management trends adopted from 1970s and '80s corporate America—almost all of which helped rationalize the expanding use of adjunct and nontenured faculty—stood some of the heaviest hitters in higher education. The American Council on Education, the Ford Foundation, and the National Center for Higher Education Management Systems gave campus leaders the green light to use PPBS. Higher education publishers like Jossey-Bass promoted MBO strategies through monographs. The University of Colorado created implementation workbooks like *MBO Goes to College* (1975). Other performance and benchmarking methods received ample support from groups such as the National Association of College and University Business Officers and the Association of Governing Boards.[18]

Of all the cost-cutting and personnel-reducing management styles of the 1980s and '90s, TQM received the most support from college reformers. From their perspective, it held the most promise. The American Council on Education (ACE) put its imprimatur on this approach to reform with the publication of *On Q: Causing Quality in Higher Education* (1992). Corporations took notice and began investing heavily in promoting TQM in colleges and universities. Funders of this campaign included companies claiming budget crises and taking extreme measures with their own personnel. Within months of firing 60,000 employees, IBM decided to spend a small fortune on spreading the word about the benefits of TQM at Georgia Institute of Technology, Oregon State University, Pennsylvania State University, University of Maryland at College Park, University of Wisconsin at Madison, and a handful of other well-established universities. IBM poured tens of millions of dollars into cash incentives, business equipment, and guest speakers to help these institutions make the "quality management" case. Some campuses even received executives on loan from IBM to help direct and implement reforms.[19]

The TQM initiatives did bring together cross-sections of 1980s and '90s campus personnel to consider ways to reduce a variety of operational expenses. But the slash-and-burn personnel practices of companies promoting TQM colored how faculty and administrators received the initiatives. The practices created assumptions about the need to reduce higher education's most expensive personnel commitments—permanent faculty—by expanding less expensive, temporary, and contingent alternatives. Pressure to do so came from a variety of sources. Joining IBM in diffusing the TQM model in higher education were Milliken, Motorola, Xerox, and Proctor and Gamble, among other corporate titans.[20]

Praise and optimism for these late twentieth-century company-sponsored initiatives in the academic labor market came from higher education leaders like Theodore J. Marchese, editor of the widely read *Change* magazine. Marchese called TQM a "possible solution" to "the way we use resources" in colleges and universities. To his mind, changes in the economy made it highly improbable that higher education could return to "business as usual." Richard Chait, later a professor of higher education at Harvard University, also gave corporate leadership of the early '90s, especially the kind appearing at IBM, a positive review. He suggested that college leaders had much to learn from the head of IBM's bold decision to eliminate jobs. Citing Gerstner, he repeated the view that these were "very tough-minded" and "highly effective" acts that could be compared to "blocking and tackling." Chait believed that college presidents should worry less about institutional "visions" and, instead, focus on "controlling costs, increasing productivity, diversifying their work forces, assessing quality, and streamlining operations." Or, put another way, college leaders might do well to "adhere" to the "sensible" management style of TQM.[21]

Opponents blamed corporate modes of thinking for the disappearance of permanent faculty positions. During the '90s Alabama A&M faced unwelcome personnel changes under the banner of corporate-style cost-cutting and efficiency. Departments across the university were told of positions that had to be eliminated. As one faculty member described the process, "We became more and more like a business and less like a university." At West Virginia University, the special assistant to the president, Robert Pedersen, fought against the slash-and-burn cost-cutting tactics occurring at peer institutions. Pedersen dubbed such fads to be "ill-suited panaceas from business." Pedersen blasted TQM in particular because it replaced the "ethical dimension of institutional management" with "statistical analysis" that offered "no guidance as to whether a given decision is either right or good, much less whether this decision will serve the broader interest." The result was "process and mechanics over the developmental" that "will only encourage the continued erosion in campus collegiality." Opponents of the business methods at Alabama A&M, West Virginia, and elsewhere perceived an unsettling distortion of collegiate values. Commitments to access and equity, they lamented, got lost in the dustup over how to define efficiency and effectiveness. Likewise, privileging statistical analyses when measuring core teaching, research, and service responsibilities, they warned, tended toward quantity over quality. With the backdrop of news reports of massive layoffs, factory closings, and global competition, opponents wondered how corporate values might irrevocably alter higher education culture.[22]

Despite faculty and administrator resistance, colleges throughout the United States implemented their own form of downsizing, or "contingifying," by replacing tenure-track lines with contingent appointments. Between 1975 and 1995, institutions nationally added more than 250,000 new part-time and non-tenure-line faculty. During the same period, fewer than 42,000 new tenured and tenure-track openings appeared.[23]

With the adjunct faculty population exploding at a rate of 600 percent more than tenure lines throughout those two decades, questions arose over how to respond. Scholars began collecting data on who these contingent faculty were, what they wanted, and what they thought about collective action. Some researchers developed taxonomies of contingent faculty to describe the variety that existed among the hundreds of thousands of new part-time instructional staff. Among them were semiretired people, graduate students, working professionals who just wanted to teach a course or two on the side, part-time faculty who hoped to gain tenure-track positions, and others. According to surveys from the 1970s and '80s, half of these individuals were under the age of 45 and had "very low" or "fairly low" morale. Seventy-six percent of part-timers working on multiple campuses wanted full-time, tenure-line positions. More than 60 percent favored collective action and bargaining to improve such things as their status, working conditions, and compensation packages. Although the US Supreme Court in *NLRB v. Yeshiva University* (1980) had put cold water on the burning question of collective action at private universities, adjunct faculty continued to organize, even if not recognized officially by universities, to call attention to their plight. As one group of researchers discovered, there was a "discomfiting universality in the feelings of part-time faculty that somehow they were being exploited, and blatantly so." This conclusion was based on interviews with nearly 500 part-time faculty, department chairs, central administrators, and faculty leaders at 18 geographically dispersed and institutionally varied colleges and universities.[24]

Knowledge Economy on FIRE

From the mid-1990s through the first decade of the twenty-first century, global trade deals contributed to the shrinking of America's manufacturing and industrial base. Thanks in large measure to the North American Free Trade Agreement and the establishment of the World Trade Organization, the production of retail goods moved to Latin America, Asia, and anywhere else US companies could find weak labor laws and an inexpensive workforce. Observers, pundits, and politicians warned that the industrial age had passed and that a new knowledge economy was on the horizon. Congress and President Bill Clinton agreed with this assessment and funded the Workforce Investment Act of 1998. The goal was to facilitate the transition to a new economy through education. Hundreds of millions of dollars went to support the retraining of displaced adult workers. Community colleges stepped in to teach new skills to those affected by the offshoring of the "old economy" jobs. Colleges became a solution, but the problem was still ill defined. No one quite knew exactly what the incoming economy would look like or which knowledge would have the most currency in it. Equally unclear was whether the new order could absorb all the new knowledge workers produced by institutions of higher education.[25]

Speculating on which jobs would rise to the top became a kind of national pastime at the turn of the twenty-first century. Would computer science majors hold the keys to the future? The field held obvious appeal as a contender for replacing the dominant skills and knowledge of the old economy. This was, after all, an age marked by the rise of Netscape and the start of the '90s internet boom. But the flood of new entrants to the field and the expanding pool of less expensive coders living abroad dampened the prospects of those who equated knowledge work with computer science. Would traditional professions—law, medicine, and business—and the technical fields that supported them continue to hold their status? Many graduate programs in those fields ended up making headlines for creating a surplus of professionals. This had the potential to produce the same conditions faced by the academics of the early '70s: eroding job prospects. What's more, a chasm existed between the skill sets, dispositions, and knowledge base possessed by factory workers and what these traditional fields demanded.[26]

While upstart and traditional careers initially had potential, they fell short of what economists and analysts now describe as the real winners of the late twentieth century's knowledge economy: finance, insurance, and real estate (FIRE). In terms of the proportion of the economy, the actual transition away from industry and manufacturing had more to do with FIRE than anything else. During the '90s, GE, GM, and other companies known for manufacturing real goods began making substantial profits through credit programs. The financialization of nonfinancial institutions turned product makers into debt distributors who also happened to make products. Increasingly sophisticated debt instruments made rehypothecation easier than ever, resulting in the increased packaging and distribution of loans and derivatives of loans. Financial institutions created these instruments, insurance companies bundled and swapped them, and real estate companies provided the collateral for high-stakes, highly speculative games in what some describe as "casino capitalism."[27]

In the closing years of the twentieth century, Wall Street speculation, corporate approaches to efficiency, and American higher education converged in the form of for-profit colleges and universities (FPCUs). The $35 billion goliath they created by the end of the first decade of the twenty-first century was built on the backs of adjunct faculty.[28]

As profit-driven corporations, FPCUs tossed aside any pretense of making long-term commitments to faculty or creating collegial academic environments at the start of the millennium. These were businesses. Traditions like shared governance, in which faculty participate in setting institutional policies, had no place in FPCUs run like publicly traded companies or the privately held playthings of equity firms. Growth, flexibility, and profitability replaced traditional approaches to teaching, research, and service. Blisteringly fast rates of growth at the turn of the twenty-first century attracted increasing numbers of investors and stimulated further expansion. Traditional nonprofits grew by 7 percent during the '90s. The FPCUs, meanwhile, averaged 266 percent growth in the same period and reached 300 percent the following decade. Stocks in for-profits went through the roof too. Investors cheered as share prices in some of these companies increased by approximately 460 percent. The University of Phoenix became the sector's poster child of financial success. It started with a mere 8 students in the '70s, but turned into an enrollment growth machine after joining forces with Wall Street financiers. By 2009, Phoenix's student population had climbed to 445,000. DeVry, Strayer, ITT Tech, Kaplan, Corinthian, Career Education Corporation, Education Management Corporation, and the many other large-scale for-profits followed a similar trajectory of astonishing growth. Collectively, their enrollments reached 2 million students, or approximately 11 percent of the overall college-going population. This same group of students also represented 44 percent of overall student loan defaults.[29]

All this expansion came out of an early twenty-first-century era swept up by flashy talk about the knowledge economy. Self-styled visionaries called for new institutions that would provide the new skill sets necessary for the workforce of tomorrow. Old, tradition-bound nonprofit colleges and universities looked like fusty relics of a bygone age to those in search of a foil. What most of these observations about higher education's future tended to overlook, however, was the way an unsettled finance sector, rather than a transformed economy, stood behind the for-profit movement. Wall Street investors wanted to move their holdings to safe, secure, and subsidized investments after the internet stock debacle of the late '90s and early 2000s. For-profit higher education looked like the best of all possible worlds: colleges run like businesses, revenues guaranteed by government-backed student aid programs, and adjunct instructors—an army of inexpensive workers—willing to accept scripted lesson plans or other deprofessionalizing employment requirements. These institutions merged corporate management values with career-oriented studies. Despite their origin as an outlet for the finance sector, large-scale FPCUs became a hallmark of a much broader, widely anticipated transformation toward a knowledge economy. They looked like the prime knowledge solution for an economy in transition—at least, that's what promoters suggested. And this industry called on the most powerful figures of the era to make such suggestions. Financial and political leaders of the FIRE economy—including Goldman Sachs, George Soros, Donald Trump, and the Clinton family—have all profited handsomely from these institutions.[30]

Adjunct faculty at for-profits—who were arguably at the commanding heights of the new economy due to their place in training future knowledge workers—gained little from the new millennium's financial upside. Although adjunct faculty often filled 90 percent or more of an FPCU's instructional staff, managers typically served them the smallest slice of the budget pie. A 2009 study of for-profits found that these institutions spent up to 500 percent more on marketing, recruitment, and profit distribution than on instruction. On average, instruction accounted for a mere 17 percent of their overall budgets. The great financial rewards of the knowledge economy weren't making their way to the adjunct faculty who were preparing the next generation of knowledge workers.[31]

Twenty-first-century contingent faculty at for-profits also had much of their professional authority stripped along the way. Complaints filed by students, former employees, and government officials in the early 2000s described the damage done by deprofessionalizing instructional staff. Litigants in a whistle-blower case against Kaplan University warned of serious consequences that occur when for-profits deny faculty their due authority. Kaplan managers, former administrators observed, took advantage of disempowered instructors when it came to student grades. If a temporary faculty member assigned students low grades, managers would override the decision in favor of a higher grade in order to keep students enrolled and revenues flowing. Contingent faculty at other FPCUs commented on the loss of the "integrity of the institution," which defies the "implicit promise made to students that college provides meaningful and legitimate learning experiences. . . . the things that have historically been of value in higher education have no place in the world of for-profit colleges." The long list of state and federal investigations, whistle-blower testimony, class action lawsuits, and shareholder litigation of the early twenty-first century corroborates these observations. Settlements of hundreds of millions of dollars in cases against Education Management Corporation, Corinthian, and others gave many reasons to believe that for-profits operated with notions of efficiency that looked very little like those found at traditional, nonprofit higher education institutions.[32]

Adjunct faculty across the institutional spectrum—from nonprofit to for-profit—organized in response to their treatment at the turn of the twenty-first century. One example is Eastern Michigan University's Lecturers Organizing Congress and its struggles since the early '90s. Year after year, the group called attention to the low wages of full-time adjunct faculty and unbenefited part-time faculty. The Michigan Employment Relations Commission assessed the adjuncts' request for recognition, and in 1999 the group won the right to unionize. Hundreds of part-timers at Roosevelt University voted to unionize the following year. The Roosevelt Adjunct Faculty Organization represented instructors who taught 60 percent of the classes at the university. With the slogan "We Want a New Deal," this organization looked to negotiate improved wages and benefits for its members. It ultimately won the right to a union contract professionalizing the adjunct faculty's status and offering them the "full freedom to conduct classes consistent with the course description or outline and established academic policies or standards."[33]

While adjunct unionization gained momentum through local efforts at Eastern Michigan, Roosevelt, and elsewhere, national efforts also picked up steam. Contingent faculty leaders from across the country met in New York for the "Scholars, Artists, and Writers for Social Justice" meeting in 2000. The group received support from such academic and labor organizations as the American Association of University Professors, the American Federation of Teachers, and the United Auto Workers. Their goal was to draft a university code of conduct for fair labor practices. Attendees were then charged with returning to their campuses with the newly created code and starting petition campaigns to get their institutions to adopt it.[34]

Adjunct organizing efforts also crossed borders in the early twenty-first century. The Coalition of Contingent Academic Labor meeting in 2001, for instance, brought together more than 150 academics from the United States and Canada. Organizers of the three-day session wanted to mobilize part-time faculty to build coalitions and lay the groundwork for collective bargaining. Tenured literature professor Cary Nelson, a longtime advocate on behalf of contingent faculty, considered the meeting an auspicious sign of things to come. "It seems we're on the verge of a national movement, and we need one," he noted. Focusing on quality of life for contingent academic labor had as much to do with improving working conditions as with "a movement to save higher education." Nelson and others at the meeting wanted to save colleges and universities from the kind of corporate model that created an underclass of instructional staff.[35]

During the opening years of the millennium, momentum at the national level received a boost with every adjunct organizing victory. Continuing education faculty at the University of Massachusetts, Boston, won the right to organize in 2001. Western Michigan University opened the door to granting tenure to nearly 1,000 of its adjunct faculty in 2002. Non-tenure-track faculty at the University of Michigan voted to unionize in 2003. The United Auto Workers got involved with the union organization efforts of teaching assistants. The American Federation of Teachers (AFT), at the time representing more than 50,000 contingent faculty, drafted "Standards of Good Practice in the Employment of Part-Time / Adjunct Faculty," which the organization called a "blueprint" for bringing equity in and taking exploitation out of the academic labor market. Citing the chasm in pay and benefits in higher education between contingent and noncontingent faculty, the AFT report described colleges and universities as "academic sweatshops."[36] Every year, the movement continued to attract increasing support from labor coalitions and academic organizations.

The organizing movement, in short, had legs, and adjunct faculty used them to walk a bit taller and a bit straighter to their seat at the boardroom negotiation table. Putting spring in their step was the fact that stocks kept climbing and real estate hit an epic boom cycle. All of this made it difficult to ignore demands from adjuncts for a greater share of the nation's wealth.

Contingency Plans for the Gig Economy

The knowledge economy, which turned out in practice to be an economy on FIRE, had run its course by the time of the economic collapse of 2007–2008. Financial deregulation begun almost a decade earlier had produced financial instruments that investor Warren Buffett called "weapons of mass financial destruction." With a declining manufacturing base and a dwindling capacity to create real goods, knowledge workers of the knowledge economy turned their energies toward speculative rather than productive interests. Financial engineers like Blythe Masters of JPMorgan Chase dreamed up increasingly complex, sophisticated, and dangerous ways to make money. They embraced rehypothecation, repackaging the work, property, and speculative arrangements of others. The income was derivative, and the multitrillion-dollar castles in the sky they built had nowhere to go but down. Mortgage-backed securities, collateralized debt obligations, and credit default swaps—these were the products of the most well-compensated knowledge workers. They're also what scholars now recognize as the main culprits in the greatest financial collapse since the Great Depression. The weapons of the knowledge economy had to be dealt with, and the Dodd-Frank bill of 2010 attempted to address some of the more pernicious elements of financial knowledge work. But the banking sector staged well-financed lobbying efforts that left the house—in this case, the Wall Street firms—the favored winner at every table in the casino. Even when held to account for illegal behavior, whether the manipulation of LIBOR (the London interbank offered rate, the benchmark rate that banks charge each other for short-term loans) or the laundering of drug cartel money, the banks could write off the settlements as tax breaks.[37]

After the global economic collapse, talk of knowledge work subsided, and protests against the most powerful 1 percent of society increased. The idea of a knowledge economy no longer commanded the same attention it had received in the pre-collapse years. Jobs, even for those who had added to their knowledge base through advanced training and education, became difficult to find. Those most affected by the scarcity of employment had reason to wonder if all the rhetoric about the knowledge economy was merely a ruse to placate opponents of deindustrialization and free trade agreements. If so, it worked. With the closing of factories, offshoring of jobs, and downsizing of once-stable employment options, talk of a knowledge economy sounded a futuristic and even exciting tone to the forward-looking. It also cast the opponents of controversial globalization policies as backward-looking Luddites. Whatever the case, employment problems increased exponentially after the collapse. Commonly cited government statistics tended to paper over the problem by failing to include those who had stopped looking for work as part of the unemployed. The context directed many unemployed or underemployed workers to find service sector, rather than knowledge-based, sources of income.[38]

Out of the ashes of the knowledge economy came a new meme: the gig economy. The founding of companies like Airbnb in 2008 and Uber in 2009 gave some people the opportunity to fill their unemployment time with occasional gigs. The temporary, unbenefited, on-demand nature of this kind of work had been long known to adjunct faculty in higher education. From the perspective of those organizing and fighting for equity and benefits, this signaled a turn in the wrong direction. It was, among other things, the "adjunctification" of the entire American workforce. Economic reports have begun forecasting an accelerating "gigification" pattern in the United States. Economists Lawrence Katz and Alan Krueger found a rapid increase in "alternative work arrangements" between 2005 and 2015. According to their study, the numbers in such types of employment rose from 10.7 percent (2005) to 15.8 percent (2015). A 2015 study by Intuit and Emergent Research estimates that 36 percent of the US workforce today is engaged in "contingent work," up from 17 percent in 1989. Researchers predict the number will rise to 43 percent by 2020.[39]

For contingent faculty, the future arrived long ago. As shown elsewhere in this volume, current estimates put their numbers at more than two-thirds of total faculty and at three-fourths of the total postsecondary instructional workforce, including graduate student instructors and all nonpermanent full- and part-time faculty who are "on demand" from semester to semester. This represents a fundamental departure from the golden era, when more than three-fourths of faculty nationally held full-time positions. Some analysts point to the rapid rise of for-profit institutions as the leading culprit in this shift. Adjunct faculty at those institutions make up more than 93 percent of the instructional staff. Kaplan University instructors in 2006 pushed back against the tenuousness of their work contracts by organizing one of the first unionization efforts in their sector. Critical of the "tremendous pressure to inflate grades" coming from the institution's management, Kaplan faculty voted to demand the right of "academic freedom." "That's something we want and don't have," one spokesperson for the movement noted.[40]

For-profits, of course, aren't alone. Public and private nonprofits rely on part-time faculty to fill their instructional lines at community colleges (65 percent) and four-year institutions (34 percent). The gigification of academic life is a present reality. Absent a significant shift in academic management practices or a robust movement toward unionization, it's one that will likely to continue in the decades ahead. But the collapse of for-profit giants like Corinthian and ITT Tech, with their combined student population of approximately 160,000 at bankruptcy, might signal such a change in practice. With the bursting of the for-profit college industry bubble, the deprofessionalization of the professoriat shows some signs of slowing.[41]

New demands emerging in the gig economy likewise have the potential to disrupt the American economy and transform American higher education as we know it. Senator Elizabeth Warren called for a reworking of labor laws in light of the expanding use of temporary workers as forecast in 2016. "The much-touted virtues of flexibility, independence, and creativity offered by gig work might be true for some workers under some conditions," she argued, "but for many, the gig economy is simply the next step in a losing effort to build some economic security in a world where all the benefits are floating to the top 10 percent." If Warren spoke for anyone, it was for adjunct faculty and for "just-in-time" and "on-demand" employees across all sectors of the economy. Policy makers like Warren continue to search for solutions to the ever-expanding adjunctification of the American workforce. And those solutions with the most promise will likely begin by recognizing the problem's origin and how social, economic, and political factors have contributed to its evolution since the postwar period.[42]

NOTES

1. Roger Geiger, "Research Universities in the Golden Age and Beyond," in his *The History of American Higher Education: Learning and Culture from the Founding to World War II* (Princeton, NJ: Princeton University Press, 2014), 491–506; John Thelin, "Gilt by Association: Higher Education's 'Golden Age,' 1945 to 1970," in his *A History of American Higher Education*, 2nd ed. (Baltimore, MD: Johns Hopkins University Press, 2011), 260–316; Malcolm Tight, "The Golden Age of Academe: Myth or Memory?" *British Journal of Educational Studies* 58 (2010): 105–16; Louis Menand, "College: The End of the Golden Age," *New York Review of Books* (Oct. 18, 2001); Richard M. Freeland, *Academia's Golden Age: Universities in Massachusetts, 1945–1970* (New York: Oxford University Press, 1992).

2. David Vacchi and Joseph Berger, "Student Veterans in Higher Education," in *Higher Education: Handbook of Theory and Research*, vol. 29, ed. Michael Paulson (Dordrecht: Springer, 2014), 96–99; Kevin Kinser, "GI Bill," in *Higher Education in the United States: An Encyclopedia*, ed. James Forest and Kevin Kinser (Santa Barbara, CA: ABC-CLIO, 2002), 276–79; V. R. Cardozier, *Colleges and Universities in World War II* (New York: Praeger, 1993), 211–29.

3. Brave New Films, *Professors in Poverty* (2015), http://www.bravenewfilms.org/professors inpoverty; "Is Academia Suffering from 'Adjunctivitis'? Low-Paid Adjunct Professors Struggle to Make Ends Meet," *PBS NewsHour* (Feb. 6, 2014), http://www.pbs.org/newshour/bb/is-academia -suffering-adjunctivitis.

4. Terry H. Anderson, *The Movement and the Sixties: Protest in America from Greensboro to Wounded Knee* (New York: Oxford University Press, 1996); Edward Berkowitz, ed., *Something Happened: A Political and Cultural Overview of the Seventies* (New York: Columbia University Press, 2007); Howard R. Bowen and Jack H. Schuster, *American Professors: A National Resource Imperiled* (New York: Oxford University Press, 1986), 176.

5. Robert Birnbaum, *Management Fads in Higher Education* (San Francisco, CA: Jossey-Bass, 2001); Bowen and Schuster, *American Professors*, 113–36.

6. Martin Filens and Benjamin I. Page, "Testing Theories of American Politics: Elites, Interest Groups, and Average Citizens," *Perspectives on Politics* 12 (2014): 564–81; Thomas Picketty, *Capital in the Twenty-First Century* (Cambridge, MA: Belknap Press at Harvard University Press, 2014); Igor Bobic, "Fed Chair Not Sure Whether to Call U.S. an Oligarchy or Democracy," *Huffington Post* (May 9, 2014), http://www.huffingtonpost.com/2014/05/09/janet-yellen-oligar chy_n_5296399.html; *Trends in the Distribution of Household Income between 1979 and 2007* (Washington, DC: Congressional Budget Office, Oct. 2011); Lawrence Summers, "Market Capitalism's Heroic Opportunity," Harvard Business School (Oct. 14, 2008), http://hbswk.hbs.edu /item/business-summit-lawrence-summers-on-market-capitalisms-historic-opportunity; Kevin Philips, *Wealth and Democracy: A Political History of the American Rich* (New York: Broadway Books, 2003); Emma Jacobs, "Workers of the Gig Economy, Unite!" *Financial Times* (Mar. 12, 2015); "New Laws for the New 'Gig Economy,'" *On Point* with Tom Ashbrook, National Public Radio (June 23, 2016); Lawrence F. Katz and Alan B. Krueger, "The Rise and Nature of Alternative Work Arrangements in the United States, 1995–2015," Mar. 29, 2016, http:// scholar.harvard.edu/files/lkatz/files/katz_krueger_cws_v3.pdf?m=1459369766.

7. Vacchi and Berger, "Student Veterans," 96–99; Kinser, "GI Bill," 276–79; Cardozier, *Colleges and Universities*, 211–29.

8. Thomas D. Snyder, ed., *120 Years of American Education: A Statistical Portrait* (Washington, DC: US Department of Education, Office of Educational Research and Improvement, 1993), 75, 83–84.

9. Phillip Lee, "The Curious Life of *In Loco Parentis* in American Universities," *Higher Education in Review* 8 (2011): 65–90; Todd Gitlin, *The Sixties: Years of Hope, Days of Rage*, rev. ed.

(New York: Bantam, 1993); William Rorabaugh, *Berkeley at War: The 1960s* (New York: Oxford University Press, 1989), 31; Robert Cohen, *Freedom's Orator: Mario Savio and the Radical Legacy of the 1960s* (New York: Oxford University Press, 2014), 459; Snyder, *120 Years*, 75, 80, 90.

10. Christopher Loss, *Between Citizens and the State: The Politics of American Higher Education in the 20th Century* (Princeton, NJ: Princeton University Press, 2014); Bowen and Schuster, *American Professors*, 176; Francis Keppel, "Higher Education Acts Contrasted, 1965–1986: Has Federal Policy Come of Age?" *Harvard Education Review* 57 (Apr. 1987): 49–68; Rupert Wilkinson, *Aiding Students, Buying Students: Financial Aid in America* (Nashville, TN: Vanderbilt University Press, 2005); Snyder, *120 Years*, 83–84.

11. Snyder, *120 Years*, 75; Michael Moffatt, *Coming of Age in New Jersey: College and American Culture* (New Brunswick, NJ: Rutgers University Press, 1989), ch. 1.

12. Bowen and Schuster, *American Professors*, 60–66. See also Emily K. Abel, *Terminal Degrees: The Job Crisis in Higher Education* (New York: Praeger, 1984); Judith Gappa and David Leslie, *The Invisible Faculty: Improving the Status of Part-Timers in Higher Education* (San Francisco, CA: Jossey-Bass, 1993).

13. Bowen and Schuster, *American Professors*, 80–112.

14. Birnbaum, *Management Fads*; Frederick Hilmer and Lex Donaldson, *Management Redeemed: Debunking the Fads That Undermine Our Corporations* (New York: Free Press, 1996); Eileen Shapiro, *Fad Surfing in the Boardroom: Managing in the Age of Instant Answers* (New York: Basic, 1996); Eric Abrahamson, "Managerial Fads and Fashions: The Diffusion and Rejection of Innovation," *Academy of Management Review* 16 (1991): 586–612.

15. Franco Gandolfi, "Unravelling Downsizing: What Do We Know about the Phenomenon?" *Review of International Comparative Management* 10 (2009): 414–26; Bob Batchelor, "The Downside of Downsizing," *History News Network* (June 28, 2004); Claire Tillman, "The 10 Biggest Corporate Layoffs of the Past Two Decades," *Fortune* (Sept. 20, 2015); Allan Sloan with Anne Underwood, "The Hit Men," *Newsweek* (Feb. 26, 1996), 44; Peter Kilborn, "New Jobs Lack the Old Security in Time of 'Disposable Workers,'" *New York Times* (Mar. 15, 1993).

16. Donald L. Thompson, "PPBS: The Need for Experience," *Journal of Higher Education* 42 (1971): 690.

17. Birnbaum, *Management Fads*, 33–61.

18. Arthur Deegan and Roger Fritz, *MBO Goes to College: Management by Objectives* (Boulder: University of Colorado, Division of Continuing Education, Bureau of Independent Studies, 1975); Birnbaum, *Management Fads*, 36–37, 82–84.

19. Daniel Seymour, *On Q: Causing Quality in Higher Education* (New York: Macmillan, 1992); Birnbaum, *Management Fads*, 97, 98–104; Daniel Seymour, *The IBM-TQM Partnership with Colleges and Universities: A Report* (Washington, DC: American Association for Higher Education, 1993); Susan Jarow and Susan Barnard, eds., *Integrating Total Quality Management in a Library Setting* (New York: Routledge, 1993), 164.

20. Jarow and Barnard, *Integrating Total Quality Management*, 164.

21. Katherine S. Mangan, "TQM: Colleges Embrace the Concept of Total Quality Management," *Chronicle of Higher Education* (Aug. 12, 1992); Richard Chait, "Colleges Should Not Be Blinded by Vision," *Chronicle of Higher Education* (Sept. 22, 1993).

22. Mangan, "TQM"; Robert Pedersen, "Letter to the Editor: The Perils of TQM for the Academy," *Chronicle of Higher Education* (Sept. 23, 1992).

23. John Curtis, *The Employment Status of Instructional Staff Members in Higher Education, Fall 2011* (Washington, DC: American Association of University Professors, 2014), 2–3, 5–6.

24. Ibid.; Bowen and Schuster, *American Professors*, 49; Abel, *Terminal Degrees*, 88; *NLRB v. Yeshiva University*, 444 US 672 (1980); Gappa and Leslie, *Invisible Faculty*, xiii.

25. Norman Caufield, *NAFTA and Labor in North America* (Urbana: University of Illinois

Press, 2009); Joseph Stiglitz, *Globalization and Its Discontents* (New York: Norton, 2002); David Bradley, *The Workforce Investment Act and the One-Stop Delivery System* (Washington, DC: Congressional Research Service, 2013); David Neumark and Deborah Reed, *Employment Relationships in the New Economy*, Working Paper 8910 (Amherst, MA: Political Economy Research Institute, 2002).

26. See, for instance, the best-selling *What Color Is Your Parachute?* series by Richard Bolles; Drew Bird and Mike Harwood, *Information Technology Careers: The Hottest Jobs for the New Millennium* (Scottsdale, AZ: Coriolis, 2000); David Leonhard, "Entrepreneurs' 'Golden Age' Is Fading in Economic Boom," *New York Times* (Dec. 1, 2000); Chris Brenner, *Work in the New Economy: Flexible Labor Markets in Silicon Valley* (Malden, MA: Blackwell, 2002); John Cassidy, *Dot Con: How America Lost Its Mind and Money in the Internet Era* (New York: Harper Perennial, 2003); Zack O'Malley Greenburg, "How Millennials Can Survive and Thrive in the New Economy," *Forbes* (Nov. 16, 2011); Robert Pear, "Doctors Assert There Are Too Many of Them," *New York Times* (Mar. 1, 1997); Lincoln Caplan, "An Existential Crisis for Law Schools," *New York Times* (July 14, 2012).

27. William Lazonick, "The Financialization of the U.S. Corporation: What Has Been Lost, and How It Can Be Regained," *Seattle University Law Review* 36 (2013): 857–909; Özgür Orhangazi, *Financialization and Capital Accumulation in the Non-Financial Corporate Sector: A Theoretical and Empirical Investigation of the U.S. Economy, 1973–2003*, Working Paper 149 (Amherst, MA: Political Economy Research Institute, 2007); Greta R. Krippner, "The Financialization of the American Economy," *Socio-Economic Review* 3 (2005): 173–208; Gerald Epstein, ed., *Financialization and the World Economy* (Northampton, MA: Edward Elgar, 2005); Hans-Werner Sinn, *Casino Capitalism: How the Financial Crisis Came About and What Needs to Be Done Now* (New York: Oxford University Press, 2012); Susan Strange, *Casino Capitalism* (1986; repr., Manchester, England: Manchester University Press, 2016).

28. A. J. Angulo, "Capital," in his *Diploma Mills: How For-Profit Colleges Stiffed Students, Taxpayers, and the American Dream* (Baltimore, MD: Johns Hopkins University Press, 2016), 109–32; Phillip W. Magness, "For-Profit Universities and the Roots of Adjunctification in US Higher Education," *Liberal Education* 102 (Spring 2016), https://www.aacu.org/liberaleducation/2016/spring/magness.

29. Angulo, *Diploma Mills*, 109–15; Michael Stratford, "Pointing a Finger at For-Profits," *Inside Higher Ed* (Sept. 11, 2015).

30. John Sperling, *Rebel with a Cause: The Entrepreneur Who Created the University of Phoenix and the For-Profit Revolution in Higher Education* (New York: Wiley, 2000); Leif Edvinsson, *Corporate Longitude: What You Need to Know to Navigate the Knowledge Economy* (New York: Prentice Hall, 2002); Paul Fain, "Digital Pink Slips," *Inside Higher Ed* (Jan. 29, 2013); Angulo, *Diploma Mills*, 115–23; Chris Kirkham, "With Goldman's Foray into Higher Education, a Predatory Pursuit of Students and Revenues," *Huffington Post* (Dec. 14, 2011), http://www.huffingtonpost.com/2011/10/14/goldman-sachs-for-profit-college_n_997409.html; Caroline Howard, "Donald Trump University Lawsuit Is Lesson for All For-Profit Colleges," *Forbes* (Aug. 27, 2013); Mina Kimes and Michael Smith, "Laureate, a For-Profit Education Firm, Finds International Success (with a Clinton's Help)," *Washington Post* (Jan. 18, 2014).

31. See *For Profit Higher Education: The Failure to Safeguard the Federal Investment and Ensure Student Success, Prepared by the Committee on Health, Education, Labor, and Pensions, United States Senate*, 4 vols. (Washington, DC: US Government Printing Office, 2012) for information about adjunct personnel and expenditures.

32. *United States ex rel. Gatsiopoulos et al. v. Kaplan*, 09-CV-21720-PAS (S.D. Fla. 2011); "Fear and Frustration: Faculty and For-Profit Colleges," *Chronicle of Higher Education* (July 10, 2011); Angulo, *Diploma Mills*, 122–32, 135–37.

33. "Eastern Michigan University Lecturers Demand Unionization," *Chronicle of Higher*

Education (Apr. 2, 1999); Alison Schneider, "Full-Time Lecturers at Eastern Michigan U. Win Right to Unionize," *Chronicle of Higher Education* (Feb. 11, 2000); Alison Schneider, "Adjuncts at Roosevelt U. Vote to Unionize," *Chronicle of Higher Education* (Apr. 14, 2000); "Agreement between Roosevelt University and the Roosevelt Adjunct Faculty," Roosevelt Adjunct Faculty Organization, IEA-NEA, 2013–2017," https://offices.depaul.edu/oaa/faculty-resources/adjunct -union-organizing/Documents/Roosevelt%20Contract.pdf.

34. Courtney Leatherman, "Scholars and Activists Approve a Fair-Labor Code for Their Universities," *Chronicle of Higher Education* (Nov. 20, 2000); Courtney Leatherman, "Union Organizers Propose Code of University Conduct," *Chronicle of Higher Education* (Dec. 1, 2000). As Timothy Cain points out in chapter 3 in this volume, adjunct faculty had been present in faculty unions throughout the twentieth century, but their concerns were often overshadowed by those of tenure-line faculty.

35. Courtney Leatherman, "Part-Time Faculty Members Try to Organize Nationally," *Chronicle of Higher Education* (Jan. 26, 2001).

36. Scott Smallwood, "Continuing-Ed Instructors Vote to Join Union at UMass-Boston," *Chronicle of Higher Education* (July 15, 2001); Piper Fogg, "Some Adjunct Faculty Members at Western Michigan U. Win Right to Earn Tenure," *Chronicle of Higher Education* (Nov. 4, 2002); "Some Adjuncts at Western Michigan U. Win Right to Tenure," *Chronicle of Higher Education* (Nov. 15, 2002); Scott Smallwood, "Non-Tenure-Track Faculty Members Vote to Unionize at U. of Michigan," *Chronicle of Higher Education* (Apr. 30, 2003); Scott Smallwood, "American Federation of Teachers Approves Standards for Treatment of Adjuncts," *Chronicle of Higher Education* (July 22, 2002); Scott Smallwood, "Faculty Union Issues Standards for Treatment of Adjuncts," *Chronicle of Higher Education* (Aug. 2, 2002).

37. James Kwak and Simon Johnson, *13 Bankers: The Wall Street Takeover and the Next Financial Meltdown* (New York: Pantheon, 2010); "Buffett Warns on Investment 'Time Bomb,'" *BBC News* (Mar. 4, 2003), http://news.bbc.co.uk/2/hi/2817995.stm; Gillian Tett, *Fool's Gold: The Inside Story of J. P. Morgan and How Wall St. Greed Corrupted Its Bold Dream and Created a Financial Catastrophe* (New York: Free Press, 2010); Jonathan Weisman and Eric Lipton, "In New Congress, Wall St. Pushes to Undermine Dodd-Frank Reform," *New York Times* (Jan. 13, 2015); Lynnley Browning, "Too Big to Tax: Settlements Are Tax Write-Offs for Banks," *News-week* (Oct. 27, 2014); Ed Vulliamy, "How a Big US Bank Laundered Billions from Mexico's Murderous Drug Gangs," *Guardian* (Apr. 2, 2011); Nicole Hong, "Banks Dealt Blow in Libor Lawsuits," *Wall Street Journal* (May 23, 2016).

38. Janet Byrne, *The Occupy Handbook* (New York: Back Bay Books, 2012); Catherine Rampell, "Comparing the Job Losses in Financial Crises," *New York Times* (Sept. 25, 2012), http://economix.blogs.nytimes.com/2012/09/25/comparing-the-job-losses-in-financial-crises.

39. Arun Sundararajan, *The Sharing Economy: The End of Employment and the Rise of Crowd-Based Capitalism* (Cambridge, MA: MIT Press, 2016); Katz and Krueger, "Rise and Na-ture of Alternative Work Arrangements"; "Intuit Forecast: 7.6 Million People in On-Demand Economy by 2020," *BusinessWire* (Aug. 13, 2015), http://www.businesswire.com/news/home /20150813005317/en.

40. For statistics on the rise of contingent faculty employment from 1989 to 2011, see appen-dix table 2 in this volume. Also see Dan Carnevale, "In an Online First, More than 50 Kaplan U. Professors Back Creation of a Faculty Union," *Chronicle of Higher Education* (Mar. 15, 2006); Dan Carnevale, "Kaplan U. Professors Seek Faculty Union," *Chronicle of Higher Education* (Mar. 24, 2006); Scott Jaschik, "Union Push in For-Profit Higher Ed," *Inside Higher Ed* (May 24, 2010); Collen Flaherty, "Union Target: For-Profits," *Inside Higher Ed* (Apr. 21, 2014); Rebecca Burns, "Kaplan Teachers Win Contract, Proving For-Profit Ed Can Be Unionized," *In These Times* (Apr. 17, 2014); Colleen Flaherty, "$15,000 per Course?" *Inside Higher Ed* (Feb. 9, 2015).

41. Magness, "For-Profit Universities"; Stephanie Gleason, "Corinthian Colleges Files for

Chapter 11 Bankruptcy," *Wall Street Journal* (May 4, 2015); "ITT Tech Is Preparing to File for Bankruptcy," *Fortune* (Sept. 15, 2016).

42. Elizabeth Warren, "Strengthening the Basic Bargain for Workers in the Modern Economy," speech at the New America Annual Conference, Washington, DC, May 19, 2016.

chapter 2

Understanding the Need for Unions

Contingent Faculty Working Conditions and the Relationship to Student Learning

ADRIANNA KEZAR AND TOM DEPAOLA

Joan Williams is a new contingent faculty member in the Department of Chemistry. She graduated two years ago and couldn't find a tenure-track job. She's now working in industry but still applying for full-time faculty work. In the interim, she's teaching part-time to get some experience. She was hired by Sunny State to teach an introductory chemistry course two weeks before the start of classes. She tried to get a copy of the syllabus, but all the department staff could find was an older copy they thought might be helpful. The text-book looks less than adequate, but she can't find any faculty to ask whether this is a good textbook or not, and the department already ordered it for the class. She missed the orientation but found some material online related to current student policies to cut and paste into her syllabus. On the first day of class, she couldn't find parking because the department failed to provide her information about getting a permit, and now she's late. The room doesn't have the basic supplies she had hoped for, so she adjusts her plan for class on the fly. The projector doesn't work, so she tells the students her slides will be posted on Blackboard, once the department gets her portion of the site up. The staff have promised it will be available any day. Class ends, and a student tells her the syllabus is covering materials they already covered last term. Joan apologizes and says she will update the syllabus. She knew that using an old syllabus was a risk; she will have to get a copy of Chemistry 101 and a current copy of Chemistry 102. Another student asks to meet with her and asks where her office is—but she doesn't have one and isn't sure what to say next. A third student, who has a learning disability, says he's confused about some material in her syllabus. Whew!—this is not the way she wanted to start the semester.

Joan hopes things will get better, but she suspects there are more surprises ahead. She can't help but think that she's not doing her best job and that the students are being shortchanged.

This story is one of many that one of the coauthors (Kezar) has collected in her research with contingent faculty members. It reflects the reality that as the numbers of contingent faculty have risen, few institutions have examined the ramifications of policies and practices related to this population. As a result, practices that would support contingent faculty remain nonexistent while those that have been proven to be detrimental to faculty and students alike continue to be utilized in their hiring and deployment. In terms of poor practices, as this story suggests, routine last-minute hiring means contingent faculty have limited or no preparation time and no standard materials about courses and students, leaving these faculty out on a limb. This story also highlights how contingent faculty often receive little or no orientation, mentoring, feedback, resources, or office space and are excluded from governance, including information about institutional and departmental learning goals. This state of affairs persists in part because of the lack of a standard set of thoughtful policies and practices to guide the use of contingent labor in the academy. We highlight Joan Williams, a part-time adjunct, for whom the situation is most dire. While contingent faculty of all stripes share some working conditions (both full-time and part-time can be terminated at will and receive lower, though varied, compensation), full-time adjuncts often enjoy access to an office, resources, information, and colleagues that are out of reach for part-time instructors, resulting in inequitable and difficult working conditions.

Researchers have documented how the rise in numbers of non-tenure-track faculty (NTTF) is resulting in negative outcomes for students—including lower graduation and retention rates, and less ability to transfer between two-year and four-year institutions.[1] Other studies document the lack of student-centered and high-quality teaching among contingent faculty compared to full-time and tenured faculty.[2]

Research published in 2013 by Kezar demonstrates how the combination of poor working conditions and lack of any supportive infrastructure has led to a phenomenon called "lack of opportunity to perform," essentially creating an environment in which contingent faculty are barred from educating to their potential and frequently experience burnout from overcompensating for their poor working conditions.[3] Joan's story clearly adheres to this pattern. It is becoming evident that the poor working conditions and lack of basic support for faculty is indeed reshaping the instructional environment for students in ways that affect the quality of learning and the overall mission of the enterprise of higher education. This chapter reviews how these various working conditions create different cultures within departments/institutions that shape faculty performance.

Unions have provided a venue, however imperfect, for rectifying or at least mitigating these poor working conditions and moving colleges and universities back to providing quality learning environments. The aim of this chapter is not to evaluate the effect of unionization on faculty working conditions, but rather to outline some key working conditions that unions ought to focus on as they seek to assert their relevance in the struggle to improve the learning environment for students and to win opportunities for all faculty to perform to their potential. Single, quick-fix practice or policy tweaks cannot be the source of change; the times call for a deeper and more wholesale reorientation of values and a thoughtful combination of policies and practices that will durably support conditions for teaching efficacy for NTTF and the success of students in every form of higher education.

Rise in the Numbers of Non-Tenure-Track Faculty

Non-tenure-track faculty are not a new phenomenon, since they have always been part of the higher education enterprise. The slow but steady rise of this workforce is linked to the fact that not much consideration had ever been given to this class of academic laborers. Policies were never created to guide their use because institutional managers preferred having the utility and flexibility to shift resources away from instruction, reassured by the fact that they had not heard many people raising concerns about contingent faculty's working conditions. Because these faculty had existed on campuses for so long without an apparent need for formal procedures, as their numbers increased there was little urgency to address how their growth might be impacting campuses and whether there was a need for new policies. Interviews with long-time adjuncts reveal situations like the following:

> I have been teaching here for 35 years. When I started, I had lots of relationships with the other faculty—I was one of two adjuncts in a department of 20 faculty. The other faculty reached out to mentor me, invited me to their house[s] for curriculum discussions, my schedule was set a year out for teaching, and I felt like part of a family. As the numbers grew—now I am one of 16 adjuncts in a department of 24 faculty—I no longer know any of the faculty. I never know

when I am teaching, classes get canceled [at the] last minute, I do not know the department goals or philosophy anymore. I decided I am not teaching anymore, it has just gotten horrible. It is really in the last ten years things got really bad—but I had this long history with the institution so I just put up with it, but not anymore.[4]

This shift over time—where a few adjuncts went from feeling they were part of a team or family to being only one of a large army of adjuncts with little connection to the department—has been described over and over. The increase in contingent faculty with poor working conditions has arguably reached a point of critical mass, creating a serious strain on institutional arrangements and taking an increasingly unbearable toll on faculty themselves.

A look at the change in numbers reveals a dramatic increase by the turn of the twenty-first century. In 1969, tenured and tenure-track positions made up approximately 78 percent of the faculty, and non-tenure-track positions were about 22 percent.[5] Forty years later these proportions had nearly flipped: in 2011 tenured and tenure-track faculty had declined to 29.2 percent, and 70.8 percent of faculty were ineligible for tenure. Of the non-tenure-track positions, 37.8 percent were full-time and 62.2 percent were part-time.[6]

Part-time faculty have experienced the most significant rate of growth since the mid-twentieth century. That population increased by 422 percent between 1970 and 2003, compared to an increase of only 70.7 percent for all full-time faculty, both tenure-track and non-tenure-track.[7] While part-time faculty are often characterized as a homogeneous class of employees, they are actually a heterogeneous group. Judith Gappa and David Leslie created a typology to describe this population, identifying four broad categories: career-enders; specialists, experts, and professionals; aspiring academics; and freelancers.[8] This heterogeneity, coupled with the lack of visibility of part-time faculty, has often led institutions to refrain from creating explicit policies related to contingent employment and support.

In 1969, full-time NTTF made up only 3.2 percent of the faculty.[9] Unlike the part-time faculty population, the number of full-time non-tenure-track faculty did not increase significantly until the early 1990s. Schuster and Finkelstein in 2006 reported that by 1993 NTTF were a majority of new full-time hires, outpacing tenure-track positions, and they reached 18 percent of all faculty by 2003.[10] While the proportion has continued to rise, it appears to have somewhat stabilized, increasing to just 19.4 percent in 2011.[11] In 2001 Baldwin and Chronister were among the first to point out that this group

Percentage Distribution of Instructional Staff by Type of Higher Education Institution, 2011

Type of institution	Part-time faculty	Full-time non-tenure-track faculty	Graduate assistants	Full-time tenured/tenure-track faculty
Research / doctorate granting	20	15	40	26
Master's universities	50	12	8	29
Private baccalaureate	42	18	0	40
Public associate's	70	14	0	16
For-profit	72	26	1	1

Source: John Curtis, *The Employment Status of Instructional Staff Members in Higher Education, Fall 2011* (Washington, DC: American Association of University Professors, 2014).
Note: Columns may not add up to 100 percent due to rounding.

even existed on campus. In fact, they continue to be downplayed or overlooked in discussions of NTTF. Baldwin and Chronister established a typology to better understand full-time non-tenure-track faculty based on the terms of their employment and specific responsibilities as teachers, researchers, administrators, and other academic professionals. They found that this kind of worker was increasingly being used for research positions in medical schools and hard sciences, for example.[12]

The shift in employment can be seen across institutional type—in research universities, in public and private comprehensive universities, in baccalaureate and community colleges—as well as across disciplines. While non-tenure-track faculty were initially based in the humanities, they now have a formidable presence in all disciplines, including mathematics, biology, chemistry, psychology, and sociology.[13] In 2011, NTTF accounted for a significant part of the faculty regardless of institutional type, though some variation is documented based on mission, priorities, and needs (table 2.1).[14]

The Impact of the Rise in NTTF on Student Learning

As the number of non-tenure-track faculty has swelled, various studies have tried to identify if and to what extent this shift is impacting student learning and success. For instance, research by the Delphi Project on the Changing Faculty and Student Success has documented some negative outcomes for students related to retention, graduation, transfer, and performance.[15] Collectively these studies provide a wake-up call for higher education that ignoring NTTF is having an impact. Although not discussed here, there are also many other negative effects of this shift, such as increased service and leadership duties for a dwindling number of tenure-track faculty, strain on shared governance, issues with curriculum development and a lack of faculty who know and can support curricular integrity and innovation, and lapses in institutional memory about key practices that support the learning environment.

Given the national urgency for increasing graduation rates, the negative impact on graduation and retention rates from increased course taking with adjuncts, particularly part-timers, should serve as an alarm and be of particular concern to institutional leaders. Ehrenberg and Zhang in 2004 and Eagan and Jaeger in 2009 found that graduation rates declined as proportions of NTTF increased.[16] Increases in part-timers have an even more pronounced impact on graduation rates and retention.[17] Harrington and Schibik published research in 2001 that tied lower retention to a disproportionate reliance on contingent faculty.[18] A study in 2017 by Ran and Xu with a state-wide data set and perhaps one of the most ambitious designs to date demonstrated that adjuncts, particularly those on short-term contracts with tenuous associations with the departments where they teach, negatively impact student performance in future courses, majoring in an area of study, and persistence in both two-year and four-year institutions.[19] In 2010 Bettinger and Long also found that younger NTTF produced more distinct negative effects, as did those in the sciences and humanities.[20] In contrast and to be fair, they also found that NTTF in technical and professional fields, including business and architecture, had a somewhat positive effect on student outcomes, yet this hardly mitigates the larger picture of learning degradation.

Another pertinent concern in higher education is the rising imperative to improve transfer between two-year and four-year institutions, particularly in connection to the need to graduate more minority and low-income students. Studies have found that students at two-year colleges that had more full-time, tenured faculty were more likely to transfer to four-year institutions.[21] In 2009, Gross and Goldhaber found a 4 percent increase in transfers to four-year institutions per 10 percent increase in the proportion of tenured faculty.[22] Similarly, Eagan and Jaeger found that increased proportions of part-time faculty were correlated with lower transfer rates.[23]

Studies also suggest that exposure to more part-time faculty can be particularly problematic in early courses in the first year, when students are still adjusting to college. In a study of college freshmen, Harrington and Schibik found that increased exposure to part-time faculty was significantly associated with lower second-semester retention rates, lower GPAs, and fewer attempted credit hours.[24] Bettinger and Long also reported that early exposure impeded students' timely selection of a major.[25]

Most studies highlight the substantial effects of the diminished time and quality of student-faculty interaction. Contact time and personal interaction between traditional faculty and students has been shown to foster student success. Unsurprisingly, researchers suggest the inverse with regard to NTTF, arguing that the inaccessibility of part-time faculty to students due to time pressures, lack of office space, and the frequent need to hold jobs at multiple locations has a proportionally negative effect on student outcomes.[26]

Furthermore, repeated studies have identified that adjuncts (often with little choice) use less engaging and student-centered pedagogies, spend less time preparing for class, and have fewer office hours, which they further may not be able to offer at a predictable time or location, stymieing students from getting advisement and building rapport.[27] Other studies have shown that adjuncts use fewer practices that are related to reliably fostering student success and learning, including active and collaborative learning strategies, culturally responsive teaching, and crafting challenging assignments that set high expectations for students while providing adequate levels of support.[28]

Several of these researchers have hypothesized that the poor working conditions of NTTF impact student learning conditions, but there is limited evidence to guide questions about whether changes in policy can make a difference or how institutional and departmental policies affect student outcomes.[29] Lest this scholarship lead to a foisting of blame on individual deficiencies among NTTF, it is important to note that none of the studies contend that non-tenure-track faculty themselves are responsible for lower student outcomes. Until recently we had little direct evidence to understand why these negative outcomes were attributable to NTTF, particularly part-time adjuncts where the findings are most pronounced. Kezar in 2013 documented the direct ways that institutional and departmental policies impact NTTF's opportunity to perform, and she discussed policies that need to be changed in order to improve student success.[30]

Problematic Working Conditions

Some policies and practices have been clearly identified in numerous studies over the years to be detrimental to learning. Studies in 2013 and 2014 by Kezar directly linked these negative policies to ways that faculty themselves describe the impacts on their performance.[31] Commentators on academic labor often quip that "faculty working conditions are student learning conditions." This slogan neatly captures what has been consistently documented in research since the 1990s: a clear relationship exists between the performance constraints imposed on a majority of the instructional force through sub-optimal conditions, and the negative outcomes associated with students who are unable to connect with their professors.

Last-Minute Hiring

In the opening anecdote in this chapter, Joan Williams's many obstacles to performing well (a livable wage, security, benefits, access to needed resources, etc.) were further compounded by the fact that she had only two weeks to fully prepare. In one survey of contingent faculty, two-thirds reported routinely receiving three weeks or less notice that they were teaching a class.[32] A large number, 38 percent, reported instances of less than two weeks to prepare for a course. These national data confirmed earlier studies of a smaller set of institutions where instances of last-minute hiring were reported as routine. Being hired at the last minute leaves little time to prepare for the term ahead by doing things such as updating course readings, defining learning goals, and developing a course plan, assuming instructors are allowed to make such decisions. In their study of part-time faculty, Gappa and Leslie in 1993 noted, "Recruitment and hiring set the tone for employment relations with part-time faculty because they are frequently the first contact between the institution and the part-timer (or non-tenure-track faculty member)."[33]

Most studies agree that colleges have no formal or systemized process for recruitment or hiring and approach the hiring of non-tenure-track faculty very casually. Researchers have found that faculty regard last-minute hiring as perhaps one of the most pernicious policies. It not only allows little if any time for course preparation, but also generally denies these faculty any opportunity to receive a formal orientation to the institution, department, colleagues, and campus policies, especially those related to instruction, grading, and students.[34] Last-minute scheduling often means they have no time to update a previously taught course, and if it is a new course with some unfamiliar material, they have no choice but to learn it alongside their students.[35] In 2013 Kezar also found that last-minute hiring precludes collaborative course scheduling. Because NTTF usually have not been hired when class schedules are created, the various class sections needing last-minute coverage can lead to wildly erratic teaching schedules that create additional commuting hardships (especially when multiple employers are involved), impacting adjunct instructors' capacity to arrive on time, to be adequately prepared, and to schedule meetings with students.[36]

Contract Renewal and Job Security

Various surveys have identified job security as one of the top concerns of existing full- and part-time NTTF.[37] To start, a persistent lack of long-term commitment from an employer can be demoralizing for professionals who regularly invest time, energy, and resources in an institution and its students.[38] Baldwin and Chronister found in 2001 that one year was the most common contract length across all institution types for full-time non-tenure-track faculty, with a limited number of institutions using multiyear contracts for these appointments.[39] As is often the case though, part-time faculty experience even more vulnerability, and while they may be hired on an ongoing basis, they typically have to be rehired each term and are informed of their reappointment only a few days before the semester begins.[40] Contract policies that provide no job security for part-time faculty result in high turnover and neglect the importance of preparation, faculty development, and quality of teaching. In effect this means the ongoing placement of teachers who, despite extensive experience on a campus, have little knowledge of their particular students, institution, and department.[41] The persistent lack of job security created by policies that constantly undermine stable employment for most of the instructional workforce fails to create conditions conducive for improving performance.

Working at Multiple Institutions

Contingent faculty describe the psychic tolls of constantly starting up at new institutions with new classes, and a never-ending cycle of diminished confidence that they will achieve success in their role. In Kezar's 2013 research, part-time faculty reported that commuting struggles impacted course time and occasionally led to class cancellation, and they also described a deeper burden of having to psychologically and physically be in so many places, each with different rules and norms that impacted classroom instruction: "The psychic burden is huge. Commute, different parking, different computer and system, different population of students, different course requirements and set up, different learning goals, different administrators and colleagues to keep up with and it makes it very difficult to be present and not fully exhausted when you meet with students. There is no real way to measure or quantify the effect and it would be hard to study the impact, but as a teacher doing it, you know it impacts your energy, presence, sense of coherence, clarity."[42]

Many of these issues are not readily apparent to someone who does not confront them regularly, and they often remain hidden in policy discussions. Meanwhile the cumulative toll of even mundane challenges like navigating institution-specific instructional and administrative platforms, managing online credentials, and correcting computer problems can quickly become overwhelming when faculty are dealing with multiple institutions and are constrained by time and space.

Orientation

Various studies have noted that non-tenure-track faculty, both part-time and full-time, are often excluded from orientation programs and workshops that are made available to other faculty and staff that convey important human resources information, provide training for work roles, and create spaces for constructive reflection and review of policies.[43] Only a small fraction of institutions distribute a handbook to NTTF, and some claim to rely on department chairs to offer a sort of welcome and socialization, although this often does not occur.[44] Orientation programming for NTTF is critical for imparting a range of know-how, including basic information on how to use classroom technology, how to guide students to different campus supports, how to communicate to students about departmental and institutional requirements or learning objectives, and how students' backgrounds and demographics shape the instructional mission and strategy, all of which could equip these faculty to more effectively support students.[45]

Professional Development

From the moment they are first hired and throughout their employment, NTTF typically lack access to mentoring, professional development programs, and funding for training and to attend conferences to support their growth as educators.[46] Non-tenure-track faculty are also routinely excluded from (or simply not invited to participate in) professional development practices that address teaching and assessment. Withholding access to professional development hinders NTTF's ability to make use of effective pedagogical strategies that inform the development of course and learning goals and the sequencing of concepts.[47] The ongoing practice of ineffective or outdated pedagogies, sustained as a by-product of an uncritical dependence on under-resourced contingent labor, creates obstacles to the intellectual stimulation of students, which can diminish their enthusiasm for learning and discourage them from connecting to course materials and topics. Without professional development or mentoring, adjunct faculty rarely receive feedback on their teaching practices.[48] This often leaves them with no sense of whether their teaching is effective and unaware of the type of professional development from which their practice could benefit.

Exclusion from Curriculum Design

Another major concern for non-tenure-track faculty is the way their teaching can be highly circumscribed by the fact that they have little if any input into curriculum design and implementation.[49] In many cases adjuncts are hired to teach "cookie-cutter" courses with predesigned lessons, a practice that reinforces the already low regard for NTTF by reducing them to warm bodies reading a script. Their skills are treated as comparable to those of a fast food worker; postsecondary instruction is valued by virtue of the efficiency with which "content" can be delivered at the lowest cost. The lack of involvement in curricular development, syllabus construction, textbook selection, and other decisions affects adjunct faculty's morale, status, and efficacy as professionals.[50] Thus whether or not they are hired with adequate time to prepare to teach, NTTF are already barred from engaging in essential dialogue and decision-making about the very content they deliver. Many are not copied on departmental communications or invited to faculty meetings where discussion of broader curricular goals and plans for pursuing them take place among faculty. As a result, NTTF, whose knowledge about the subjects they teach is comparable to that of tenure-track faculty, are restricted from making meaningful contributions to academic and curricular planning. They may even be asked to teach courses using another instructor's syllabus and materials or course plans that have not been updated or are misaligned with current institutional learning goals.[51]

By preventing non-tenure-track faculty from participating in curriculum design or by imposing rigid, prefabricated course guidelines, department chairs and others may be forgoing utilization of the expertise and talents NTTF bring, leading to courses created without students' capabilities and interests in mind, the adoption of textbooks that do not serve learning objectives, having to work with goals and courses that are misaligned, and missed opportunities for capturing and cultivating the unique strengths of NTTF.[52] When contingent faculty are excluded from departmental communications, such as emails or meetings, their contact with tenured faculty may be scarce or nonexistent, meaning they enjoy no professional dialogue. The absence of an inclusive conversation about courses and the curriculum creates the opportunity for instruction and teaching materials to unwittingly become misaligned with the objectives and policies officially established by the department or institution.[53]

Inadequate Resources

It would be naïve to believe that faculty do not need access to instructional resources, space on campus, and administrative or support personnel in order to be successful as instructors. Yet the existence of these resources for individual NTTF on a campus or in an academic unit is highly uneven,[54] and as already mentioned, basic resources and support are often missing. Faculty needs may vary, but certain basics are universally helpful, such as sufficient office space for preparing the day's lessons, grading papers, meeting with students and colleagues, and attending to other responsibilities, for instance managing graduate assistants or arranging field placements.[55] Like any other faculty, they need a bare minimum of clerical support to assist with instructional and administrative duties, and they also need access to a computer, photocopier, projector, phone, fax machine, and other basic office equipment. Consistently having to make do with inadequate materials and equipment affects class preparation and organization and discourages instructors from designing activities that depend on institutional assistance. A lack of office space also reduces faculty members' opportunities to brainstorm with or seek advice from colleagues, effectively preventing them from building professional networks and social capital that could enhance courses and instructional quality.[56]

Since part-time faculty may find it difficult to be on campus when they are not teaching, and many teach evening classes, they may never have the opportunity to utilize support services provided by the university or department personnel who only work during regular business hours.[57] When access to resources and staff is not ensured, non-tenure-track faculty have little recourse but to procure their own resources, go without them, or get creative in finding alternatives. This arbitrary encumbrance steals time away from teaching and supporting students.[58] Unlike their tenure-track counterparts, NTTF do not usually have the power to appoint teaching assistants to help with coursework, which can be particularly challenging for those teaching large classes. Often they are simply expected to personally handle every aspect of a course without assistance, regardless of the number of students enrolled.[59]

Many more practices remain in use that are problematic, including poor to no processes of evaluation by department heads; the high-stakes use of student evaluations, which confine instructors to a "customer satisfaction" model of teaching; a lack of involvement in campus-wide governance; and last-minute course cancellation without remuneration. This sample of items at the very least provides a clear link between faculty working conditions and the quality of the student learning environment. In addition, these working conditions are becoming ingrained into campus cultures, deeply entrenching a systemically undersupportive learning environment into the structures of academic programs and institutions.

Research also indicates that these conditions are increasingly causing depression, anxiety, and other forms of psychological suffering among NTTF.[60] This compounds all of the problems already outlined, as faculty resilience is eroded by sustained exposure to negative conditions, in addition to the mental stress already wrought by unstable, insufficient income and a lack of insurance or other benefits. A somewhat perverse set of circumstances has been observed whereby contingent faculty who identify with and are committed to the campuses they work for are precisely the ones most injured by the stress generated by negative working conditions.[61] We discuss this more extensively in the next section, but it is worth noting that this sense of commitment is one of the qualities that enable professors to excel in their performance, and yet the current paradigm frequently discourages it.

Unfortunately, altering policies and practices alone is insufficient, because it does not address the underlying values of faculty or departmental chairs and staff. Research suggests that underlying values are what drive the success or failure of new policies, and if values remain unexamined and unchanged then toxic working conditions for NTTF are likely to persist.[62] Policy implementation is complicated and can lag or dilute the original policy to the point of irrelevance, and a critical reevaluation of one's own practice is hard to compel with only a superficial mandate. Thus, addressing the values at the root of practice—how other faculty fundamentally conceive of and regard their non-tenure-track colleagues—is critical to the establishment and maintenance of working conditions that affirm the basic dignity of contingent academic labor.

Opportunity to Perform: Departmental Cultures of Success or Failure

In 1982 Blumberg and Pringle suggested that to thoroughly understand workers' performance, it is important to understand their capacity, willingness, and opportunity to perform. "Capacity to perform" is defined as a worker's background knowledge, skills, intelligence, and level of education. "Willingness to perform" is defined as a worker's motivation, satisfaction, attitude, and feelings of equity at work. "Opportunity to perform" is defined as the set of conditions that facilitate successful work, including necessary resources, required equipment, appropriate materials, the actions of coworkers, leader behavior, mentoring, and organizational policies, rules, procedures, norms, and information. Opportunity to perform is most heavily influenced by the organization, which also shapes capacity but to a lesser degree.[63]

In studies of non-tenure-track faculty, four cultures have been identified within departments that affect the faculty's opportunity to perform: destructive, neutral or invisible, inclusive, and learning. Each of these cultures shapes a very different learning environment for students and represents a different set of values related to NTTF. These four cultures impact NTTF's willingness to perform at a high level, their capacity, and their opportunities to create a high-quality teaching and learning environment.[64]

In the destructive culture, non-tenure-track faculty perceive disrespect and hostility from their tenure-track colleagues. They are actively excluded from professional development activities and departmental meetings, and their role is not perceived as a professional one. The hiring of NTTF in the destructive culture is haphazard, random, and last-minute, with little attention given to matching faculty with courses in their area of expertise or to accommodating their schedules if they also teach at other institutions. The salary and benefits for NTTF are grossly inequitable. They are not given the resources they need to succeed, such as an orientation to campus; mentoring from other faculty; office space or supplies; advance access to syllabi, curricula, and learning goals; or information to correctly advise students. While research has found that the purely destructive culture is less common than the other cultures discussed here, it does exist in pockets on most campuses.[65]

In the neutral or invisible culture, NTTF perceive no respect or inclusion from their departmental colleagues; while there is no active disrespect, NTTF are typically ignored or treated as temporary teachers or mechanisms for content delivery. Contingent faculty in the neutral/invisible culture are typically not included in faculty meetings or professional development. Hiring is generally random and last-minute, though occasionally some intentionality may occur around hiring someone with specific subject matter expertise. Pay is generally inequitable, and NTTF preferences are typically not taken into account when scheduling courses. In the neutral/invisible culture, NTTF may have some basic office supplies and equipment and access to some type of office space that allows them to perform their basic teaching function; however, it is unlikely that they receive orientation to campus policies, mentoring from other faculty, or formal evaluations, and they have no significant input into course syllabi, textbooks, or curricula. Research indicates that most academic departments have a neutral/invisible culture.[66]

In the inclusive culture, NTTF perceive that they are respected and included by their departmental colleagues. They are typically invited to attend faculty meetings and events and are included in on-campus professional development activities. Contingent faculty in the inclusive culture are acknowledged as professionals, though often in another profession or job (e.g., lawyer, businessperson). Attempts are made in the inclusive culture to approach equity in the salaries of tenure-track and non-tenure-track faculty. Hiring typically occurs intentionally to select people with the best expertise for a particular course; the scheduling of courses occurs in advance of the beginning of the semester and typically includes NTTF input. In the inclusive culture, NTTF typically have shared office space on campus and the basic materials and equipment to do their jobs. They generally receive a formal or informal orientation to campus policies and are sometimes given input into their course syllabi or textbooks. Yet, the policies and practices are not created in ways that reflect NTTF's contribution to the learning environment. There is no formal understanding of how certain practices negatively impact (or could positively impact) student learning. An inclusive culture helps NTTF feel better about their work, even if they are not always able to translate this to improved performance.[67]

In the learning culture, NTTF perceive a positive atmosphere of respect and inclusion; they are treated as professional equals by their tenure-track colleagues. In the learning culture, policies and practices are developed for the purpose of supporting NTTF's role in creating a positive and effective learning environment. They are invited and encouraged to attend faculty meetings and events, and they are given opportunities to participate in on-campus and off-campus professional development activities. Department chairs in the learning culture actively work to promote equity in salary and benefits for NTTF. Hiring is thoughtful and intentional to select faculty with the teaching and professional expertise for each course. Hiring occurs well in advance of the beginning of the semester, and openings are few since turnover is low in the learning culture. Scheduling is done collaboratively to ensure that NTTF are well prepared to teach their courses and to minimize any scheduling conflicts. Contingent faculty in the learning culture share office space with colleagues who teach similar courses, allowing for collaboration and discussion around teaching and learning. They receive a formal orientation to campus, formal or informal mentoring, evaluations, and feedback. Supplies are pro-actively acquired by the department chair, and NTTF are always given input into syllabi, textbooks, and curricula. Non-tenure-track faculty in the learning culture are often asked to participate in campus governance or play a departmental leadership role.[68]

Departments can craft an environment and a set of working conditions that allow NTTF to perform optimally and can work to foster such environments. But to do so requires self-assessment and leadership.

Conclusion

In the opening of this chapter, we sketched the experience of Joan Williams, whose impediments to performing well at her job and building a fulfilling professional career are all too typical of the experience of contingent faculty across the postsecondary spectrum. The accumulated disadvantages she must consistently weather are intimately familiar to a great swath of academic laborers, and the simple truth is that conditions are unlikely to change without organized collective action. As Joan finds other faculty members who also are stymied from successfully educating and supporting their students, they may find themselves emboldened and ethically compelled to push their institutions to make changes.

Unions in the twenty-first century have been actively expanding their efforts to recruit contingent faculty, as demonstrated by the growing momentum behind (to cite one notable example) the SEIU's Faculty Forward campaign, and they have reached an opportune moment to broaden the conversation to encompass a fuller range of faculty concerns about which unions offer a viable mechanism to do something. In this chapter we have reviewed a web of interconnected concerns that are currently underutilized as a basis for galvanizing non-tenure-track faculty around the project of unionization. By presenting both the story of Joan Williams and the data and research showing the linkages between academic labor conditions and student outcomes, we hope to have highlighted the unsustainable nature of the status quo. There is plainly the necessity for some type of action to move working conditions and campus cultures in a direction that is more intentional about supporting learning and success. There are many thousands of faculty just like Joan; they are a potential wellspring of collective power if only they can be galvanized effectively. The California Faculty Association, for example, has in recent years given more attention to building its contingent faculty ranks and fighting for protections, which has produced one of the most robust NTTF agreements in the nation, including retirement benefits and sick leave provisions that far exceed what is typically extended to part-time faculty. Union organizers seeking ways to boost membership and parlay early victories into a durable and effective instrument of collective agency would do well to draw strategic inspiration from the California Faculty Association and the SEIU, and more deeply integrate the ranks and concerns of contingent labor into their bargaining missions.

NOTES

1. Eric P. Bettinger and Bridget T. Long, "Does Cheaper Mean Better? The Impact of Using Adjunct Instructors on Student Outcomes," *Review of Economics and Statistics* 92 (Aug. 2010): 598–613.

2. Roger G. Baldwin and Matthew R. Wawrzynski, "Contingent Faculty as Teachers: What We Know, What We Need to Know," *American Behavioral Scientist* 55 (May 2011): 1485–1509; Ernst Benjamin, "Reappraisal and Implications for Policy and Research," *New Directions for Higher Education* 123 (2003): 79–113; Paul D. Umbach, "How Effective Are They? Exploring the Impact of Contingent Faculty on Undergraduate Education," *Review of Higher Education* 30 (Winter 2007): 91–123; Paul D. Umbach and Matthew R. Wawrzynski, "Faculty Do Matter: The Role of College Faculty in Student Learning and Engagement," *Research in Higher Education* 46 (Mar. 2005): 153–84.

3. Adrianna Kezar, "Examining Non-Tenure Track Faculty Perceptions of How Departmental Policies and Practices Shape Their Performance and Ability to Create Student Learning at Four-Year Institutions," *Research in Higher Education* 54 (Aug. 2013): 571–98.

4. This quote is excerpted from unpublished data gathered as part of Adrianna Kezar, "Departmental Cultures and Non-Tenure-Track Faculty: Willingness, Capacity, and Opportunity to Perform at Four-Year Institutions," *Journal of Higher Education* 84 (Mar.–Apr. 2013): 153–58.

5. Jack H. Schuster and Martin J. Finkelstein, *The American Faculty: The Restructuring of Academic Work and Careers* (Baltimore, MD: Johns Hopkins University Press, 2006).

6. American Association of University Professors, *The Employment Status of Instructional Staff Members in Higher Education, Fall 2011* (Washington, DC: American Association of University Professors, 2014), https://www.aaup.org/sites/default/files/files/AAUP-InstrStaff2011 -April2014.pdf.

7. Schuster and Finkelstein, *American Faculty*.

8. Judith M. Gappa and David W. Leslie, *The Invisible Faculty: Improving the Status of Part-Timers in Higher Education* (San Francisco, CA: Jossey-Bass, 1993).

9. Schuster and Finkelstein, *American Faculty*.

10. Ibid.

11. American Association of University Professors, *Employment Status of Instructional Staff*.

12. Roger G. Baldwin and Jay L. Chronister, *Teaching without Tenure: Policies and Practices for a New Era* (Baltimore, MD: Johns Hopkins University Press, 2001).

13. American Association of University Professors, *Employment Status of Instructional Staff*.

14. Ibid.

15. This section draws heavily on "Review of Selected Policies and Practices and Connec-

44   Adrianna Kezar and Tom DePaola

tions to Student Learning," Delphi Project on the Changing Faculty and Student Success, Pullias Center for Higher Education, https://pullias.usc.edu/wp-content/uploads/2013/07/Delphi-NTTF _Conditions-Student-Summary_2013WebPDF.pdf (accessed Sept. 8, 2017).

16. Ronald G. Ehrenberg and Liang Zhang, *Do Tenured and Non-Tenure Track Faculty Matter?* National Bureau of Economic Research, Working Paper 10695 (2004), http://www.nber .org/papers/w10695.pdf; M. Kevin Eagan and Audrey J. Jaeger, "Effects of Exposure to Part-Time Faculty on Community College Transfer," *Research in Higher Education* 50 (Mar. 2009): 168–88.

17. Daniel Jacoby, "The Effects of Part-Time Faculty Employment on Community College Graduation Rates," *Journal of Higher Education* 77 (Nov.–Dec. 2006): 1081–1103.

18. Charles Harrington and Timothy Schibik, "Caveat Emptor: Is There a Relationship between Part-Time Faculty Utilization and Student Learning Outcomes and Retention?" Association for Institutional Research, 2001, http://files.eric.ed.gov/fulltext/ED456785.pdf.

19. Florence X. Ran and Di Xu, *How and Why Do Adjunct Instructors Affect Students' Academic Outcomes? Evidence from Both Two-Year and Four-Year Colleges,* CAPSEE Working Paper (2017), http://capseecenter.org/wp-content/uploads/2017/01/how-and-why-do-adjunct -instructors-affect-students-academic-outcomes.pdf.

20. Bettinger and Long, "Does Cheaper Mean Better?"

21. Bethany Gross and Dan Goldhaber, *Community College Transfer and Articulation Policies: Looking beneath the Surface,* Center on Reinventing Public Education, Working Paper 20091 (2009), https://www.crpe.org/sites/default/files/wp_crpe1R_cc2_apr09_0.pdf.

22. Ibid.

23. Eagan and Jaeger, "Effects of Exposure."

24. Harrington and Schibik, "Caveat Emptor."

25. Bettinger and Long, "Does Cheaper Mean Better?"

26. Benjamin, "Reappraisal and Implications"; Center for Community College Student Engagement, *Contingent Commitments: Bringing Part-Time Faculty into Focus* (2014), http://www .ccsse.org/docs/PTF_Special_Report.pdf; Eagan and Jaeger, "Effects of Exposure"; Jacoby, "Effects of Part-Time Faculty."

27. Baldwin and Wawrzynski, "Contingent Faculty as Teachers"; Benjamin, "Reappraisal and Implications"; Umbach, "How Effective Are They?"; Umbach and Wawrzynski, "Faculty Do Matter."

28. Umbach and Wawrzynski, "Faculty Do Matter."

29. Baldwin and Wawrzynski, "Contingent Faculty as Teachers"; Eagan and Jaeger, "Effects of Exposure"; Ehrenberg and Zhang, *Do Tenured and Non-Tenure Track Faculty Matter?*

30. Kezar, "Examining Non-Tenure Track Faculty Perceptions."

31. Delphi Project on the Changing Faculty and Student Success, Pullias Center for Higher Education, "Review of Selected Policies and Practices and Connections to Student Learning," http://www.uscrossier.org/pullias/wp-content/uploads/2013/07/Delphi-NTTF_Conditions -Student-Summary_2013WebPDF.pdf (accessed Feb. 8, 2017); Kezar, "Examining Non-Tenure Track Faculty Perceptions"; Kezar, "Departmental Cultures and Non-Tenure-Track Faculty"; Adrianna Kezar and Dan Maxey, "Faculty Matter: So Why Doesn't Anyone Think So?" *Thought and Action* 30 (Fall 2014): 29–44.

32. Steve Street et al., "Who Is Professor 'Staff'? and How Can This Person Teach So Many Classes?" (2012), Center for the Future of Higher Education, https://www.insidehighered.com /sites/default/server_files/files/profstaff(2).pdf.

33. Gappa and Leslie, *Invisible Faculty*, 145.

34. John G. Cross and Edie N. Goldenberg, *Off-Track Profs: Nontenured Teachers in Higher Education* (Cambridge, MA: MIT Press, 2009); Gappa and Leslie, *Invisible Faculty*.

35. Adrianna Kezar, *Embracing Non-Tenure Track Faculty: Changing Campuses for the New*

Faculty Majority (New York: Routledge, 2013); Kezar, "Departmental Cultures and Non-Tenure-Track Faculty."

36. Kezar, *Embracing Non-Tenure Track Faculty*.

37. Center for Community College Student Engagement, *Contingent Commitments*; American Association of University Professors, *Employment Status of Instructional Staff*.

38. Cross and Goldenberg, *Off-Track Profs*.

39. Baldwin and Chronister, *Teaching without Tenure*.

40. Gappa and Leslie, *Invisible Faculty*.

41. Kezar, *Embracing Non-Tenure Track Faculty*.

42. Kezar, "Examining Non-Tenure Track Faculty Perceptions," 583.

43. Valerie M. Conley and David W. Leslie, *Part-Time Instructional Faculty and Staff: Who They Are, What They Do, and What They Think* (Washington, DC: National Center for Education Statistics, 2002); Gappa and Leslie, *Invisible Faculty*; Eileen Schell and Patricia L. Stock, eds., *Moving a Mountain: Transforming the Role of Contingent Faculty in Composition Studies and Higher Education* (Urbana, IL: National Council of Teachers of English, 2001).

44. Baldwin and Chronister, *Teaching without Tenure*; Gappa and Leslie, *Invisible Faculty*.

45. Kezar, "Examining Non-Tenure Track Faculty Perceptions"; Kezar, "Departmental Cultures and Non-Tenure-Track Faculty"; Kezar, *Embracing Non-Tenure Track Faculty*.

46. Baldwin and Chronister, *Teaching without Tenure*; Adrianna Kezar and Cecile Sam, *Understanding the New Majority of Non-Tenure-Track Faculty in Higher Education* (San Francisco, CA: Jossey-Bass, 2010).

47. Kezar, "Departmental Cultures and Non-Tenure-Track Faculty."

48. Kezar, "Examining Non-Tenure Track Faculty Perceptions."

49. Kezar and Sam, *Understanding the New Majority*.

50. Baldwin and Chronister, *Teaching without Tenure*.

51. Ibid.

52. Kezar, "Departmental Cultures and Non-Tenure-Track Faculty"; Kezar, *Embracing Non-Tenure Track Faculty*.

53. Kezar, "Departmental Cultures and Non-Tenure-Track Faculty."

54. Kezar and Sam, *Understanding the New Majority*.

55. Baldwin and Chronister, *Teaching without Tenure*; Gappa and Leslie, *Invisible Faculty*.

56. Kezar, "Examining Non-Tenure Track Faculty Perceptions"; Kezar, "Departmental Cultures and Non-Tenure-Track Faculty."

57. Kezar and Sam, *Understanding the New Majority*.

58. Kezar, "Departmental Cultures and Non-Tenure-Track Faculty."

59. Kezar and Sam, *Understanding the New Majority*.

60. Gretchen Reevy and Grace Deason, "Predictors of Depression, Stress, and Anxiety among Non-Tenure Track Faculty," *Frontiers in Psychology* 5 (July 2014): 1–17.

61. Ibid.

62. Kezar, "Departmental Cultures and Non-Tenure-Track Faculty."

63. Melvin Blumberg and Charles D. Pringle, "The Missing Opportunity in Organizational Research: Some Implications for a Theory of Work Performance," *Academy of Management Review* 7 (Oct. 1982): 560–69.

64. Kezar, "Departmental Cultures and Non-Tenure-Track Faculty."

65. Ibid.

66. Ibid.

67. Ibid.

68. Ibid.

chapter 3

A Long History of Activism and Organizing

Contingent Faculty, Graduate Students, and Unionization

TIMOTHY REESE CAIN

Faculty unionization in American higher education traces its roots to the November 1918 founding of the American Federation of Teachers (AFT) Local 33 at Howard University. It took on new importance amid the economic and political struggles of the mid- to late 1930s, with faculty from more than 60 college campuses joining union locals. In the 1960s and early 1970s, unionization changed fundamentally with widespread collective bargaining that helped structure faculty working conditions and remuneration. Despite some setbacks in the ensuing decades—the US Supreme Court's 1980 decision in *NLRB v. Yeshiva University* being the most significant[1]—unionization has continued as a key, underappreciated element of American higher education. Indeed, college and university instructional staff are among the most unionized workers in the United States, with more than 400,000 faculty and graduate students—including 27 percent of the faculty—covered by bargained contracts as of 2012.[2] Importantly, non-tenure-line instructors and graduate students have been present in the unions throughout. From substantial, and at times controversial, membership in early nonbargaining locals through the contemporary organizing campaigns, these key and growing sectors of the instructional workforce have been part of that broader history of unionization in American higher education.

The focus of this chapter is the history of contingent faculty and graduate students in labor unions from 1918 through the modern period. I trace the early history of small, activist union locals, which were fragile but could still influence institutional policies, local situations, and national policy development. I highlight the rise of collective bargaining and the conflict over unit composition, including whether part-time instructors should be members of broader unions of full-time faculty; legal authorities, college administrators, and the unions themselves were often unsure. Many were also unclear as to whether inclusive unions were best able to represent all of the interests of their diverse constituents. This chapter also considers the struggles over the rights of graduate students to collectively bargain, beginning with efforts in the 1960s and including the stark disagreements at the end of the century. I conclude with the expansion of unions serving contingent faculty in the early twenty-first century.

Early Attempts to Unionize Faculty

It is necessarily true that non-tenure-line faculty were in the first faculty unions in the United States. Before the widespread adoption of the "1940 Statement of Principles on Academic Freedom and Tenure"—a joint statement of the American Association of University Professors (AAUP) and the Association of American Colleges—there was no modern tenure system. Established faculty at leading institutions had the expectation of continuance but no formal protections, as the numerous dismissals of educational workers in the decades before World War II demonstrated. Faculty were at-will employees.[3] Yet despite the lack of procedural protections and the lack of a ladder system of promotion, there were differences in rank, authority, and job security. And the earliest unions drew from multiple places in the academic hierarchy, from the most elite—such as Columbia University philosopher John Dewey, the leading educator of his day and holder of AFT card number 1—to the instructors at the lowest rungs.

Founded in 1916, the AFT was designed to promote and protect the interests of K-12 teachers, although it did include members of the Wilson Normal School as part of the Washington, DC, local. A summer of 1918 revision to the organization's constitution broadened membership eligibility, including allowing for the formation of locals for college faculty.[4] The AFT's issuance of a charter to a group of 29 educators at Howard University in the weeks after the conclusion of World War I initiated faculty organizing in American higher education. That initial group of 29 was diverse, including both established faculty and the leading social and political activist Mary Church Terrell. Most of its members, though, were instructors in the undergraduate portion of the institution, the division that was most beleaguered and where teaching loads were the highest. The main focuses of the local included uniting instructors and faculty from across Howard, providing for their greater input in university affairs, and lobbying the US Congress for increased appropriations to the institution.[5]

The precedent at Howard was soon followed at numerous other institutions, with 20 separate locals formed explicitly for or including significant numbers of college and normal school faculty by the end of 1920. Prefiguring the modern push to organize non-tenure-track faculty, several locals were organized on city-wide bases. When the second campus local— at the University of Illinois—was founded in early 1919, its leader, Arthur C. Cole, noted, "Unlike the followers of most professions, instructors generally are without democratic voice in determining the conditions under which they perform their services to the public. This has caused a widespread academic unrest."[6] Yet, the desire to affiliate with labor was not widespread nor readily understood even though financial conditions for faculty had worsened since the turn of the twentieth century. At Illinois, there was even confusion about for whom the local was intended—some believed it was to be an organization of instructors, rather than the entire faculty, even though union leadership believed that including professors and department heads among the membership was crucial for gaining influence and support. Still, in its early recruiting efforts, the union failed to appeal to those at the top of the academic hierarchy. The rank and status divisions within the faculty ultimately proved difficult to overcome at Illinois, as did the incredulity that faculty would align themselves with laborers, a decision assumed by many to eschew the privileges of professional status—privileges that unionized faculty claimed that they had already lost.[7]

These first campus locals were all short-lived. The Howard local closed in the face of administrative pressure amid concerns over communism on campus and the effects that the union could have on congressional funding of the institution. At Illinois, administrative pressure was likewise applied. Almost all of its union leaders soon left the institution as university president David Kinley pushed out heterodox faculty. Indeed, one of the themes across these early union locals is the insecurity of the instructors and professors who belonged to them. The local at the Milwaukee State Normal School was the only one to survive the 1920s, but even it struggled from its very founding. In his letter to the AFT office acknowledging the receipt of its charter, local president Lucius T. Gould suggested that he and his colleagues may have acted too hastily in requesting the charter since the institution's president was opposed to unionization.[8] Within a few months, Gould was dismissed in a move that he and the union attributed to his political and organizing activity. The local's standing was so shaky, however, that not only did it not act on Gould's behalf, but it requested that the AFT national assiduously avoid the suggestion that the local had sought his reinstatement or campaigned for tenure more broadly. Noting that the request was "*most* important," local member Edith B. White wrote, "the decision not to act as a Federation committee was . . . prompted by the conviction that we could accomplish nothing, under existing circumstance, if we acted under that label. We also felt that even the impression that we were so acting might endanger the life of the local. We found this to be a correct prophecy; and though the danger is now safely past, we shall have to be very quiet indeed for some weeks to come."[9] Indeed, a primary pattern in this first wave of faculty unions was the tenuousness of the locals and the faculty who founded them. While most early locals had larger purposes, such as bringing the faculty into greater contact with labor, democratizing education broadly, and building shared governance, this lack of security both gave educators reasons to organize and made any decision to do so risky.[10]

A second pattern that is particularly relevant here was the mixed but limited membership of the early locals. Although membership records are sparse and rarely include enough details to fully identify individuals and their positions, the existing evidence points to a variety of faculty in the locals. Some were founded by long-standing professors, others by instructors at the lowest levels of the academic hierarchy. It appears that many had a full range of positions represented. Only at the University of Montana was the AFT local able to convince the majority of the faculty to join, but amid institutional and state-wide political pressure it, too, was short-lived. The local at the University of Missouri is perhaps indicative of the larger situation. It was founded in late October 1919 and within a few weeks had 39 members: 19 professors, 5 associate professors, 5 assistant professors, 9 instructors, and an assistant. The local engaged in public debates with AAUP leadership over the appropriateness of unionization in higher education, and sought to improve the conditions and professional status of both K-12 and college teachers. At one point it counted roughly 40 percent of the instructional staff among its membership, but the faculty as a whole was opposed to the union, arguing that its very existence would diminish the institution in the eyes of the legislature and work against the university's efforts to garner increased funding. In response, the local folded in November 1920; almost all of the other initial college locals would do the same in the next few years.[11]

The Second Wave

The AFT's unionization efforts receded for much of the 1920s amid internal disagreements, external attacks, and the American Federation of Labor's withdrawal of support, but the union was reinvigorated at the end of the decade and even more so in the 1930s. In 1934 the union counted 7,500 members— only three-quarters of its total in 1919 but three times its membership for much of the 1920s; by 1940 membership had grown to 32,000.[12] Small groups of faculty at Yale University, the University of Wisconsin, and a collection of colleges in western Massachusetts received AFT charters in 1928, 1930, and 1931. In the tumultuous 1930s, unionization spread among college faculties, with more than 60 locals including substantial numbers of college faculty formed by the end of the decade. This reemergence of the AFT was influenced by larger, Depression-related changes in American society and labor, as well as the larger political concerns of the old left. Unionization across sectors experienced substantial gains, especially after the 1935 National Labor Relations Act provided some workers with the rights to form unions and collectively bargain. Between 1930 and 1940, the percentage of the US labor force in unions jumped from 12.3 to 27.6.[13] The establishment of the Congress of Industrial Organizations (CIO) and the industrial strikes in the late 1930s further changed the nature, experience, and perception of unions in the United States.

These broad economic and societal changes were joined by issues specific to higher education in causing some faculty to turn to unionization; among the latter were the rising numbers of junior faculty and continued use of part-time and graduate student instructors. An examination of faculty rank at colleges and universities in New York found a reduction of the percentage of full professors over the first half of the twentieth century and a concomitant increase in assistant and associate professors; the percentage of instructors and tutors remained largely constant at just over 25 percent, with slight increases to over 30 percent in the 1930s. Approximately one-fifth more were generally classified as "other."[14] The Depression caused hardships for institutions and their employees, especially those at the lowest end of the wage scale, some of whom were kept on staff largely to protect them from further difficulties. Still, with the standard tenure system not yet established and few openings for new instructional staff, the "plight of the academic underclass," in Walter Metzger's terms, included "heavy workloads at cut-rate pay, and turned the currently employed into supplicants for continued favor."[15] In his 1942 landmark study,

Academic Man, Logan Wilson likewise described the "unadmitted exploita-tion" of instructors whose "teaching load is usually the heaviest and most oner-ous." Further problematic were the difficulties in undertaking research and the "vague and conflicting criteria" by which instructors' work was judged.[16]

The college locals that were founded in this period were politically active but, as with their predecessors, only attracted a minority of the faculty on their campuses. They fought for academic freedom, tenure, and the rights of educators across sectors and across ranks. Indeed, many of the locals were formed explicitly to aid K-12 teachers or to speak to issues faced by graduate students and other academic laborers on tenuous appointments. Some locals had little focus from their start and struggled to find activities that would generate interest and membership. Still, as the locals multiplied and some grew stronger, many did become more active, attending to internal institu-tional issues and broader campaigns for societal change. By the late 1930s, college faculty were prominent in AFT leadership positions, with Yale's Jerome Davis assuming the presidency in 1936 and Columbia University's George S. Counts succeeding him three years later. They were joined by numerous vice presidents from higher education. Many of the locals were at the left edge of their campus faculties and the left edge of the AFT, which caused increasing difficulties as concerns about communist infiltration in the union spread: Davis himself was frequently accused of being at least a fellow traveler and perhaps a Communist Party member. Counts's election began a multiyear ef-fort to counter communism within the union, which ultimately resulted in the 1941 expulsion of three locals: the Philadelphia Teachers Union, the New York Teachers Union, and the New York College Teachers Union. The last, which drew membership from across the city but was especially strong in the public colleges, was by far the largest college local in the country.[17]

The expulsions were a key step in reducing the role of faculty in the union, and the union in faculty affairs. Yet in the years that preceded the purge, the locals could and did influence both local and national conditions, including those that affected the most tenuous of faculty. Much of the union's appeal was to the youngest and most underserved members of the instructional staff, a fact that was lost on neither the AFT nor the AAUP. Some in the for-mer began to question the role played by college faculty in the larger union, believing that they were steering the union away from the interests of the majority of its members. Moreover, while members of the AFT were excited to have the prestige that renowned college faculty such as Dewey or Counts could provide, they were dismayed that most of the college members were instructors and assistants who lacked the reputations that were most desired. The AAUP had been founded in 1915 by and for elite faculty, and many of its early activities emphasized established faculty at reputable institutions. The devastation of the Depression helped attune the association to the needs of the broader instructional staff; so too did the encroachments of the AFT into higher education. The two organizations clashed over academic freedom in the late 1930s, both claiming credit for the partial success in the defense of Jerome Davis after his dismissal from Yale. Most important, those differing approaches and the AFT's appeal to younger instructors and faculty both set the context and provided an impetus for the AAUP to engage in negotiations with the Association of American Colleges. The eventual result was the "1940 Statement" and modern understandings of academic freedom and tenure. It was the pressure of the AFT that caused the AAUP to shorten its proposed years of probation before tenure from ten to five, eventually agreeing to seven in the "1940 Statement," which has become the norm in four-year colleges and universities.[18]

Often highly political, and occasionally largely inactive, the 1930s locals sometimes played important roles in their institutional contexts. At Howard, the local's efforts to have its president, Henry Arthur Callis, reinstated were unsuccessful but led to formalized, written tenure policies at the institution. Faculty unionists helped achieve a more democratic administration at the City College of New York (CCNY) but, at the same time, struggled to protect heterodox faculty in the face of institutional pressure and a legislative inquiry into communism at the institution. In 1936, CCNY president Frederick Robinson dismissed communist English tutor Morris U. Schappes along with several other low-ranked staff members. After mass student and union protest on Schappes's and the others' behalf, they were reinstated, and the board extended tenure protections for instructors with three years of service. In 1940–1941, however, the state's Rapp-Coudert Committee investigated communism in public education, focusing much of its effort on CCNY and its members in the New York College Teachers Union. Ultimately, more than 30 faculty and staff were fired or forced to resign by the Board of Higher Education for their refusal to testify or for what they said under oath; numerous others were quietly not renewed. Among those dismissed was Schappes, who spent more than 13 months in jail for perjury after denying knowing of members of the Communist Party still on campus.[19]

At times, locals focused a significant portion of their efforts on what was often known as the "subfaculty"—the collection of instructors, assistants, associates, and others who made up sizable portions of institutions' instructional staffs. The University of Washington Teachers Union, for example, was especially concerned about this group, which made up as much as half of the institution's instructional staff in some years. Despite fulfilling vital teaching roles, members of the subfaculty received meager pay and were denied permanence, a say in institutional decision-making, and the recognition that would lead to retirement benefits. Course assignments were contingent upon student enrollment and subject to last-minute cancellation. The union attempted to intervene on behalf of the subfaculty and attracted many of its members, campaigning to increase their influence, arguing for more equitable salaries, and challenging the president's clear disregard of the group. It was, according to one member, "the only organization on campus that represented my interests as an Associate."[20] The University of Wisconsin Teachers Union was likewise concerned with instructors, as well as with the graduate students who, it argued, taught almost one-third of the undergraduate classes. The union's founding purposes included addressing the "exploitation of graduate assistants," and one of its initial committees was dedicated to addressing their concerns. As the university cut salaries because of severe budget reductions, the union argued that the salaries of those at the lowest ranks needed to be protected. It used political connections in the statehouse to apply pressure on the institution. Although the union was unable to achieve all that it wanted, the resulting salary scale was more favorable for instructors than it otherwise would have been. Even without the ability to bargain—and faced with a larger faculty opposed to its idea that graduate assistants were employees—the union was able to raise important issues and provide a voice for those on the instructional staff who lacked one.[21]

The 1941 expulsions and the larger split of the American left took tolls on faculty unionization. The challenges of World War II, which diverted many faculty from campuses and occupied the time of others, exacerbated the difficulties and caused many faculty unions to wither. Some shut down while others were held together by skeletal groups. Only a handful remained relevant after the war. The local at the University of Wisconsin rebounded dramatically, however, and through a series of reports on the conditions of the faculty was instrumental in securing increased remuneration before closing in the early 1950s, a victim of its own success.[22] The Washington local survived until 1949, when an anticommunist purge at the institution led to the dismissal of faculty and the AFT's expulsion of the local.[23] That same year, the AFT received a request from members of the Cornell University faculty to revoke the charter of Local 608 at that institution. The writers complained that the local was populated only by instructors and assistants, that it was dominated by communists, and that it was allied with Stalinist-affiliated organizations. The AFT did not act immediately against Local 608, but when the local fell behind in its dues payments two years later, the AFT quickly revoked its charter and did not allow it to reaffiliate. The AFT was largely quiescent in higher education.[24]

The Rise of Collective Bargaining in US Higher Education

American higher education changed significantly in the decades after World War II, with tremendous growth in student populations, educational opportunities, and facilities. In part these changes were spurred by shifting notions of college-going that were an outgrowth of the Servicemen's Readjustment Act of 1944.[25] Junior colleges transformed into community colleges and exploded in popularity. Enrollment in public two-year colleges rose from 168,043 in 1950, to 393,553 in 1960, to 2.1 million in 1970.[26] The creation of state systems helped coordinate higher education, although they did little to combat stratification; at times, these systems explicitly promoted it. Moreover, racial and gender discrimination remained rampant in student access and faculty hiring. The growth in higher education, particularly in public higher education, resulted in substantial growth of the faculty—a doubling from 1940 to 1960, and another by 1970. For a brief period, faculty jobs were relatively plentiful and salaries increased. The tenure system became normalized in four-year colleges and universities even if it failed to protect heterodox faculty from the challenges of McCarthyism, and in established institutions, tenure-line faculty gained increasing influence.[27] And yet, in a growing and diversifying system, the advantages were not spread evenly.

The immediate postwar period was a difficult one for AFT college locals, although there were a handful of successful union activities, including those at the University of Wisconsin. Additionally, in late 1947, faculty at Tri-State College in Indiana negotiated a new salary scale that might be considered the first AFT contract of its type, though details are scarce and the agreement only existed for a short time.[28] In part due to the conflict within the AFT, some faculty had already looked elsewhere for organizing assistance, including the expelled New York unionists, who maintained their locals and joined the CIO-affiliated State, County, and Municipal Workers of America, which merged with the United Federal Workers of America (UFWA) in 1946 to become the United Public Workers of America (UPWA). At Howard University, shortly after local leader and former AFT national vice president Doxey Wilkerson resigned and announced his membership in the Communist Party in 1942, the AFT local was replaced by a UFWA local, which covered the entire range of employees at the institution. In 1945, the nonteaching members of the union voted 203–0 in favor of collective bargaining; they agreed to their first contract five months later. In a February 1947 vote overseen by the National Labor Relations Board (NLRB), the teaching faculty of the UPWA voted 130–1 in favor of bargaining. The contract, agreed to in May, was the first of its kind in American higher education and included grievance procedures, protections for tenure, dues checkoff, and salary increases. The institution as a whole operated under UPWA contracts until 1950, when the university allowed the contract to expire after the CIO expelled the union over charges of communist domination. A similar fate befell faculty at Fisk University who bargained a contract shortly after those at Howard.[29]

The early contracts foretold the significant shift in higher education unionizing in the 1960s and beyond. Inspired by successful strikes and bargaining among schoolteachers, aided by enabling legislation at the state and federal levels, and encouraged by the larger social movements of the times, college faculty followed K-12 teachers into wide-scale collective bargaining. The AFT began its push toward bargaining in the mid-1950s and gained traction with the United Federation of Teachers' schoolteachers strike in New York in 1960 and victory in a representation election in 1961. A second strike in 1962 resulted in a contract with wage increases and amnesty for the strikers. The New York successes contributed to a great spread in teacher organizing across the nation and increased the competition among the groups hoping to represent them. By the mid-1960s, the National Education Association (NEA), a professional association whose leaders had long opposed unionization, was acting like a union, although it emphasized "professional negotiations" over collective bargaining and rejected union status. It openly committed to bargaining in the early 1970s. The AAUP likewise reconsidered its historic stance that unionization was antithetical to professionalism. It first allowed bargaining in select circumstances in the late 1960s and then, in 1972, embraced bargaining as a way of securing faculty rights and improving working conditions.[30]

Bargaining in higher education returned in 1963 at the Milwaukee Vocational and Adult School and moved into four-year colleges with faculty at the US Merchant Marine Academy organizing in 1966 and ratifying a contract two years later. Rhode Island's Bryant College of Business Administration reached a contract agreement with its faculty union in 1967. A lengthy 1966–1967 strike by the United Federation of College Teachers (AFT Local 1460) at St. John's University in New York helped attract substantial attention to unionization, as did the 1967 signing of a contract for faculty at the City Colleges of Chicago. Many of the early successes in bargaining were at two-year institutions, which were often outgrowths of K-12 systems that lacked shared governance, but the 1969 contracts at the City University of New York, Central Michigan University, and Southeastern University in Florida brought bargaining more fully to four-year institutions. By June 1972, there were 158 recognized bargaining units, 119 of which were at two-year colleges. More than half were affiliated with the NEA: 72 at two-year colleges and 11 at four-year institutions. The AFT represented faculty at 52 institutions: 38 at two-year colleges and 14 at four-year. The AAUP, having been led into bargaining in 1967 by faculty at Belleville Junior College in southwestern Illinois, was likewise involved with 12 bargaining units, 11 of which were in four-year institutions. Unionization then exploded and, by the end of the decade, more than 25 percent of college faculty and 20 percent of institutions in the United States were covered by bargained contracts.[31] Although not nearly as widespread, graduate student bargaining traces its beginnings to this period as well.

The roles and status of part-time faculty—an imperfect match with non-tenure-line faculty but with significant overlap—in these early bargaining locals were at times unsettled. With tenure systems in place, it was unclear whether they shared a "community of interest" with full-time faculty and, therefore, if they should be in the same bargaining units. Indeed, the early efforts to unionize involved a wide range of potential constituencies, including full- and part-time faculty, librarians, full-time researchers, student personnel administrators, and graduate teaching assistants. At Central Michigan, for example, instructors were included in a unit with tenure-line faculty, and their support of collective bargaining helped win a close election.[32] At CUNY, lecturers and adjuncts were initially represented by the AFT's United Federation of College Teachers; other faculty were represented by the NEA-affiliated Legislative Conference. In 1972, they merged into the Professional Staff Congress (PSC), a broader unit covering a wide range of professionals, including librarians and graduate assistants.[33]

In these and other public institutions, the determination of bargaining units—which organizers and institutions often contested on both philosophical and pragmatic grounds—was and is ruled by state legislative provisions and state board rulings. These not only vary across states but also can be inconsistent within them. The original bargaining units at CUNY were separate because of a 1968 New York State Public Employment Relations Board (PERB) determination that the roughly 50 percent of the faculty who were ineligible for tenure did not primarily identify as college faculty but instead as graduate students, high school teachers, or other professionals. Three years later, all parties reversed course. The unions, which had initially argued for separate units, claimed that there should be only one representative for all faculty. The university shifted from favoring a single bargaining representative to separate ones. Rather than enforcing either, the PERB allowed the faculty to vote. In between these rulings, the PERB approved a different, even more expansive unit at the State University of New York, including all professional staff at all of its campuses. Even though neither the unions nor the university sought their inclusion, 2,000 part-time faculty members were made part of the bargaining unit.[34]

As New York and other states ruled on unit inclusion in seemingly conflicting ways, they increasingly looked to the NLRB, which oversees bargaining in private colleges and universities, for guidance. As Gregory M. Saltzman notes in chapter 4 of this volume, the NLRB was also inconsistent due to both its changing membership and the specifics of individual cases. In a series of rulings beginning with a pair addressing organizing at two campuses of Long Island University in 1971, the NLRB at first acknowledged that there were differences between full-time and "regular" part-time faculty but decided that their basic teaching functions and qualifications were the same. Subsequent cases at Fordham University, the University of New Haven, and the University of Detroit likewise pointed to differences between part-time and full-time faculty, including tenure eligibility and governance roles, but reached the same conclusion. The Detroit ruling took the further step of defining "irregular" faculty ineligible to join, providing a formula that equated to teaching less than a one-quarter of a load, often three credit hours. Yet many full-time faculty felt that their interests could be undermined by the inclusion of any part-time faculty, who already composed significant portions of many institutions' instructional staffs; at the University of New Haven, they were two-thirds of the faculty. In recognition of such concerns, the NLRB soon used a case involving the unionization of faculty at New York University to revisit the issue, ultimately determining that part-time and full-time faculty did *not* share a community of interest. The differences in their compensation, governance roles, working conditions, and tenure eligibility were too great.[35]

The concerns of full-time faculty about being outnumbered may have influenced the NLRB's NYU decision, but a competing concern was also true: including part-time and adjunct faculty in a larger unit could work against *their* interests. At CUNY, for example, the initial contract for non-tenure-line faculty included preferential rehiring for part-time faculty who were let go due to enrollment declines, financial difficulties, or curricular changes. The first PSC contract for full- and part-time faculty did not include such provisions. While part-time faculty did achieve some gains, they also experienced significant losses, including tuition waivers and workload limits. The results were such that David Y. Allen, the leader of an adjunct advocacy group at the institution, contended that "even union leaders have admitted publicly that part-timers were clobbered," and he filed an unsuccessful claim against the union with the PERB.[36] In 1974, the Newt Davidson Collective, a group of faculty and students from across CUNY, offered a stinging critique of the university, the union, and higher education more broadly, arguing that the PSC did too little for the most underprivileged members of the faculty. The collective pointed to the high dues that limited adjunct participation and the shortcomings in the first contract, claiming that adjuncts were the "chief victims of current union policy."[37] In ensuing years, many adjunct faculty continued to decline membership in the union, thereby limiting their influence in decision-making. A 1978 change in voting and election eligibility procedures limited their influence even further and contributed to the concerns over fair representation that would, a decade later, lead to decertification attempts.[38]

The inclusion of graduate students in the first CUNY contract for part-time faculty points to another front of organizing in higher education. Though not nearly as widespread as faculty organizing in the 1960s and 1970s, graduate teaching assistants at a handful of universities likewise looked to collective bargaining as a route to improving their working conditions while also pursuing broader changes in higher education. With links to student protests in the turbulent 1960s, as well as the shifting conditions in higher education, graduate students staked a claim to employee status and agitated for change. In 1964, graduate students at the University of California, Berkeley—who taught nearly a third of undergraduate classes—formed the Graduate Coordinating Council as a wing of the free speech movement. It raised concerns about teaching and research assistant compensation, equitable hiring, and academic quality, among other issues. A one-week strike in December 1964 led to the chartering of an AFT local two months later. The early union members were torn over whether to emphasize professional matters related to their work at the university or take on broader social and political issues; for a short period, they decided on the former and soon lobbied to prevent legislative efforts to cut funds for teaching assistant salaries. The AFT local engaged in negotiations for better conditions in several academic departments and the university library, claiming victories in improved communications and procedures, if not formal agreements. The union struck several more times, including in 1966, and then, after moving further left, in 1969 in support of the Third World Liberation Front. In 1972, it was part of a larger coalition's bargaining effort between the Alameda County Labor Council and the University of California. While the resulting agreement included a 10 percent raise, a fee refund, and improved grievance procedures, the union played little role in the negotiations and the primary issues involved non-university workers. Moreover, by that time its membership had already dropped from 400 only a few years earlier to 300; within three years it would have barely any members left.[39]

The Teaching Assistants Association (TAA) at the University of Wisconsin was more effective and long lasting. It was formed in 1966, successfully fought for a student's reinstatement to her position in 1967, and received some concessions on grievance procedures the following year. It achieved new strength in 1969 when many more teaching assistants joined as the legislature considered eliminating tuition waivers over concerns that out-of-state graduate students were fomenting protests. That year, the university recognized the union, even though it was not legally required to do so. Following a strike by the TAA, the two sides agreed to a contract in 1970, though it fell short of the local's goals, especially on issues involving graduate teaching assistants' influence in curricular issues.[40] The local's president, Steven Zorn, later noted that the contract "made virtually no concessions on the educational planning issue. These arguments for input into educational planning were central to the union, which argued not just for bread and butter issues but for professional rights as the educators in charge of many undergraduate classes. The first contract, however, set up an impartial grievance procedure, gave teaching assistants a guarantee of long-term appointments, and improved working conditions to some degree."[41]

The TAA operated as the graduate students' bargaining agent throughout the 1970s, affiliating with the AFT in 1974 and winning further concessions, including on benefits. Yet it continued to be frustrated in its demands for additional input into educational issues. These demands for participation in shared governance caused friction with the faculty and administrators, as did the union's grievances, which were seen to infringe on faculty educational responsibilities. That friction was exacerbated by an April 1980 strike pursued in hopes of forcing a new contract. When talks that summer broke down over faculty authority in educational decision-making, the new chancellor withdrew recognition of the union. The TAA's bargaining was halted until 1985 when state legislation provided graduate student employees with legally protected bargaining rights.[42]

Graduate students at private institutions, including Columbia, Georgetown, and Yale, also began organizing in the early 1970s but were unsuccessful in achieving bargaining rights. Rulings by the NLRB kept graduate students out of faculty unions, and in the mid-1970s additional NLRB rulings prevented organizing in discrete units.[43] In public higher education, though, graduate students were incorporated into a larger unit at Rutgers University and formed their own units at the Universities of Michigan and Oregon. At Michigan, students founded a union of teaching assistants in 1970, which was denied bargaining rights by the Michigan Employment Relations Commission (MERC). When merged with a broader union that included research and staff assistants, the university granted a certification election, which the union won in April 1974. A month-long strike the following year led to a contract that included affirmative action provisions, an agency shop, and a nondiscrimination policy for gay and lesbian graduate students. Difficult negotiations for a second contract the following year led to a lengthy legal battle—which cost the union its research assistant members when the MERC ruled that they were students, not employees. In November 1981, the university finally signed the contract that had been negotiated more than five years earlier.[44] Graduate teaching fellows at Oregon began organizing in 1975, affiliated with the AFT in 1976, achieved recognition in 1977, and agreed to a first contract—which included salary increases, grievance procedures, standardized workloads, and written appointment criteria—in 1978.[45] While these unions would soon be joined by three at public universities in Florida, at most institutions graduate students did not join unions either by choice or because they were precluded from doing so. Additionally, even where there were organizing drives leading to elections, such as at the University of Minnesota, unions sometimes failed to garner majority support.[46]

Organizing after the *Yeshiva* Ruling

The great growth of faculty bargaining slowed in the late 1970s and then suffered a significant setback with the US Supreme Court's 1980 decision in *NLRB v. Yeshiva University*. Finding substantial faculty oversight and authority on curricula, admissions, faculty hiring and promotion, and other matters, the court ruled that the faculty were managerial employees and ineligible for collective bargaining. Although the court noted that the findings were specific to Yeshiva University, the ruling was applied widely, severely limited bargaining in private higher education. New union locals were almost impossible to found at private institutions, and most existing ones soon lost bargaining rights.[47] For the rest of the twentieth century, unionism spread in higher education but at slower rates than in the 1970s. It was also even more localized in the two-year and public sectors than it had been.

When the Supreme Court issued its *Yeshiva* ruling, the unionization of contingent faculty was almost exclusively undertaken through locals that also included tenure-line faculty—only part-time faculty at Nassau Community College and at Long Island University's C. W. Post campus had contracts as discrete bargaining units at the time—suggesting that organizing non-tenure-line faculty might be difficult. Instead, part-time and adjunct bargaining units gained new traction, though mostly in public higher education. By 1988, 20 separate units were certified as bargaining agents, with several covering faculty at multiple campuses or entire systems. Enabled by a 1982 NLRB ruling that part-time faculty at the University of San Francisco could form their own unit, a handful of these were at private institutions. Continuing to spread, there were 35 units specifically for part-time and contingent faculty on almost 90 campuses in 1996. Together, they had almost 18,000 members; many more adjuncts were in the more than 200 units that included both tenure-line and non-tenure-line faculty.[48]

Part of this increase in adjunct union locals was a result of the great increase in the number and percentage of non-tenure-line faculty in American higher education (see A. J. Angulo, chapter 1 in this volume). As the growth area in college faculty, it was likewise the growth area for unionization. The increase was also influenced by enabling legislation and strategic local decision-making that shaped the nature of bargaining units; at times these pushed toward inclusive units, and at times they fostered separate ones. Among some union organizers, there was continuing concern that units that included a broad range of faculty did a disservice to those at the lowest levels of the academic hierarchy, including adjunct and other non-tenure-line faculty. Even advocates for inclusive unions pointed to potential conflicts since many tenure-line faculty positioned non-tenure-line faculty as less integral to their institutions.[49] Indeed, Gary Rhoades's extensive analysis of union contracts in the mid-1990s demonstrated the shortcomings in provisions for part-time faculty; many contracts included few such provisions, and those that did often worked against part-timers' interests in favor of full-timers.[50] Later analysis pointed to some improvements in contractual language while also highlighting the ongoing limitations on protections and benefits for adjuncts in many agreements.[51]

The debates over appropriate units continued into the twenty-first century, even as the AFT, the AAUP, and the NEA recognized the importance of organizing adjunct faculty—in part due to efforts of groups such as the Coalition of Contingent Academic Labor (COCAL), formed in 1998. All three issued revised statements and dedicated additional resources to organizing contingent faculty. As adjunct activist Joe Berry noted in 2011, "Contingent faculty have been a substantial percentage of the faculty for decades, and it is only in the last 10 years—and in many ways less—that unions have actually come up with national strategies for dealing with this." He credited unions with finally doing so, but also noted, "They are late to the game."[52] Some locals initiated significant shifts in how adjuncts were included and served. The Massachusetts Community College Council, for example, changed its long-standing policy of giving part-time faculty, the majority of its membership, only one-quarter of a vote in union elections, finally providing them with full voting rights and the power to shift the union. At CUNY, adjuncts who had challenged the union's representation of their interests worked outside of the union and then within it to gain influence and improve their treatment. Despite these improvements, tensions and disagreements remain, and other situations, including those involving part-time faculty in the state of Washington, highlight the ongoing potential for conflict and concerns about fair representation.[53]

A key aspect in the unionization of contingent faculty in the twenty-first century has been the emergence of other unions as important advocates and organizers. The Service Employees International Union (SEIU) has been especially active on campuses across the country, organizing non-tenure-line faculty at a range of institutional types. One significant part of its strategy has been organizing on a metropolitan basis, an approach that has historical antecedents in early nonbargaining locals and was unsuccessfully pursued by COCAL in Boston at the turn of the century. Using this strategy, the SEIU has sought to apply city-wide market pressure across institutions, even beyond those that unionize, and has gained bargaining victories in DC, Boston, and elsewhere.[54] The International Union, United Automobile, Aerospace and Agricultural Implement Workers of America, better known as the United Auto

Workers (UAW), has also been active, leading much of the organizing of post-doctoral researchers. The UAW-affiliated postdocs at the University of California formed the first such union in 2005 and garnered their first contract five years later. With more than 6,500 members, it represents more than 10 percent of the postdoctoral workers in the country. Postdocs at the University of Massachusetts and Rutgers University have likewise successfully bargained contracts.[55]

The 1990s and early 2000s also saw increased activity around graduate student organizing, highlighted by contentious battles for bargaining rights at private universities and more successful efforts in public higher education. Unions were formed and contracts signed at public universities in Florida, Iowa, Kansas, Massachusetts, Michigan, Oregon, and Wisconsin. Graduate student units at two large multicampus universities, the State University of New York in 1993 and the University of California in 1999, were also recognized, dramatically increasing the number of unionized students in American higher education. In the first five years of the twenty-first century, they were joined by more than 6,000 students in the California State University system—the second largest group after that at UC—and students at eight other public institutions.[56] At the same time, challenges remained, including in Wisconsin, where 2011 anti-union legislation stripped numerous public employees of bargaining protections and made the process so onerous that the University of Wisconsin's TAA abandoned bargaining.[57] Moreover, the struggles for recognition at private institutions demonstrated the vastly differing views on whether teaching assistants are primarily students, primarily employees, or both. At Yale University, for example, students in the late 1980s organized TA Solidarity, which transformed into the Graduate Employees and Students Organization in 1990. Early walkouts and a 1995–1996 grade strike generated significant national attention, as well as allegations of administrative and faculty threats against striking students. The strikes did not, though, result in recognition by the university.[58]

At NYU, graduate students who affiliated with the UAW in 1997 campaigned for bargaining rights and, when the institution denied an election, petitioned the NLRB. The NYU administration fought against the unit, appealed the unanimous ruling that graduate students could unionize, and threatened a federal lawsuit to nullify the ruling. In the end, though, the two sides negotiated and in 2002 agreed to the first graduate student contract at a private university. The NYU efforts spurred organizing at other private universities, but one of those drives soon undid some of the graduate students' gains at NYU. In 2004, the NLRB found that graduate workers at Brown University were primarily students and not covered for bargaining. The ruling not only denied Brown students the right to bargain, it removed protections at NYU and forestalled graduate student bargaining more broadly.[59] It would take almost another decade of activism—until late 2013—before NYU agreed to bargain again, this time without legal mandate but in the face of significant political pressure. By the actual start of bargaining a few months later, graduate students at Columbia, inspired in part by the NYU situation, were considering unionizing. Those considerations led to UAW affiliation, an organizing drive, and a petition for recognition to the NLRB. The full NLRB ruling in August 2016—that graduate student instructors and research assistants at Columbia were employees—changed the landscape of graduate student unionization and energized organizing efforts at private institutions across the nation. As of this writing, union advocates and activists are simultaneously excited about the possibilities and worried that the NLRB under President Donald Trump will overturn the ruling and once again deprive graduate students of bargaining rights.[60]

Conclusion

With one-quarter of faculty and graduate students in bargaining units and many more otherwise affiliated with labor, faculty unionization is a central feature of US higher education, though it is too often missing from both treatments of modern conditions and studies taking a historical view. More faculty are in unions than ever before—and more adjunct faculty and graduate students are likewise—but the phenomenon has deep roots; at least some faculty have been in unions for a century. Throughout, a portion of unionized faculty has been composed of contingent employees working without the protections, security, and benefits of tenure or the ability to earn them. In non-bargaining locals before and after the creation of the formal tenure system, in broader bargaining units at midcentury and beyond, and finally in stand-alone units founded in the more recent past, contingent faculty and graduate students have advocated for their own rights and benefits, as well as for larger educational improvements. These efforts have frequently been contested by those opposed to unions in higher education writ large and those who questioned the roles and rights of non-tenure-line faculty specifically. The rights of graduate students have been even more controversial. Still, adjuncts and graduate students have taken center stage in the unionization of instructional workers through the efforts of the three historic faculty unions and newer entrants, such as the SEIU; the UAW; the American Federation of State, County, and Municipal Employees; and the Communication Workers of America. Adjuncts and graduate students constitute more than half of organized instructional workers and, barring a dramatic and unexpected reversal in faculty staffing, they will continue to do so.

NOTES

1. *NLRB v. Yeshiva University*, 444 US 672 (1980); Judith Wagner DeCew, "The *Yeshiva* Decision and Unions at Private Institutions," in her *Unionization in the Academy: Visions and Realities* (Lanham, MD: Rowman and Littlefield, 2003), 45–56.

2. Curtis R. Sproul, Neil Bucklew, and Jeffery D. Houghton, "Academic Collective Bargaining: Patterns and Trends," *Journal of Collective Bargaining in the Academy* 6 (2014), http://the keep.eiu.edu/cgi/viewcontent.cgi?article=1315&context=jcba; Joe Berry and Michelle Savarese, *Directory of Faculty Contracts and Bargaining Agents in Institutions of Higher Education* (New York: National Center for the Study of Collective Bargaining in Higher Education and the Professions, Hunter College of the City University of New York, 2012), vi.

3. Timothy Reese Cain, *Establishing Academic Freedom: Politics, Principles, and the Development of Core Values* (New York: Palgrave, 2012); Cain, "The Old Normal: Casualization and Contingency in Historical Perspective," *Thought and Action* 31 (Summer 2015): 23–38.

4. Marjorie Murphy, *Blackboard Unions: The AFT and the NEA, 1900–1980* (Ithaca, NY: Cornell University Press), 83–84; V. B. Turner, "The American Federation of Teachers," *Monthly Labor Review* 9, no. 2 (1919): 247–55.

5. Timothy Reese Cain, " 'Only Organized Effort Will Find the Way Out!': Faculty Unionization at Howard University, 1918–1950," *Perspectives on the History of Higher Education* 29 (2012): 113–50, 116–18.

6. "Illinois University Teachers' Union," *Christian Science Monitor* (Mar. 28, 1919).

7. Timothy Reese Cain, " 'Learning and Labor': Faculty Unionization at the University of Illinois, 1919–1923," *Labor History* 51, no. 4 (2010): 543–69.

8. Lucius Gould to F[reeland] G. Stecker, May 17, 1919, ser. 4, box 13, folder 79, American Federation of Teachers Inventory Part I, Archive of Labor and Urban Affairs, Walter P. Reuther Library, Wayne State University, Detroit, MI (hereafter AFT Inventory).

9. Edith B. White to L. V. Sampson, Feb. 18, 1920, ser. 4, box 13, folder 79, AFT Inventory.

10. Timothy Reese Cain, "The First Attempts to Unionize the Faculty," *Teachers College Record* 112, no. 3 (2010): 875–913.

11. Cain, "First Attempts," 895–97; H. Wade Hibbard to Charles B. Stillman, Nov. 16, 1919, ser. 4, box 18, folder 126, AFT Inventory; Harry G. Brown to Freeland G. Stecker, Nov. 25, 1920, ser. 4, box 18, folder 126, AFT Inventory.

12. Murphy, *Blackboard Unions*, 107–8, 150.

13. Walter Galenson and Robert S. Smith, "The United States," in *Labor in the Twentieth Century*, ed. John T. Dunlop and Walter Galenson (New York: Academic, 1978), 31.

14. George J. Stigler, *Employment and Compensation in Education* (New York: National Bureau of Economic Research, 1950), 40, http://www.nber.org/books/stig50-1.

15. Walter P. Metzger, "The 1940 Statement of Principles on Academic Freedom and Tenure," *Law and Contemporary Problems* 53, no. 3 (1990): 3–77, 69.

16. Logan Wilson, *The Academic Man: A Study in the Sociology of a Profession* (New York: Oxford University Press, 1942), 61–62.

17. Timothy Reese Cain, "Unionised Faculty and the Political Left: Communism and the American Federation of Teachers on the Eve of the Second World War," *History of Education* 41, no. 4 (2012): 515–35.

18. Cain, *Establishing Academic Freedom*, 140–75.

19. Cain, "Only Organized Effort," 125–27; Abraham Edel, *The Struggle for Academic Democracy: Lessons from the 1938 "Revolution" in New York's City Colleges* (Philadelphia: Temple University Press); Marjorie Heins, *Priests of Our Democracy: The Supreme Court, Academic Freedom and the Anti-Communist Purge* (New York: New York University Press, 2013), 38–66.

20. Margaret A. Hall, "A History of Women Faculty at the University of Washington, 1896–1970," PhD diss., University of Washington, 1984, 165–75, 171.

21. Timothy Reese Cain and Philip Wilkinson, "On Wisconsin: Generations of Faculty and Graduate Student Unionization," paper presented at the Association for the Study of Higher Education Annual Meeting, Denver, CO, Nov. 2015.

22. Ibid.

23. Jane Sanders, *Cold War on the Campus: Academic Freedom at the University of Washington, 1946–64* (Seattle: University of Washington Press, 1979).

24. Jeannette Lester, "The American Federation of Teachers in Higher Education: A History of Union Organization of Faculty Members in American Colleges and Universities, 1916–1966," PhD diss., University of Toledo, 1968, 162–64.

25. Daniel Clark, "'The Two Joes Meet: Joe College, Joe Veteran': The G.I. Bill, College Education, and Postwar American Culture," *History of Education Quarterly* 38, no. 2 (1998): 165–89.

26. John R. Thelin, *A History of American Higher Education*, 2nd ed. (Baltimore, MD: Johns Hopkins University Press, 2011), 299–300.

27. Philo A. Hutcheson and Ralph Kidder, "In the National Interest: The College and University in the United States in the Post–World War II Era," in *Higher Education: Handbook of Theory and Research*, vol. 26, ed. John C. Smart and Michael B. Paulson (New York: Springer), 221–64; Martin J. Finkelstein, Valerie Martin Conley, and Jack H. Schuster, *The Faculty Factor: Assessing the American Academy in a Turbulent Era* (Baltimore, MD: Johns Hopkins University Press, 2011), 44–45; Howard R. Bowen, "Faculty Salaries: Past and Future," *Educational Record* 49, no. 1 (1968): 9–21.

28. Lester, "American Federation of Teachers," 152–55.

29. Cain, "Only Organized Effort," 131–39.

30. Murphy, *Blackboard Unions*, 209–31, 252–55; Philo Hutcheson, *A Professional Professoriate: Unionization, Bureaucratization, and the AAUP* (Nashville, TN: Vanderbilt University Press, 2000), 112–26, 136–37.

31. Ronald L. Johnstone, *The Scope of Faculty Collective Bargaining: An Analysis of Faculty Union Agreements at Four-Year Institutions of Higher Education* (Westport, CT: Greenwood, 1981), 4; Hutcheson and Kidder, "In the National Interest," 234–35; E. D. Duryea, Robert S. Fisk, and Associates, *Faculty Unions and Collective Bargaining* (San Francisco, CA: Jossey-Bass, 1973), 14; Joseph W. Garbarino and John Lawler, "Faculty Union Activity in Higher Education," *Industrial Relations* 18 (1979): 244–46.

32. John C. Helper, "Timetable for a Take-Over," *Journal of Higher Education* 42, no. 2 (1971): 103–15.

33. F. K. Barasch, "Collective Bargaining at CUNY," *Change* 5, no. 6 (1973): 14–16.

34. Ronald B. Head and David W. Leslie, "Bargaining Unit Status of Part-Time Faculty," *Journal of Law and Education* 8, no. 3 (1979): 361–78, 368–69.

35. Ibid., 365–66; Kathleen E. Shannon, "Labor Law—Determination of the Appropriate Faculty Bargaining Unit in a Private University—New York University," *Boston College Law Review* 15, no. 2 (1973): 423–42.

36. Vincent Tirelli, "The Invisible Faculty Fight Back: Contingent Academic Labor and the Political Economy of the Corporate University," PhD diss., City University of New York, 2007, 261–65, 264.

37. Newt Davidson Collective, *Crisis at CUNY* (New York: Newt Davidson Collective, 1974), 103, http://cdha.cuny.edu/files/original/1974_NDC_CrisisAtCUNY.pdf.

38. Tirelli, "Invisible Faculty Fight Back," 265–76.

39. Sidney Ingerman, "Employed Graduate Students Organize at Berkeley," *Industrial Relations* 5, no. 1 (Oct. 1965): 141–50; Robert Dubin and Frederic Beisse, "The Assistant: Academic Subaltern," *Administrative Science Quarterly* 11, no 4 (1967): 521–47; American Federation of Teachers Local 1570, *AFT Local 1570: A Union for Student Employees* (San Francisco, CA: American Federation of Teachers, 1970); Bill Aussieker, "Student Involvement with Collective Bargaining," *Journal of Higher Education* 46, no. 5 (1975): 533–47, 538–40.

40. Gregory M. Saltzman, "Union Organizing and the Law: Part-Time Faculty and Graduate Teaching Assistants," *NEA 2000 Almanac of Higher Education* (2000): 43–55; Judith S. Craig, "Graduate Student Unionism: The Teaching Assistants Association at the University of Wisconsin–Madison, 1970–1980," PhD diss., University of Wisconsin, Madison, 1986; Nathan P. Fensinger and Eleanore J. Roe, "The University of Wisconsin, Madison Campus—TAA Dispute of 1969–70: A Case Study," *Wisconsin Law Review* 1971, no. 1 (1971): 229–74.

41. Steven Zorn, "Unions on Campus," in *Academic Supermarkets: A Critical Case Study of a Multiversity*, ed. Philip G. Altbach, Robert S. Laufer, and Sheila McVey (San Francisco, CA: Jossey-Bass, 1971), 288–302, 299.

42. Barry Mitzman, "Union Power for Teaching Assistants," *Change* 7, no. 5 (1975), 17–19; Craig, "Graduate Student Unionism"; Saltzman, "Union Organizing," 46.

43. John Rinschler, "Students or Employees? The Struggle over Graduate Student Unions in America's Private Colleges and Universities," *Journal of College and University Law* 36, no. 3 (2010): 615–40.

44. Saltzman, "Union Organizing"; Daniel C. Tsang, "Echoes of Ann Arbor in UC's Fight with Graduate Students," *Los Angeles Times* (Dec. 6, 1998), M6, http://articles.latimes.com/1998/dec/06/opinion/op-51126; "A Narrative History of GEO," http://www.geo3550.org/about-geo/a-narrative-history-of-geo (accessed Dec. 8, 2016).

45. "History of GTFF," http://gtff3544.net/about/history-of-gtff (accessed Dec. 8, 2016).

46. Mario F. Bognanno and Edward L. Suntrup, "Graduate Assistants' Response to Unionization: The Minnesota Experience," *Labor Law Journal* 27, no. 1 (1976): 32–37.

47. DeCew, *Unionization in the Academy*, 45–49.

48. Joel M. Douglas with Steven Kramer, *Directory of Faculty Contracts and Bargaining Agents in Institutions of Higher Education*, vol. 8 (New York: National Center for the Study of Collective Bargaining in Higher Education and the Professions, Baruch College, City University of New York, 1982); Joel M. Douglas with Beth Genya Cohen, *Directory of Faculty Contracts and Bargaining Agents in Institutions of Higher Education*, vol. 14 (New York: National Center for the Study of Collective Bargaining in Higher Education and the Professions, Baruch College, City University of New York, 1988); Richard Hurd and Amy Foerster with Beth Hillman Johnson, *Directory of Faculty Contracts and Bargaining Agents in Institutions of Higher Education*, vol. 23 (New York: National Center for the Study of Collective Bargaining in Higher Education and the Professions, Baruch College, City University of New York, 1997).

49. David W. Leslie, Samuel E. Kallams, and G. Manny Gunne, *Part-Time Faculty in American Higher Education* (New York: Praeger, 1982), 59–63; Christine Maitland, "Temporary Faculty and Collective Bargaining in Higher Education in California," *Journal of Collective Negotiations* 16, no. 3 (1987): 233–57.

50. Gary Rhoades, "Reorganizing the Faculty Workforce for Flexibility: Part-Time Professional Labor," *Journal of Higher Education* 67, no. 6 (1996): 626–59; Rhoades, *Managed Profes-*

sionals: Unionized Faculty and Restructuring Academic Labor (Albany: State University of New York Press, 1998).

51. Christine Maitland and Gary Rhoades, "Bargaining for Contingent Faculty," *NEA 2005 Almanac of Higher Education* (2005): 75–83.

52. Peter Schmidt, "Unions Confront the Fault Lines between Adjuncts and Full-Timers," *Chronicle of Higher Education* (Nov. 20, 2011), http://www.chronicle.com/article/Unions-Confront-Fault-Lines/129836.

53. Ibid.

54. Gary Zabel, "A New Campus Rebellion: Organizing Boston's Contingent Faculty," *New Labor Forum* 6 (Spring–Summer 2000): 90–98; Peter Schmidt, " 'Metro' Unionizing Strategy Is Viewed as a Means to Empower Adjunct Faculty," *Chronicle of Higher Education* (Dec. 3, 2012), http://www.chronicle.com/article/Metro-Unionizing-Strategy-Is/136101.

55. Gary Rhoades and Blanca M. Torres-Olave, "Academic Capitalism and Secondary Labor Markets: Negotiating a New Academy and Research Agenda," in *Higher Education: Handbook of Theory and Research*, vol. 30, ed. Michael B. Paulsen (New York: Springer, 2015), 383–430, 411–17.

56. Berry and Savarese, *Directory of Faculty Contracts*, xii–xiv, 50–54.

57. Scott Jaschik, "Negotiating No More," *Inside Higher Ed* (Aug. 22, 2011), https://www.insidehighered.com/news/2011/08/22/union_for_teaching_assistants_at_wisconsin_madison_votes_not_to_certify_for_collective_bargaining.

58. Parbudy Singh, Deborah M. Zinni, and Anne F. MacLennan, "Graduate Student Unions in the United States," *Journal of Labor Research* 27, no. 1 (2006): 55–73.

59. "Unions at NYU, 1971–2007," in *The University against Itself: The NYU Strike and the Future of the Academic Workplace*, ed. Monika Krause et al. (Philadelphia, PA: Temple University Press, 2008), 115–22.

60. Vimal Patel, "Graduate-Student Union Efforts Gain Momentum, Despite New Uncertainties," *Chronicle of Higher Education* (Dec. 13, 2016), http://www.chronicle.com/article/Graduate-Student-Union-Efforts/238659.

chapter 4

Union Organizing and the Law

Contingent Faculty and Graduate Teaching Assistants

GREGORY M. SALTZMAN

Many who teach in US higher education are not part of the tenure track. Between 1969 and 2009, the fraction of faculty appointments at American colleges and universities held by persons ineligible for tenure tripled, rising from 21.7 percent to 66.5 percent. Contingent faculty appointments have become particularly common at community colleges. By 2009, 68.7 percent of faculty at public two-year colleges held part-time, non-tenure-track appointments, while another 13.8 percent held full-time, non-tenure-track appointments. At research universities, a substantial fraction of undergraduate instruction is done by teaching assistants (TAs), who typically teach part-time while pursuing a graduate degree.[1]

A surge in union activity in the twenty-first century among contingent faculty and TAs has increased the need for contingent faculty, TAs, and higher education administrators to understand the legal rules regarding union organizing. This chapter updates an earlier survey of labor law issues related to organizing among contingent faculty and TAs.[2] Depending on the type of institution and its location, contingent faculty and TAs might or might not have a legally protected right to organize labor unions and bargain collectively. Where unionization is protected, however, there is considerable uniformity in the procedures for settling questions of union representation.

Private versus Public

Labor law varies by jurisdiction. Most private-sector employees are covered by the National Labor Relations Act (NLRA) of 1935, as amended by the Taft-Hartley Act of 1947. The NLRA protects the right of employees to en-

gage in concerted activities and bans unfair labor practices (ULPs) that inter-
fere with this right. The NLRA provides for secret-ballot elections to determine whether unions have majority support, and it requires employers to
bargain collectively with unions that win such elections. The National Labor
Relations Board (NLRB) enforces the ban on ULPs and conducts union representation elections; its five-member board interprets the statute, while its
regional directors investigate ULP charges and file ULP complaints in cases
deemed meritorious.

For-profit colleges and universities and private nonprofit institutions generally fall under the jurisdiction of the NLRB. The board addressed in 2014
and 2016 two controversial issues of jurisdiction, both described in depth later
in this chapter. First, to what extent does the NLRB have jurisdiction over
religiously affiliated colleges and universities? Second, are TAs statutory employees for purposes of the NLRA and thus covered by federal labor law?

The NLRA does not apply to state and local public employees, but state
public-sector bargaining statutes give union rights to many public employees.
Most public-sector bargaining statutes are patterned after the NLRA, minus
the right to strike. There was a surge in enactment of such statutes in the 1960s
and 1970s, and empirical evidence indicates that these statutes were important causes of the spread of public-sector bargaining.[3] By 1998, most states in
the Northeast, the Midwest, and the West Coast plus Hawaii and Alaska had
laws protecting the right of public college or university employees to organize
and bargain, though Indiana, Missouri, and North Dakota were exceptions.
Most states in the Mountain West and the South still have no public-sector
bargaining statutes today; some southern states expressly ban public-sector bargaining, while Florida, Montana, and New Mexico protect it.[4]

Union Rights of Contingent Faculty at Private Institutions

In private colleges and universities, union organizing among tenure-track faculty has been severely constrained by the US Supreme Court's 1980 decision
in the *Yeshiva* case.[5] The Court ruled that tenure-track faculty at Yeshiva University were managers and, hence, were not statutory employees for the purposes of the NLRA. They had no protected right to organize, nor did their
employer have any obligation to engage in collective bargaining with their
representative. Tenure-track faculty could still win union recognition by striking, as many blue-collar workers had prior to the enactment of the NLRA in
1935,[6] but tenure-track professors generally lack the militancy to do so. Thus,
Yeshiva generally has thwarted unionization among tenure-track faculty at

private colleges and universities. There have been some rare exceptions, including the decision in 2016 by Notre Dame de Namur University in California to recognize the Service Employees International Union (SEIU) as the representative of tenure-track faculty in addition to the SEIU's established role as the representative of part-time faculty.[7]

Contingent faculty usually have much less role in institutional governance than do tenure-track faculty. Even so, when the SEIU filed a petition with the NLRB to represent 176 contingent faculty members at Pacific Lutheran University, the university administration argued that the 39 who worked full-time were managers and therefore not protected by the NLRA. The NLRB unanimously rejected that argument in their 2014 *Pacific Lutheran University* ruling.[8] The three Democratic members of the board went further, adopting (despite the dissent of the two Republican members) a new test for the managerial status of faculty. Although the board lacks authority to overturn the Supreme Court's *Yeshiva* ruling, the new test makes it easier for the NLRB to distinguish the factual situation at many colleges and universities from the factual situation that was the basis for *Yeshiva*. The *Pacific Lutheran* test for managerial status is based on the faculty role in five policy areas:

> [W]here a party asserts that university faculty are managerial employees, we will examine the faculty's participation in the following areas of decisionmaking [sic]: academic programs, enrollment management, finances, academic policy, and personnel policies and decisions, giving greater weight to the first three areas than the last two areas. We will then determine, in the context of the university's decision making [sic] structure and the nature of the faculty's employment relationship with the university, whether the faculty actually control or make effective recommendation over those areas. If they do, we will find that they are managerial employees and, therefore, excluded from the Act's protections.[9]

The board stated, "[T]he party asserting managerial status must prove actual—rather than mere paper—authority. . . . A faculty handbook may state that the faculty has authority or responsibility for a particular decision-making area, but it must be demonstrated that the faculty exercises such authority *in fact.* . . . [T]o be 'effective,' [faculty] recommendations must almost always be followed by the administration."[10] The "almost always" language makes it difficult to prove that faculty are managers.

Because of *Pacific Lutheran*, the *Yeshiva* decision will almost never strip contingent faculty of their protected legal right to organize and bargain collectively. The *Pacific Lutheran* standard for managerial status, combined with the increasing corporatization of higher education, which reduces faculty authority, will also make it easier for tenure-track faculty at private colleges and universities to unionize.

In addition to establishing a new test for managerial status, *Pacific Lutheran* addressed the issue of the NLRB's jurisdiction over religiously affiliated institutions. In 1979, the US Supreme Court ruled in *NLRB v. Catholic Bishop of Chicago* that the NLRB did not have jurisdiction over lay teachers at Catholic high schools because of the First Amendment ban on interference with the free exercise of religion.[11] The US Court of Appeals cited *Catholic Bishop* in 2002 when it declined to enforce an NLRB order in *University of Great Falls v. NLRB.*[12] In *Pacific Lutheran*, the board tried to limit the impact of *University of Great Falls* by adopting a new test for when the NLRB would decline jurisdiction on First Amendment grounds.

By a 3–2 party-line vote (with the two Republicans dissenting), the board asserted NLRB jurisdiction unless the institution demonstrated "that it holds out the petitioned-for faculty members as performing a religious function."[13] To avoid interfering with First Amendment rights, the board declined to "examine whether faculty members *actually perform* a religious function."[14] Instead, the board ruled, "We rely on the institution's own statements about whether its teachers are obligated to perform a religious function, without questioning the institution's good faith or otherwise second-guessing those statements. . . . However, general or aspirational statements, without specificity as to how the requirement affects actual job functions, will not suffice."[15] Because Pacific Lutheran University did not claim that its contingent faculty performed a religious function, the board's majority asserted jurisdiction.

The NLRB's regional directors subsequently applied the *Pacific Lutheran* standard for jurisdiction to contingent faculty cases at other religiously affiliated institutions. The administrations of both Seattle University and St. Xavier University appealed regional director decisions, and the board ruled on both appeals in 2016.[16] In both cases, the board refused to review the regional directors' decision that the NLRB had jurisdiction. In *Seattle University*, the majority opinion asserted: "Uncontested evidence shows that the vast majority of contingent faculty are not hired to advance the religious goals of the institution. For example, calculus teachers are hired based on their ability to teach calculus. They are not required to be Catholic or to take any part in any religious activities on or off campus; religion is not mentioned in their employment contracts."[17] Still, in both cases, the board agreed to exclude from the bargaining unit those faculty members teaching religious studies or theology, on the grounds that the university administration claimed that these faculty members maintained the university's religious educational environment.

The exclusions authorized in *Seattle University* and *St. Xavier University* are narrow. For as long as the board's *Pacific Lutheran* decision stands, most contingent faculty at private colleges or universities—whether secular or religiously affiliated—will have a protected right to organize and bargain under the NLRA. But when the NLRB regional director announced, after the 2016 board ruling in *Seattle University*, that a majority of the adjuncts had voted to unionize, the university president announced his intention to challenge the result on religious freedom grounds.[18] Since employers cannot directly challenge representation decisions by the NLRB, Seattle University can obtain review of that decision only by refusing to bargain with the union. If the board orders Seattle University to bargain in good faith, then the administration could appeal that order to the US Circuit Court of Appeals for the DC Circuit, thus gaining an opportunity to raise in court the underlying issue of whether the NLRB has jurisdiction over religiously affiliated colleges and universities.

Union Rights of Teaching Assistants at Private Institutions

Just as the status of faculty as statutory employees for the purposes of the NLRA was challenged on the grounds that they are managers, that of TAs was challenged on the grounds that they are students. The NLRB has twice reversed its policy on whether TAs at private universities have a protected right to organize and bargain. Statutory interpretation depends on who is on the board.

A Democratic NLRB majority ruled in 2000 that New York University TAs are protected by the NLRA.[19] A new Republican NLRB majority overturned this precedent in the 2004 *Brown University* decision, ruling that TAs and research assistants are primarily students, not employees.[20] In 2016, a Democratic NLRB majority overturned *Brown University* with the *Columbia University* ruling that TAs do have a protected right to organize and bargain.[21]

In the *Columbia* case, the union petitioned for a bargaining unit of all graduate and undergraduate TAs plus all graduate research assistants (RAs), including those compensated through training grants. The board found in *Columbia* that "[t]he *Brown University* Board's decision . . . deprived an entire category of workers of the protections of the Act, without a convincing justification in either the statutory language or the policies of the Act."[22] In *Colum-*

bia, the board dismissed the argument that simultaneous status as a student precludes an employee from coverage under the NLRA: "Statutory coverage is permitted by virtue of an employment relationship; it is not foreclosed by the existence of some other, additional relationship that the Act does not reach."[23] The board concluded that "affording student assistants the right to engage in collective bargaining will further the policies of the Act, without engendering any cognizable, countervailing harm to private higher education. Accordingly, we overrule *Brown University* and hold that student assistants who have a common-law employment relationship with their university are statutory employees entitled to the protections of the Act."[24]

Though the *Columbia* decision echoed the *New York University* decision of 2000, it went further by including in the bargaining unit RAs funded by external grants. Overruling a 1974 NLRB ruling that Stanford University RAs were not covered by the NLRA, the board ruled in *Columbia* that "the fact that a research assistant's work might advance his own educational interests as well as the University's interests is not a barrier to finding statutory-employee status."[25]

In December 2016, Columbia's TAs and RAs voted overwhelmingly to unionize.[26] The university administration filed objections to the election, asking the board to invalidate the vote conducted by the regional director.[27] By the time the NLRB rules on this request, President Donald Trump may have appointed an anti-union majority to the board.

Union Rights of Contingent Faculty and Teaching Assistants at Public Institutions

Though public-sector bargaining laws are patterned after the NLRA, they have only rarely applied the *Yeshiva* doctrine to faculty at public colleges and universities. In states that grant most public employees the right to organize and bargain, faculty members and TAs at public institutions generally have that right too. Less often, RAs have protected union rights. In 2013, the Oregon Employment Relations Board ruled that RAs at Oregon State University were employees covered by Oregon's public-sector bargaining law, even though the university administration asserted that RAs did research primarily in their capacity as students rather than as employees.[28]

In the wake of Tea Party victories in the 2010 elections, Ohio and Wisconsin severely limited the union rights of public employees, including those at public colleges and universities, but the anti-union statute in Ohio was overturned by a 2011 referendum.[29] In 2012, Indiana and Michigan passed "right-to-work" laws banning the requirement that all employees covered by a collective bargaining contract pay a "fair share" service fee for union representation, and Wisconsin passed a "right-to-work" law in 2015.[30] In 2016, the US Supreme Court was widely expected to declare fair share arrangements unconstitutional in the public sector, via the *Friedrichs* case. But the death of conservative justice Antonin Scalia led to a 4–4 tie that upheld the lower court ruling, which had upheld the constitutionality of fair share fees.[31]

Union Representation Procedures

The NLRA established secret-ballot elections as the procedure for deciding whether a group of employees want to be represented by a labor union. State public-sector bargaining statutes typically have patterned their union representation procedures after the NLRA. In 2012, the office of the NLRB general counsel issued a detailed guide to law and procedure in representation cases.[32] To summarize briefly, if at least 30 percent of a group of employees sign union authorization cards, then the union can petition the NLRB to conduct a secret-ballot union representation election. The NLRB will certify the union as the exclusive bargaining representative if a majority of those voting in the election vote for the union.

A 2016 law review article by University of Michigan law professor Kate Andrias began by stating, "American labor unions have collapsed. While they once bargained for more than a third of American workers, unions now represent only about a tenth of the labor market and even less of the private sector. In the process, the United States has lost a core equalizing institution in politics and the economy."[33] In part, she blamed this collapse

> on how the governing rules of union elections fail to protect workers' statutory right to organize in the face of concerted management opposition. Among its many problems, the law provides employers with great latitude to dissuade employees from self-organization, while offering unions few rights to communicate with employees about unionization's merits. Unions are denied physical access to the workplace during an organizing campaign, but employers are permitted to compel employee presence for antiunion communication. Meanwhile, the NLRB's election machinery is extraordinarily slow; employers are able to defeat organizing drives through delay and attrition. Perhaps most important, the NLRB's remedial regime is too protracted and its penalties too meager to protect employees against employer retaliation. One study found that about twenty-five percent of employers illegally discharge workers for union activity;

more than one-half make illegal threats to close all or part of a plant. When such illegal activity occurs, remedies are too little, too late.[34]

Access to the workplace during organizing campaigns is less of a problem for higher education unions than for most other unions because of the open nature of most college and university campuses. And the NLRB adopted new rules, effective April 2015, that are designed to shorten the time between the filing of a union representation petition and the holding of the representation election.[35]

But the other concerns raised by Andrias are quite relevant to higher education. For example, the Duquesne University administration filed an appeal to the NLRB in June 2015 that included text interpreted by the union as a threat to fire two adjuncts for testifying before the NLRB.[36] It is not unusual for employers to make illegal threats of reprisals for union activity, but putting such a threat in an appeal document that the employer filed with the NLRB was extraordinary. In October 2015, Duquesne announced that several adjuncts, including one of the two threatened in the NLRB filing, were being terminated as of the end of the semester.[37] The resolution of a ULP charge alleging unlawful discharge for union activity was still pending at the time this chapter was written.[38] If the Court of Appeals for the DC Circuit overturns the NLRB's assertion of jurisdiction over religiously affiliated institutions, then the ULP charge against Duquesne (a Catholic university) will be dismissed.

Appropriate Bargaining Unit

Sometimes, union representation elections are delayed by employer objections to the bargaining unit proposed by the union. The bargaining unit defines which employees are allowed to vote in the union representation election and which employees are covered by the union contract if the union wins. Employers may seek to make it harder for the union to win the election by excluding pro-union groups or including anti-union groups. Employers may also object to a proposed unit in order to exclude key employees whose participation in a strike would increase the union's bargaining power.

When the employer and the union cannot agree on the bargaining unit, the NLRB has the discretion to choose an appropriate unit. Unit determination is typically based on the concept of "community of interest." Among the considerations in evaluating a community of interest are the following: "a. Degree of functional integration. . . . b. Common supervision. . . . c. The nature of employee skills and functions. . . . d. Interchangeability and contact among employees. . . . e. Work situs. . . . f. General working conditions. . . . g. Fringe benefits."[39] If the NLRB decides that two employee groups do not share a community of interest, then the NLRB will not include them in the same bargaining unit.

Labor relations agencies sometimes weigh the specifics of a community of interest against the high cost per worker of negotiating separate contracts for each employee group. Small public school districts sometimes have "wall-to-wall" units combining teachers, aides, cafeteria workers, and bus drivers, even though their job duties are disparate. But in large school districts with many employees, professional and nonprofessional employees are almost always in separate units. One would expect a similar pattern in higher education, with units at huge universities that are more homogeneous occupationally than those at small colleges.

The NLRB has excluded TAs from bargaining units of university faculty since 1972.[40] The *Yeshiva* doctrine reinforced the policy of separate units for TAs at private research universities since the tenure-track faculty there were not deemed to be covered by the NLRA. State labor boards and legislatures have usually also put TAs in separate units, though TAs were included in larger faculty bargaining units at the City University of New York and at Rutgers.[41]

Another key issue in unit determination is whether to include contingent faculty in the same bargaining unit as tenure-track faculty. In the early 1970s, unions sometimes sought units including all faculty members, both tenure-track and contingent. The NLRB decided in 1973, however, that adjunct and part-time faculty did not have sufficient community of interest with tenure-track faculty to be included in the same bargaining unit.[42] But despite this precedent, the NLRB and a federal circuit court subsequently upheld a combined unit of full-time and part-time faculty at the Kendall School of Design.[43]

The same issue has arisen in public-sector cases. Tenure-track and contingent faculty at the University of Illinois, Chicago, petitioned for a combined bargaining unit. Although the university administration prevailed in 2012 "in a legal battle to keep the two types of faculty members from being represented in the same collectivebargaining unit, their separate bargaining units nonetheless belong to the same union for the campus and share a negotiating team."[44] At the University of Oregon, the administration filed objections in 2012 to a proposed unit combining non-tenure-track instructors and tenure-track professors, but it withdrew these objections a few weeks later.[45]

At the University of Minnesota's flagship Twin Cities campus, the SEIU petitioned in January 2016 for a union representation election for a unit of 2,500 faculty members, including both tenure-track and contingent faculty. A newspaper reported:

> One of the goals is to improve job security and pay for more than 1,100 contingent faculty members who are not on the tenure track. . . . [T]he last faculty unionizing effort on the Twin Cities campus, in 1997, was rejected by 26 votes. At the time, many faculty members were up in arms about a proposal to weaken tenure protections, which ultimately was abandoned. This time, says . . . [a professor who helped lead the union drive], her colleagues are worried about different kinds of threats to their profession. "The threat to tenure is not a threat to those of us who have it," she said. "It's a threat to those who are never going to get it."[46]

The university administration contested the proposed unit, arguing that contingent faculty should not be included in the same unit as tenure-track faculty, but the state's Bureau of Mediation ruled in September 2016 that the combined unit was appropriate.[47] In October 2016, the university administration appealed the ruling. The Minnesota Court of Appeals ruled in favor of the university in September 2017.[48]

Duty of Fair Representation

For bargaining units that combine contingent and tenure-track faculty, a potential concern arises about the duty of fair representation:

> In 1944, the U.S. Supreme Court ruled that exclusive representation rights established by statute implied a duty of fair representation [*Steele v. Louisville & Nashville R.R.*, 323 US 192 (1944)]. A union whose constitution excluded Blacks from membership won exclusive representation rights for a bargaining unit that included a substantial number of Black workers. In 1940, the union proposed new contract language that would ultimately have excluded Blacks from employment on the 21 railroads covered by the contract. The union did not inform the Black workers about the proposal or give them a chance to be heard.
>
> The Supreme Court ruled that a union could negotiate contracts favoring some members of the bargaining unit over others, if the favoritism were based on seniority, the type of work performed, or individual skill. But the union could not discriminate on the basis of race in contract negotiations, and the

employer was not bound by, nor entitled to benefit from, a contract that violated the union's duty of fair representation.[49]

A fair representation issue could arise in a combined unit of contingent and tenure-track faculty if, for example, the union sought severe limits on the employment of contingent faculty in order to maintain job opportunities for tenure-track faculty. The issue could also arise if a union dominated by contingent faculty ignored the interests of tenure-track faculty who were in the same bargaining unit. On the other hand, where tenure-track faculty have strong feelings of solidarity with contingent faculty, a combined unit may enable contingent faculty to win favorable terms of employment that they lacked the power to win on their own.

Union Hiring Hall as an Alternative Model

Collective bargaining with individual employers is the standard model for unions in higher education, but it is not the only possible model. The SEIU Local 500 organized about 80 percent of the adjunct faculty members in the Washington, DC, area, and the local's executive director expressed interest in replacing campus-by-campus bargaining with a single collective bargaining contract for all adjuncts in the metropolitan area.[50] The SEIU also has metrowide adjunct organizing campaigns in Boston, Los Angeles, Philadelphia, and Seattle; the American Federation of Teachers has one in Philadelphia; and the United Steelworkers has one in Pittsburgh.[51] Joe Berry, a labor educator then living in Chicago who advocated the metro organizing strategy, proposed that unions establish union hiring halls where local colleges and universities would recruit contingent faculty.[52] Historically, union hiring halls set labor standards in several industries.

A classic law review article by David Feller analyzed the union hiring hall approach, though not in the context of higher education.[53] Feller noted, "Until the turn of the twentieth century, most of the trades in which worker organization was successful did not engage, or even seek to engage, in collective bargaining. Their relationships with employers involved, rather, the attempt to secure acquiescence in the rules the members unilaterally established as the ones under which they would agree to work."[54] The union could fine members who worked for employers who paid less than the union pay scale. The American Federation of Musicians still unilaterally set prices for music gigs at the time Feller wrote his article in the early 1970s.[55]

"The essential characteristic of union-created rules," Feller wrote, "is that they are part of union government."[56] The "constitution of the American Federation of Musicians gives each local the authority to try members, even of another local, for violations of local or federation law occurring within its territorial jurisdiction. Fines, penalties, and, in extreme cases, expulsion may be imposed for violations."[57] "Fines and expulsions as sanctions can secure compliance with the rules only if union membership is a prerequisite of employment. The closed shop [in which employers may only hire union members] or its functional equivalent is therefore essential to the effectiveness of union regulation," Feller noted.[58]

A union of contingent faculty could adopt a similar approach, establishing a union hiring hall through which colleges and universities would hire contingent faculty for short-term teaching gigs. For this to work, however, the faculty union would need to organize a large fraction of the potential labor supply. Moreover, there is a legal problem identified by Feller: "Industrial relations systems in which any substantial part of the employment relationship is governed by union rule are essentially inconsistent with the National Labor Relations Act."[59] Though the NLRB "adopted a 'hands off' policy with regard to the construction industry," in which unions unilaterally set some work rules, the Taft-Hartley Act undermined the ability of construction unions to enforce union rules by banning the closed shop and secondary boycotts (in which construction union members refuse to work on the same site as nonmembers).[60] Emulating the American Federation of Musicians approach therefore might be quite difficult for contingent faculty unions.

Likely Changes under President Donald Trump

There has long been a tendency for Democratic presidents to appoint pro-union majorities to the National Labor Relations Board and for Republicans to appoint anti-union majorities.[61] In the twenty-first century, there have also been fierce partisan battles in the Senate over confirming any nominees to the board, who typically serve five-year terms. A Democratic Senate blocked Republican president George W. Bush's board nominees in 2008, and the Republican minority in the Senate blocked Democratic president Barack Obama's nominees in 2009.[62] In 2013, a filibuster by Senate Republicans of Obama's nominees to the NLRB led to a Democratic threat to end the filibuster; the Republicans backed down.[63] In 2016, Senate Republicans (having gained a majority in the 2014 elections) took no action on Obama's reappointment of a pro-union board member whose term was scheduled to end in August of that year.[64] By the end of Obama's second term, there was a 2–1 pro-union majority on the board, with two vacant positions.

The election of Donald Trump as president in 2016 and continued Republican control of the US Senate are likely to lead to a 3–2 anti-union majority on the NLRB by the time this chapter is published. Trump nominated two candidates to vacant board positions. The Senate confirmed one on August 2, 2017, and confirmed the other in September 2017.[65] Moreover, the term of the pro-union NLRB general counsel expired in November 2017,[66] and his replacement is likely to be anti-union. Though the board and the general counsel are bound by the statutory language of the NLRA, Trump appointees are likely to interpret and enforce the law in a way unfavorable to labor unions.

Two board decisions may be overturned as a result of the 2016 election: the 2016 *Columbia University* ruling that reestablished the right of TAs to organize and bargain, and the 2014 *Pacific Lutheran University* ruling that limited the ability of religiously affiliated colleges and universities to refuse to bargain with adjunct faculty. Other pro-union NLRB rulings not specific to higher education may also be overturned. Although the NLRB has no jurisdiction over public colleges and universities, unions representing contingent faculty or TAs at private colleges and universities will face a challenging legal environment during the next few years.

Finally, the refusal of Senate Republicans to consider President Obama's nomination of Merrick Garland to the US Supreme Court seat previously held by Antonin Scalia gave President Trump the opportunity to nominate Neil Gorsuch to the Court. In April 2017, Senate Republicans exercised the "nuclear option" and eliminated the 60-vote requirement for ending filibusters against Supreme Court nominees, clearing the way for Gorsuch to be confirmed.[67] Justice Gorsuch may vote with the four conservative justices on a new case similar to *Friedrichs*, thereby ending the fair share fees that finance some of the activity of labor unions at public colleges and universities.

The Supreme Court could, for example, choose to hear an appeal of the March 2017 decision in *Janus v. AFSCME*, in which the US Court of Appeals for the Seventh Circuit ruled that Illinois state government employees can lawfully be required to pay union service fees. Judge Richard Posner's decision noted that the circuit court was bound by the 1977 Supreme Court ruling in *Abood*,[68] which declared fair share fees in the public sector to be constitutional. "Of course, only the Supreme Court has the power, if it so chooses, to overrule *Abood*," Posner wrote.[69] A conservative journalist commented, "That's what right-to-work advocates are betting on."[70]

NOTES

1. Adrianna Kezar and Daniel Maxey, "The Changing Academic Workforce," *Trusteeship* 21 (2013), http://agb.org/trusteeship/2013/5/changing-academic-workforce. For the proportion of graduate assistants teaching at research universities, see table 2.1 in this volume.

2. Gregory M. Saltzman, "Union Organizing and the Law: Part-Time Faculty and Graduate Teaching Assistants," *NEA 2000 Almanac of Higher Education* (2000): 43–55.

3. Gregory M. Saltzman, "Public Sector Bargaining Laws Really Matter: Evidence from Ohio and Illinois," in *When Public Sector Workers Unionize*, ed. Richard B. Freeman and Casey Ichniowski (Chicago: University of Chicago Press, 1988), 41–79.

4. Gregory M. Saltzman, "Legal Regulation of Bargaining in Colleges and Universities," *NEA 1998 Almanac of Higher Education* (1998): 45–63.

5. *NLRB v. Yeshiva University*, 444 US 672 (1980).

6. A prominent labor historian noted, "The strike wave that erupted in the summer of 1933, and especially those strikes that proved most difficult to settle, concerned the right to organize and union recognition in the steel, automobile, and electrical manufacturing industries." Melvyn Dubofsky, *The State and Labor in Modern America* (Chapel Hill: University of North Carolina Press, 1994), 116. The NLRA, by providing union representation elections and establishing a duty of employers to bargain with unions that win such elections, rendered recognition strikes unnecessary for most private-sector employees. But the NLRA does not cover public employees. New York City K-12 teachers, for example, struggled to win union recognition even after their strike on November 7, 1960. Henry Mayer, "School Board Criticized: Denial of Teachers' Right to Union, Collective Bargaining Charged," *New York Times*, June 16, 1961, 32. After a delay of more than a year, the school board finally held a representation election in December 1961, which the union won. Ralph Katz, "Federation Wins in Teacher Vote: Gets Two-Thirds of Ballots in 3-Way Election to Pick Bargaining Agent Here," *New York Times*, Dec. 17, 1961, 1, 67.

7. Colleen Flaherty, "Notre Dame de Namur Recognizes Tenured Faculty Union," *Inside Higher Ed*, June 1, 2016, https://www.insidehighered.com. According to Donna R. Euben and Thomas P. Hustoles, between 1980 and 1997, the NLRB allowed elections for at least seven private institutions. See Euben and Hustoles, "Collective Bargaining Revised and Revisited" (2001), https://www.aaup.org/issues/collective-bargaining/collective-bargaining-revised-and-re visited-2001.

8. *Pacific Lutheran University and Service Employees International Union, Local 925*, 361 NLRB No. 157 (2014).

9. Ibid., 20.

10. Ibid., 18, emphasis in original.

11. *NLRB v. Catholic Bishop of Chicago*, 440 US 490 (1979).

12. *University of Great Falls v. NLRB*, 278 F.3d 1335 (DC Cir. 2002).

13. *Pacific Lutheran University*, 1.

14. Ibid., 6, emphasis in original.

15. Ibid., 9.

16. *Seattle University and Service Employees International Union, Local 925*, 364 NLRB No. 84 (2016); *Saint Xavier University and St. Xavier University Adjunct Faculty Organization, IEA-NEA*, 364 NLRB No. 85 (2016).

17. *Seattle University*, 2.

18. Colleen Flaherty, "Seattle U Says It Will Challenge Adjunct Union Vote," *Inside Higher Ed*, Oct. 3, 2016, www.insidehighered.com.

19. *New York University and International Union, United Automobile, Aerospace, and Agricultural Implement Workers of America*, 332 NLRB No. 1205 (2000).

20. *Brown University and International Union, United Automobile, Aerospace and Agricultural Implement Workers of America*, 342 NLRB No. 483 (2004).

21. *Trustees of Columbia University in the City of New York and Graduate Workers of Columbia—GWC, UAW*, 364 NLRB No. 90 (2016).

22. Ibid., 1.

23. Ibid., 2.

24. Ibid., 13.

25. Ibid., 17.

26. Elizabeth A. Harris, "Grad Students at Columbia Vote for Union," *New York Times*, Dec. 10, 2016, A21.

27. Elizabeth A. Harris, "At Columbia, Unionization Debate Grows," *New York Times*, Dec. 21, 2016, A22.

28. Bennett Hall, "Grad Assistants Are Employees, State Rules," *Corvallis Gazette-Times*, Jan. 10, 2013, http://www.gazettetimes.com/news/local/grad-assistants-are-employees-state-rules/article_0266209a-5ac1-11e2-8d6c-001a4bcf887a.html.

29. Gregory M. Saltzman, "An Anti-Union Tide: The 2011 Attacks on Public Employees' Bargaining Rights," *NEA 2012 Almanac of Higher Education* (2012): 39–50.

30. Gregory M. Saltzman, "Contested Terrain: Developments in Labor Law Affecting Higher Education since 2012," *NEA 2016 Almanac of Higher Education* (2016): 31–38.

31. *Friedrichs v. California Teachers Association*, 136 S. Ct. 1083 (2016).

32. Office of the General Counsel, National Labor Relations Board, *An Outline of Law and Procedure in Representation Cases* (Washington, DC: US Government Printing Office, 2012), https://www.nlrb.gov/sites/default/files/attachments/basic-page/node-1727/representation_case_outline_of_law_4-16-13.pdf.

33. Kate Andrias, "The New Labor Law," *Yale Law Journal* 126 (2016): 2–100, 5.

34. Ibid., 25–26.

35. National Labor Relations Board, "Representation—Case Procedures: Final Rule," *Federal Register* 79 (Dec. 15, 2014): 74308–490.

36. Moshe Z. Marvit, "Duquesne's NLRB Filing Reads as a Brazen Threat to Adjunct Union Organizers," *In These Times*, Aug. 3, 2015, http://inthesetimes.com/working/entry/18266/duquesnes_nlrb_filing_reads_as_a_brazen_threat_to_adjunct_union_organizers; Bill Schackner, "Footnote in Legal Brief Adds to Labor Rift at Duquesne University," *Pittsburgh Post-Gazette*, Aug. 6, 2015.

37. Moshe Z. Marvit, "In the Midst of Union Battle, Duquesne University Just Laid Off All but One of Its English Adjuncts," *In These Times*, Oct. 28, 2015, http://inthesetimes.com/working/entry/18547/duquesne-adjunct-faculty-union-firings-english-department.

38. National Labor Relations Board, "Duquesne University of the Holy Spirit," Case 06-CA-163073, filed Oct. 30, 2015, https://www.nlrb.gov/case/06-CA-163073.

39. Office of the General Counsel, NLRB, *Outline of Law*, 136.

40. *Adelphi University and Adelphi University Chapter, American Association of University Professors*, 79 LRRM 1545 (NLRB 1972).

41. Saltzman, "Union Organizing," 48.

42. *New York University and New York University Chapter, American Association of University Professors*, 205 NLRB 4 (1973).

43. *Kendall School of Design v. NLRB*, 866 F.2d 157 (6th Cir. 1989).

44. Peter Schmidt, "U. of Illinois at Chicago Strike Showed Unusual Support for Contingent Faculty," *Chronicle of Higher Education* (Feb. 21, 2014).

45. Diane Dietz, "UO's Union Objections Withdrawn," *Register-Guard* (Eugene, OR), Apr. 25, 2012.

46. Maura Lerner, "University of Minnesota Faculty to File for Union Vote," *Star Tribune*, Jan. 19, 2016, http://www.startribune.com/maura-lerner/10645281.

47. Josh Verges, "UMN Faculty Can Form a Single Union, Ruling Says," *Pioneer Press*, Sept. 20, 2016, http://www.twincities.com/2016/09/20/umn-faculty-single-union-ruling-bureau -mediation-tenure-track-contingent-professors.

48. Rilyn Eischens, "UMN Union Can't Include Both Faculty and Lecturers, Court Says," *Minnesota Daily*, Sept. 5, 2017, http://www.mndaily.com/article/2017/09/umn-union-cant-in clude-both-faculty-and-lecturers-court-says.

49. Saltzman, "Legal Regulation," 55–56.

50. Justin Miller, "When Adjuncts Go Union," *American Prospect* 26 (Summer 2015): 46–51.

51. Peter Schmidt, "Power in Numbers: Adjuncts Turn to Citywide Unionizing as Their Best Hope," *Chronicle of Higher Education* (Apr. 14, 2014).

52. Joe Berry, *Reclaiming the Ivory Tower: Organizing Adjuncts to Change Higher Education* (New York: Monthly Review Press, 2005), 103.

53. David E. Feller, "A General Theory of the Collective Bargaining Agreement," *California Law Review* 61 (1973): 663–856.

54. Ibid., 726.

55. Ibid.

56. Ibid., 727.

57. Ibid., 728.

58. Ibid., 729.

59. Ibid., 734.

60. Ibid., 734–35.

61. Gregory M. Saltzman, "Rights Revoked: Attacks on the Right to Organize and Bargain," *NEA 2006 Almanac of Higher Education* (2006): 49–62.

62. Steven Greenhouse, "Labor Panel Is Stalled by Dispute on Nominee," *New York Times*, Jan. 15, 2010, A16.

63. Jonathan Weisman and Jennifer Steinhauer, "Senators Reach Agreement to Avert Fight over Filibuster," *New York Times*, July 17, 2013, A1.

64. "PN1397—Kent Yoshiho Hirozawa—National Labor Relations Board," https://www.con gress.gov/nomination/114th-congress/1397 (accessed Dec. 22, 2016).

65. "Senate Confirms Trump NLRB Nominee Marvin Kaplan; Delays Nomination of William Emanuel," *National Law Review*, Aug. 3, 2017, https://www.natlawreview.com/article /senate-confirms-trump-nlrb-nominee-marvin-kaplan-delays-nomination-william-emanuel. "Members of the NLRB," https://www.nlrb.gov/who-we-are/board/members-nlrb-1935 (accessed Dec. 31, 2017).

66. "Richard F. Griffin Jr.," National Labor Relations Board, https://www.nlrb.gov/who-we -are/general-counsel/richard-f-griffin-jr (accessed Dec. 22, 2016).

67. Matt Flegenheimer, "Republicans Gut Filibuster Rule to Lift Gorsuch," *New York Times*, Apr. 7, 2017, A1.

68. *Abood v. Detroit Board of Education*, 431 US 209 (1977).

69. *Mark Janus and Brian Trygg v. American Federation of State, County, and Municipal Employees, Council 31*, 16–3638 (US Ct. App., 7th Cir. Mar. 21, 2017), 3.

70. M. D. Kittle, "Appeals Court Tosses Forced Union Dues Lawsuit, Next Stop Supreme Court," Mar. 21, 2017, http://watchdog.org/291557/appeals-union-supreme-court.

PART II

Unionization in Private and Public Institutions

chapter 5

A Just Employment Approach to Adjunct Unionization

The Georgetown Model

NICHOLAS M. WERTSCH AND JOSEPH A. MCCARTIN

The movement for adjunct unionization appears to have reached a crossroads. As the ranks of adjunct professors multiplied and their grievances proliferated, they began organizing in increasing numbers in the wake of the Great Recession. One survey published in October 2014 found that adjuncts were organizing in 22 states.[1] Adding momentum to their movement was a December 16, 2014, decision by the National Labor Relations Board (NLRB) in a case involving Pacific Lutheran University, which made clear that the union rights of adjunct professors at most religiously affiliated universities are protected by the National Labor Relations Act (NLRA).[2] Given the green light by the *Pacific Lutheran* decision, many unions expanded their organizing campaigns. Some, such as the Service Employees International Union (SEIU), had already embarked on a "metro strategy" in an effort to unionize the labor markets of adjunct-dense cities, such as Boston and Washington, DC.[3] Union efforts were further bolstered on August 23, 2016, when the NLRB reversed a Bush era decision dating to 2004 by ruling in a case involving Columbia University that graduate assistants at private institutions could also unionize. That decision made graduate assistants natural campus allies for adjunct unionists.[4]

No sooner had adjunct unionization begun to gain momentum, however, than the results of the 2016 presidential election threatened to derail the movement. Republican Donald J. Trump was elected to the presidency despite the nearly unanimous opposition of the nation's labor unions. As Gregory Saltzman notes in chapter 4 in this volume, if the partisan patterns of the past hold, President Trump is likely to shift the balance of power within the

NLRB and federal courts to the disadvantage of workers—including adjuncts—who seek to win collective bargaining under the NLRA. It seems likely that a Trump-appointed NLRB will revise the board's decisions in the *Pacific Lutheran* and *Columbia University* cases and that Trump-appointed Supreme Court justices will be more inclined to rule that faculty at religiously affiliated institutions cannot invoke NLRA coverage, no matter how secular their disciplines or how distant their work from religious instruction.

If, as most observers predict, federal protection for collective bargaining rights diminishes under Trump, adjuncts would be wise to look to other forms of law and policy through which to justify their claims for the right to a collective voice in negotiating the terms of their labor. In this respect, the experiences of adjuncts at Georgetown University, the nation's oldest Catholic university, which was founded by the Society of Jesus (the Jesuits), is instructive.

Georgetown's adjuncts achieved unionization in 2013 not by leveraging NLRA rights in a contentious battle with university administrators, but instead by affirming the justice of their unionization campaign in the context of the university's own moral framework for employment relations, Georgetown's Just Employment policy (JEP). The very existence of that policy, which is based on more than a century of Catholic social teaching, led Georgetown administrators to take an approach to the question of adjunct unionization that was starkly different from that of other private institutions, including many that share its Catholic and Jesuit heritage. Whereas many other Catholic universities (including some Jesuit ones) have taken the position that the religious character of their institutions should exempt them from coverage by the NLRA, Georgetown amicably recognized its adjunct union and refused to contest the applicability of the NLRA. The key difference at Georgetown was that the institution did not see adjunct unionization in a compartmentalized way, but rather approached the question through the lens of a comprehensive policy meant to align its labor relations with the university's values and mission.

Georgetown adopted its Just Employment policy in 2005 in response to student activism and the desire for campus custodial workers, who were employed by a subcontractor, to achieve a living wage. Through its JEP, Georgetown committed to ensuring that all campus workers, whether directly employed by the university or by its subcontractors, will be paid a living wage (calculated at $16.45/hour in 2016), that their rights to organize and bargain collectively will be respected, and that they will be guaranteed a safe and harassment-free workplace.

When the SEIU began organizing Georgetown adjuncts in 2012, it did so realizing that the university was already on record as supporting workers' right to decide for themselves whether to unionize. The university made clear at the beginning of the process that it would abide by its JEP, and it refused to contest the adjuncts' organizing effort. The union was successfully organized and its contract was negotiated amicably and ratified in October 2014. The organizing process avoided the divisive arguments that have pitted adjuncts against administrators at many other universities. Indeed, it ended up being a community-building exercise.

The Georgetown Context

In many respects, Georgetown resembles other research-oriented universities of its size and rank. Since the 1980s, as tenure-line faculty were expected to produce more scholarship and garner more research leaves, adjunct professors played an increasingly important role in the life of the university. As university officials struggled to restrain ballooning costs—tuition exceeded $50,000 in 2017 and has risen over the last 30 years at a level comparable to the national average[5]—adjuncts provided a cost-effective supplementary labor force. Georgetown did pay its adjuncts at a higher rate than other Washington, DC, area institutions, including George Washington University, American University, Howard University, the University of the District of Columbia, George Mason University, and the University of Maryland. This was not saying much, however, for the metropolitan Washington, DC, labor market for adjunct professors was saturated with potential adjuncts, and many took jobs paying less than $4,000 per course.

When SEIU Local 500 began an effort to organize on multiple campuses in metropolitan DC in 2012, it put Georgetown high on its list of priority campuses. This was unusual in that unions rarely target the highest-paying employer early in a multiemployer organizing campaign, for that employer can most easily dismiss union demands by arguing that it is already paying above the market rate. What made the Georgetown context different and much more congenial for adjunct unionists is that, unlike other universities, it had encoded a Just Employment policy rooted in the teachings of the Catholic Church, and the university was led by enlightened administrators who sought to uphold that policy's principles.[6] The JEP sets a living wage standard for all direct employees and contract employees working on Georgetown's campuses, which is updated annually to keep pace with inflation; it asserts the right to appropriate grievance procedures and access to campus resources, like the library, ESL (English as a Second Language) programs, and transportation shuttles; and it states that all workers have "the right to freely associate and organize." It also includes provisions for a standing university committee—the Advisory Committee on Business Practices (ACBP)—that is charged with seeking to efficiently implement the policy.[7]

It is important to note that the JEP was not born without struggle and conflict. Its origins date back to campus activism that began stirring in 1998, when students at Georgetown and other campuses began to demand that their universities refuse to allow apparel bearing the university's logo to be made in exploitative sweatshops either in the United States or abroad. A January 1999 sit-in at the office of Georgetown's president, orchestrated by student activists of the Georgetown Solidarity Committee (GSC), led to the creation of the campus Licensing Oversight Committee to review the status of the university's apparel licenses. After pressure was brought to bear by a new national organization called United Students against Sweatshops, in which GSC members played a prominent role, Georgetown joined other institutions, including Duke, in April 2000 as a charter member of the Worker Rights Consortium, a university-funded monitoring group that policed labor standards in factories making goods bearing university logos.

Having achieved their immediate goals in the anti-sweatshop movement, GSC members turned their attention to the plight of campus workers. In 2002, the GSC began to build relationships with contracted janitorial workers and to bring workers' concerns to the attention of the university administration. Students were especially surprised to learn that janitors who worked for P&R Enterprises, one of the university's subcontractors, many of whom were immigrants who held more than one job to provide for their families, earned substantially less than those who worked directly for the university. Students and workers organized for the following three years with a strategy of gradually escalating their organizing tactics to pressure the university to raise workers' wages. At the same time, a standing university committee that included students, faculty, and administrators explored how to foster a better environment for campus workers. In January 2005 this standing committee created a Living Wage Subcommittee whose mandate was to provide the deeper attention necessary for deciding how to arrive at a figure for a living wage, and ultimately this subcommittee created a draft Just Employment policy for the larger standing committee.[8]

Student activists felt that this draft policy was still not strong enough, and the coalition of students involved in the living wage campaign launched a hunger strike in March 2005. The hunger strike combined a public fast by students, outreach to faculty members and DC community leaders for support,[9] and an intensive media campaign to draw attention to the issue. Appealing to the university's Catholic and Jesuit identity, organizers timed the hunger strike to coincide with the Holy Week leading up to Easter, and they employed the language and concepts of Catholic social teaching to explain their demands.[10] During the hunger strike, the Living Wage Subcommittee continued to meet and to work toward a consensus on what an acceptable JEP could look like.

As mounting public pressure lent increased intensity to the deliberations of the Living Wage Subcommittee, a resolution was reached. The university announced in late March 2005 a comprehensive policy relating to wages and other rights of campus workers.[11] Under this policy, the lowest compensation rate went up from $11.33 an hour to $13 an hour by July 2005 and to $14 an hour by July 2007.[12] The students considered the result an important victory.[13]

While most observers focused on the wage increases, the policy that the university adopted included more than a commitment to ensuring that full-time workers could earn a living wage. The JEP affirmed five basic rights for workers, whether directly employed by the university or by its on-campus contractors. These provisions, firmly rooted in the tradition of Catholic social teaching, were as follows:

- Living wage: The JEP announced a schedule for increasing workers' pay to the new living wage standard, indexing this wage to inflation, and providing that the living wage would apply to both Georgetown employees and full-time contract workers on campus.
- Safe environment: The university committed to a "safe and harassment-free environment" for "everyone in the Georgetown community"— including workers.
- Free association: It was affirmed that workers have the right "to freely associate and organize, and that the University [would] respect the rights of employees to vote for or against union representation without intimidation, unjust pressure, undue delay or hindrance in accordance with applicable law."
- Full-time work: The university would provide "full-time jobs when possible and part-time or temporary work only when necessary," and it pledged to seek similar commitments from its contractors.

- Oversight: A standing committee—the Advisory Committee on Business Practices—would be established to oversee the ongoing implementation of the policy.[14]

Following the adoption of the JEP, the campus saw a union organizing drive quickly emerge at one of its key contractors. The janitors who worked for P&R Enterprises expressed an interest in joining SEIU Local 32BJ. Students provided support for that organizing effort.[15] While the GSC pushed the administration to demand that P&R accept a card-check recognition of the union's certification in lieu of an NLRB-supervised election, the university refused, citing the employer's right to seek an election under the NLRA. However, the university made clear that it did not oppose card-check union recognition by P&R or its other contractors: "Any of our contractors are free to adopt a card-check (unionization) process if they decide to do so."[16] Moreover, the university made clear that it expected its contractors would adhere to the principles of the JEP and refrain from mounting an anti-union campaign. The union was certified in 2006. The JEP not only survived its first important test, it proved to be a valuable framework for ensuring an amicable settlement of a union campaign.

A few years later, the JEP would be put to a second test. During the spring of 2010 food service workers employed by the campus dining hall contractor, the Aramark Corporation, began organizing a union with the help of students and organizers from UNITE HERE Local 23.[17] Because Aramark's local managers were known to oppose unionization, the effort to organize the Aramark workers unfolded secretly through the fall of 2010; student organizers reached out to workers as their shifts were ending and followed up with them in home visits. Once Aramark workers and Georgetown students publicly announced their intention to gain union representation on campus in January 2011, many workers cited instances of abusive behavior by managers or decisions to cut back the number of working hours for the most visible union supporters.[18]

While Georgetown never directly involved itself in the negotiations between the workers and Aramark management, the university administration took steps to ensure that all parties would be guided by the provisions of its JEP, including the protection of a safe and harassment-free workplace. At a crucial moment after the campaign surfaced and instances of discrimination against union supporters were reported, Assistant Vice President for Business Policy and Planning LaMarr Billups and Associate Vice President for

Auxiliary Services Margie Bryant sent a letter to Aramark CEO Joseph Neu-
bauer demanding that his company abide by Georgetown's JEP. On February
3, 2011, they wrote: "As you know, Georgetown University's mission as a
Catholic and Jesuit institution includes principles and values that support
human dignity in work, and respect for workers' rights. We expect the leadership of the companies we engage to provide services on our campuses to
inform their managers, supervisors and employees of the JEP provisions in
a timely manner. . . . We appreciate the partnership we have enjoyed with
Aramark, and urge you to remain open to respectful dialogue with your employees."[19] Aramark quickly responded with a statement that the company
was "neither anti-union, nor pro-union" and made a point to highlight that
"for half a century, Aramark has enjoyed excellent relationships with the 35-
plus different unions that represent [its] employees."[20] An escalation of conflict in this organizing effort was averted, and what followed was a respectful
process. By the end of March 2011 workers had voted for a union, and Aramark had officially recognized UNITE HERE Local 23 as the representative
of its food service workers at Georgetown.

Despite this success, it would be almost another year before the union and
Aramark concluded the collective bargaining process and arrived at a contract. In the meantime, students and workers managed to keep public attention on the importance of a fair contract for workers,[21] and the JEP helped
once again to set a tone for the bargaining process. After the conclusion of the
negotiations, a university spokesperson noted that Georgetown was "pleased
that Aramark and the union worked collaboratively to reach an agreement
that honors Georgetown University's Just Employment Policy."[22]

Having been put to the test in two union organizing drives, the JEP was
becoming an increasingly important feature of Georgetown's labor-management culture by 2012. It proved useful once again when alleged instances of
abuse were reported by another group of subcontracted workers on campus.
Workers hired by a different food service contractor brought lawsuits against
their employer in 2010 and in 2012, alleging "wage theft" because they had
not been paid legally mandated overtime rates.[23] Ultimately, that contractor
settled with its workers out of court, but not before the court found that
the workers' claims were legitimate.[24] Concerned students soon learned from
workers that the lawsuits had not ended the abusive practices of this contractor, and they brought evidence of ongoing violations to Georgetown's ACBP,
the committee responsible for overseeing the JEP. The ACBP in turn pressed
the university to hold the contractor accountable. The university acted, asking

the contractor to submit to payroll audits, allow Georgetown officials to conduct a workers' rights training with the contractor's employees, and pledge that henceforth it would abide by the JEP.[25]

Although the Georgetown administration had been pushed into promulgating the JEP in 2005 after a contentious student and worker-led campaign, it embraced the policy and worked to perfect it in subsequent years. The university featured a short video explaining the JEP on its website and ensured that all new employees were briefed on the policy's content.[26] Moreover, the university improved the policy, developing a protocol to ensure confidentiality for workers reporting JEP violations and detailing the investigative and reporting mechanisms that would be employed to follow up on complaints.[27] Over time, Georgetown had in effect developed its own internal system of labor law grounded in the principles of Catholic social teaching, principles that acknowledged workers' rights under law, protecting workers' dignity and promising them a collective voice on the job should they desire one.

Georgetown's Adjuncts Organize

It was in this context that Georgetown's adjunct professors began to organize in the fall of 2012 and the spring of 2013. While Georgetown paid its adjuncts more than other schools in the area did, its adjuncts faced many of the same challenges that confronted part-time faculty in other university settings. Their pay remained low and could vary by department; they had limited or nonexistent office space; they lacked employer-provided health-care benefits and faculty enrichment funds; they carried heavy teaching loads; and they suffered chronic job insecurity. Thus, like adjuncts elsewhere, they decided to organize to address these issues.[28]

Dr. Kerry Danner, an adjunct professor of theology, noted the difficulties of conducting research as an adjunct professor. "A full-time professor normally gets a research budget. The University will pay for them to travel to academic conferences. They usually teach one or two classes a semester and so they're also paid and expected to be researching for the college," she said. "What happens with the adjunct staff [is that] if you're getting paid so little, you have to work more classes, so you don't have time to keep up your publications because it is like you're working multiple jobs."[29] The low pay also "inhibits a deeper presence and engagement with students on campus because of the additional commuting costs or, for those with caregiving obligations, babysitting or elder care costs."[30] Danner decided to support the union organizing efforts, because she realized that she had little retirement savings and no college savings for her daughter.[31]

Danner's concerns were shared by many others. Dr. Mark Habeeb, an adjunct in Georgetown's School of Foreign Service, explained his support for the union as a combination of his existing political leanings and a sense that the lowest-paid adjuncts were not receiving a fair amount of money for the work required of them. Though Georgetown offered a higher minimum pay per course than other universities in the area, Habeeb pointed out the challenges facing adjuncts at the bottom of the pay scale who were dependent on their income from teaching. Although the national discussion of how adjuncts were treated in higher education had already caught his attention, seeing the rate for the lowest-paid adjuncts at Georgetown motivated Habeeb to take an active role in supporting the union organizing efforts on campus.[32]

Habeeb and Danner both pointed to a desire for greater predictability and stability in their work relationship with the university. With adjunct contracts usually terminating after each semester, it was difficult to make any longer-term plans based on continued employment. "Everyone talks about tenure-track [faculty] as the norm [in higher education], but that's not the norm any more," noted Danner when discussing the lack of job security. "There's a lot of frustration with that."[33] Both Habeeb and Danner saw stabilizing the relationship between adjuncts and the university as an important step toward achieving more respectful treatment for their adjunct colleagues, who generally lacked any support for their professional development and who often felt like the faculty's second-class citizens.

Local 500 of the SEIU, which was also organizing adjuncts at George Washington and American Universities, sent organizers to meet with Georgetown's adjuncts. Soon, the local had engaged a number of adjunct professors at the university and received vocal support from individual students and one of the main student newspapers.[34]

Yet as Georgetown's adjuncts began to organize, they were mindful of the hostility that adjuncts in other universities around the country were experiencing in their attempts to unionize.[35] They knew that the leaders of other Catholic and Jesuit universities were contesting the rights of adjuncts to organize and arguing that their institutions' religious affiliation exempted them from the coverage of the NLRA and the jurisdiction of the NLRB. The adjuncts were well aware of Georgetown's JEP, but they also understood that up to that point the policy had never been invoked in connection with directly employed university staff, let alone those engaged in classroom instruction. Whether Georgetown would continue to adhere to its JEP when it was put to the test on adjunct unionization was an open question.

It did not remain open for long. Once it became known in September 2012 that SEIU Local 500 had organizers on campus talking with Georgetown adjuncts, the university's top-level leadership met to review the situation. That meeting produced a clear consensus. "This seems like a straightforward issue for us to deal with," argued one of the administrators in that meeting. "This is not a complicated decision, because we've thought through the principles on this already." Georgetown had a policy about which it was justifiably proud, the university's leaders agreed, and it would apply that policy in this case just as it had in the cases involving janitors and food service workers.[36]

On September 28, 2012, Executive Vice President and Provost Robert M. Groves sent an email to all Georgetown faculty members that addressed the administration's position on the nascent organizing drive. The message made clear that Georgetown would not fight an effort by its adjuncts to organize. Instead, referring to the JEP, Groves affirmed the adjuncts' right to unionize if they chose to do so. "The university has a long history of working productively with . . . unions," Groves wrote. "As stated in Georgetown's Just Employment Policy, our University respects employees' rights to free[ly] associate and organize, which includes voting for or against union representation without intimidation, unjust pressure, undue delay or hindrance in accordance with applicable law." Groves went on to say that representatives of SEIU Local 500 would be allowed on campus and in buildings open to the public, like members of other outside organizations, as long as they did not disturb classes. Moreover, the provost encouraged adjunct faculty to gather information on the union, the representation process, and the rights of adjuncts under federal labor law. Not only did Georgetown refrain from hiring an anti-union law firm to fight the adjuncts' organizing effort, but Groves's letter concluded by sharing links to the NLRB's website and providing the phone number for the NLRB's Washington office for those who had questions about the organizing process.[37]

Even though Georgetown administrators took a neutral stance, many adjuncts still feared they would be discriminated against by their department chairs if they were seen as openly pro-union.[38] The prevalence of such fears indicated how precarious the adjuncts' situation was, even in the best of circumstances. As it happened, however, no instances of intimidation materialized, and the organizing campaign proceeded smoothly.

Provost Groves sent another message to all Georgetown faculty on March 25, 2013, describing the pending union election process. Again, he cited the principles of the JEP and provided links to the NLRB website for further questions.[39] The union election took place from April 12 to May 3, and 70 percent of those who cast ballots voted in favor of the union.[40] Groves announced the results on May 14, once again citing the JEP and making clear that the university looked forward to "productive negotiations" with the adjuncts' union.[41]

Observers noted that Georgetown had "lived up to its promise to remain neutral"[42]—distinguishing it from other universities facing adjunct organizing campaigns. Local SEIU spokesperson Christopher Honey praised Georgetown's administration for its respectful handling of the situation, saying, "They were not just neutral but very cooperative throughout the entire process. They really upheld their social values."[43]

Following the certification of SEIU Local 500 as the representative of Georgetown's adjuncts, the university and the adjuncts began the bargaining process. Six part-time faculty members were part of the bargaining committee for the union, including Kerry Danner and Mark Habeeb. The administration's bargaining team included Senior Advisor to the President for Faculty Relations Lisa Krim, Deputy Dean of the School of Continuing Studies Walter Rankin, and Director of Faculty Affairs and Assistant Provost Cynthia Chance.

In September 2014, the bargaining committee reached a tentative agreement. Groves and adjunct members of the union negotiating team sent a message to all university faculty to announce the details on October 9, 2014, saying they were "hopeful that, through this agreement, and through our continued work together, part-time faculty members in our community will feel as welcomed and valued as other faculty members." The joint message cited Georgetown's Catholic and Jesuit beliefs and how these faith traditions would be manifested in the first collective bargaining agreement with the part-time faculty.[44] On October 28, 2014, the union's members voted to approve the pact.[45]

The deal included several significant improvements for adjuncts. Union negotiators had focused on setting a higher floor for adjunct compensation rates and on formalizing adjunct rights in the workplace. Key provisions addressed the need for greater job security.[46] The contract would provide "good faith consideration" to adjunct faculty who had taught at Georgetown regularly over the prior two years or more and a small raise for those adjunct faculty who were earning above the minimum compensation rate but below $6,000 per course. The minimum compensation rate for a three- or four-credit course was set at $4,300 for the spring 2015 semester and would go up to $4,700 by the fall of 2016.[47] According to Mark Habeeb, this represented a significant increase in pay for the roughly 25 percent of adjuncts who were earning approximately $2,300 to $3,000 per course before the agreement.[48]

The agreement also mandated a $300 course cancellation fee to be paid to adjuncts if a course was canceled 21 days before classes began, and it established a "just cause" standard for the disciplining or dismissal of an adjunct faculty member.[49] Furthermore, the agreement codified existing benefits for adjuncts, like voluntary contribution retirement plans (nonmatching), and revamped the evaluations process for adjuncts in order to increase transparency and fairness.[50] Finally, it created a $35,000 professional development fund for adjunct faculty members. This pool of funding was viewed as "a real win-win" because it helped adjuncts advance their careers by presenting their research at conferences, while in turn enhancing the university's reputation. Perhaps most important, this showed that the university "respects [adjuncts] as legitimate scholars. It says that it's worth it for [the university] to send [adjuncts] to a conference as scholars, [that an adjunct is not] just a person who drops in to teach once a week on campus."[51]

Both sides agreed that the unionization of adjuncts would foster positive pedagogical outcomes. By raising pay and increasing job stability, Georgetown invested in improving retention among its adjunct faculty, and studies have shown that improving faculty retention tends to also improve student outcomes.[52] Each side also saw the agreement as the beginning of a new and more productive relationship. Adjuncts viewed it as a first step in a longer process to improve the conditions of their jobs. The university viewed it as the beginning of an ongoing dialogue about building a more inclusive work environment. In the same manner that the organizing and union certification process had been more amicable at Georgetown than at other institutions, the contract negotiations also exemplified a strong working relationship built on mutual respect between the university and the adjunct union.

Both sides credited the JEP for shaping the positive tone of the campaign, negotiations, and ongoing relationship. Lisa Krim, one of the university's lead negotiators, observed that the JEP "created a foundation for the university's position in the negotiations because the policy clearly stated the values of the institution."[53] She also noted that the participants in the bargaining process "built trust and mutual respect through open and respectful dialogue."[54] Anne McLeer, the director of higher education and strategic planning at SEIU Local 500, also praised the JEP: "Georgetown stands out as a model for collaboration with their faculty for, first of all, not opposing the organizing to begin with and in collaboration with the adjuncts, negotiating a really good contract."[55]

Lessons and Implications

Ultimately, the adjunct unionization process and contract negotiations at Georgetown became a unifying moment for the campus community and did not produce the division and rancor that have prevailed on many other campuses. Leaders of some other Catholic and Jesuit institutions have raised concerns over whether collective bargaining with adjuncts would undermine their institutional mission. The Georgetown experience suggests that such fears are unfounded. Collective bargaining with adjuncts did not bankrupt Georgetown's finances, undermine working relationships in academic departments, or compromise the university's religious identity. To the contrary, wrestling with the labor question in a principled way allowed Georgetown to further reinforce the religious ideals at the heart of its mission of *cura personalis*—the care and education of the whole person.

Through the struggles to define and implement the Just Employment policy, including the adjunct organizing campaign, students from many faith backgrounds and those who identified with no faith were introduced to the principles of Catholic social teaching in ways that are bound to affect them no matter what walk of life they enter. They have seen not only that institutions of higher learning can provide top-quality education *and* respect the dignity of workers, but that these two goals are deeply complementary.

Two factors made a difference at Georgetown. First, the university saw the adjunct question from the beginning as one part of a larger issue of just employment relations. Having previously made commitments to defending the dignity and rights of low-waged janitorial and food service workers, Georgetown administrators were more likely to respond similarly to the demands of adjunct professors. Second, Georgetown had a policy in place before adjuncts began to organize, which helped ensure that adjunct rights would be respected.

The lessons of the Georgetown experience are obviously applicable to every university that claims a Catholic affiliation. How seriously can such universities take their religious affiliation if they have not adopted and begun to implement a policy rooted in Catholic social teaching, like Georgetown's JEP? As a first step toward defending workers' rights at these universities, adjuncts and their supporters should consider joining with students and other campus workers—both directly employed and subcontracted—in demanding their own Just Employment policies. Such policies will not only help campus workers win dignity, they will promote the educational mission of these institutions.

And the implications of Georgetown's experience have the potential to transcend the world of religiously affiliated universities. All universities extol their virtues as "communities." Few, however, have delineated the principles of their "community" when it comes to workers' rights to living wages and a collective voice on the job. Their students and faculty should call upon them to do so. As influential employers and engines of economic development, universities act as anchor institutions whose labor practices inevitably influence the labor practices of their surrounding cities and towns. What they do matters, and we all have an interest in ensuring that these institutions elevate rather than depress labor standards.

In an era when aggrieved workers can expect little help from government, the time is ripe for worker rights advocates to focus on building a supplemental rule of law on the nation's university campuses, one that ensures that these institutions of learning, individual development, and upward mobility do not themselves reproduce exploitation and inequality. If Georgetown's experience is any measure, spreading campus Just Employment policies might do more than help adjuncts win their rights. It might help us turn our universities into incubators of a more just, sustainable, and democratic future.

NOTES

1. Joe Berry and Helena Worthen, "22 States Where Adjunct Faculty Are Organizing for Justice," *In These Times*, Oct. 9, 2014, http://inthesetimes.com/working/entry/17233/wave_of _contingent_faculty_organizing_sweeps_onto_campuses.

2. *Pacific Lutheran University and Service Employees International Union, Local 925*, 361 NLRB No. 157 (2014); Bruce Bagley, "New NLRB Determination Makes It Easier for Unions to Organize Faculty at Universities and Colleges," *Pennsylvania Labor and Employment Blog*, Jan. 20, 2015, http://www.palaborandemploymentblog.com/2015/01/articles/unions/new-nlrb-de termination-makes-it-easier-for-unions-to-organize-faculty-at-universities-and-colleges.

3. Peter Schmidt, "'Metro' Unionizing Strategy Is Viewed as a Means to Empower Adjunct Faculty," *Chronicle of Higher Education* (Dec. 3, 2012), http://www.chronicle.com/article/Metro -Unionizing-Strategy-Is/136101.

4. *Trustees of Columbia University in the City of New York and Graduate Workers of Columbia—GWC, UAW*, 364 NLRB No. 90 (2016); Colleen Flaherty, "NLRB: Graduate Students at Private Universities May Unionize," *Inside Higher Ed*, Aug. 24, 2016, https://www.insidehighered.com/news/2016/08/24/nlrb-says-graduate-students-private-universities-may-unionize.

5. Georgetown tuition rates are available at https://finaid.georgetown.edu/cost-of-attendance/undergraduate. On rising tuition generally, see Michelle Jamrisko and Ilan Kolet, "College Costs Surge 500% in U.S. since 1985," *Bloomberg News*, Aug. 26, 2013, https://www.bloomberg.com/news/articles/2013-08-26/college-costs-surge-500-in-u-s-since-1985-chart-of-the-day.

6. Georgetown University, Office of Public Affairs, "Just Employment Policy," updated Jan. 1, 2015, http://publicaffairs.georgetown.edu/acbp/just-employment-policy.html.

7. Ibid.

8. Virginia Leavell and Kathleen Maas Weigert, "Working towards a Just Employment Policy," *Hoya*, May 20, 2005, http://www.thehoya.com/working-towards-a-just-employment-policy.

9. Sudarsan Raghavan, "GU Activists Go Hungry to Help Janitors," *Washington Post*, Mar. 21, 2005, http://www.washingtonpost.com/wp-dyn/articles/A52340-2005Mar20.html.

10. United Students against Sweatshops and the Student Labor Action Project, "Case Studies: Georgetown University Hunger Strike," Student Worker Solidarity Center, ca. July 2005, http://www.livingwageaction.org/workshops_action_cases.htm#2.

11. Susan Kinzie, "GU Protestors Savor a Win—and a Meal," *Washington Post*, Mar. 25, 2005, http://www.washingtonpost.com/wp-dyn/articles/A62829-2005Mar24.html.

12. Ibid.

13. Ibid.

14. Georgetown University, "Just Employment Policy."

15. Voice Staff, "Wages and Unions: Living Wage Revival," *Georgetown Voice*, Mar. 2, 2006, http://georgetownvoice.com/2006/03/02/wages-and-unions-living-wage-revival.

16. Ibid.

17. Lauren Weber and Laura Engshuber, "Aramark Workers' Union Certified," *Hoya*, Mar. 31, 2011, http://www.thehoya.com/aramark-workers-union-certified.

18. Molly Redden, "Aramark Workers at GU Push to Unionize," *Georgetown Voice*, Feb. 17, 2011, http://georgetownvoice.com/2011/02/17/georgetown-aramark-workers-push-to-unionize.

19. Ibid.

20. Ibid.

21. Matthew Strauss, "Workers Union, Aramark Strike Deal," *Hoya*, Feb. 10, 2012, http://www.thehoya.com/workers-union-aramark-strike-deal.

22. Ibid.

23. Upasana Kaku, "Employees File Suit against Epicurean and Co.," *Hoya*, July 31, 2012, http://www.thehoya.com/employees-file-suit-against-epicurean-and-co.

24. Christopher Zawora and Annie Chen, "Activists March on Epicurean," *Hoya*, Nov. 12, 2013, http://www.thehoya.com/activists-march-on-epicurean.

25. Kenneth Lee, "Epicurean Owner Responds to Solidarity Committee Petition," *Georgetown Voice*, Dec. 5, 2013, http://georgetownvoice.com/2013/12/05/epicurean-owner-responds-solidarity-committee-petition.

26. Georgetown Events, *Reflections on Georgetown University's Just Employment Policy*, Oct. 31, 2013, https://www.youtube.com/watch?v=CATEqRwXPd4.

27. Georgetown University, Office of Public Affairs, "Protocol for Reporting Concerns related to the Just Employment Policy," Oct. 2013, https://publicaffairs.georgetown.edu/acbp/jep-compliance.html.

28. Lucia He, "'Second-Class Faculty': The Hidden Struggles of Georgetown's Adjunct Professors," *Georgetown Voice*, Oct. 17, 2013, http://georgetownvoice.com/2013/10/17/second-class-faculty-hidden-struggles-georgetowns-adjunct-professors.

29. Ibid.

30. Kerry Danner, interview with Nicholas M. Wertsch, Mar. 23, 2015.

31. Colleen Flaherty, "'Critical' Organizing," *Inside Higher Ed*, Mar. 25, 2014, https://www.insidehighered.com/news/2014/03/25/union-event-focuses-adjuncts-role-changing-their-own-working-conditions.

32. Mark Habeeb, interview with Nicholas M. Wertsch, May 25, 2017.

33. Kerry Danner, interview with Nicholas M. Wertsch, May 25, 2017.

34. Sydney Browning, "Part-Time Professors Deserve Their Full-Time Rights," *Georgetown Voice*, Feb. 6, 2013, http://georgetownvoice.com/2013/02/06/part-time-professors-deserve-their-full-time-rights; Editorial Board, "Adjunct Unionization Efforts Deserve Support," *Georgetown Voice*, Apr. 4, 2013, http://georgetownvoice.com/2013/04/04/adjunct-unionization-efforts-deserve-support.

35. After Manhattan College adjuncts had cast their ballots for a union in 2010, the college claimed it was religiously exempt from US labor laws that would force it to recognize the adjunct union. Other religiously affiliated universities soon followed suit, including Seattle University, a Jesuit institution.

36. Opening remarks, Robert M. Groves, "Ten Years of the Just Employment Policy," Nov. 5, 2015, https://vimeo.com/157315075.

37. Robert Groves, "A Message regarding Adjunct Faculty Organizing Campaign," Sept. 28, 2012, email.

38. Danner interview, Mar. 23, 2015.

39. Robert Groves, "Important Update regarding Adjunct Faculty Union Election," Mar. 25, 2013, email.

40. Madison Ashley, "Adjuncts Vote in Favor of Union," *Hoya*, May 5, 2013, http://www.thehoya.com/adjuncts-vote-in-favor-of-union.

41. Robert Groves, "Update regarding Adjunct Faculty Election," May 14, 2013, email.

42. Alexandra Bradbury, "Adjunct Faculty, Now in the Majority, Organize Citywide," *Labor Notes*, May 30, 2013, http://www.labornotes.org/2013/05/adjunct-faculty-now-majority-organize-citywide.

43. Ashley, "Adjuncts Vote in Favor."

44. Robert Groves and adjunct members of the union negotiating team, "Tentative Agreement with the Union," Oct. 9, 2014, email.

45. Clayton Sinyai, "A Sign of Hope at Georgetown: Adjuncts Ratify Union Contract," *America: The Jesuit Review*, Nov. 13, 2014, https://www.americamagazine.org/content/all-things/sign-hope-georgetown-adjuncts-ratify-union-contract.

46. Shalina Chatlani, "Adjunct Professors Reach Settlement Agreement with the University," *Georgetown Voice*, Sept. 18, 2014, http://georgetownvoice.com/2014/09/18/adjunct-professors-reach-settlement-agreement-with-the-university.

47. "Collective Bargaining Agreement between Georgetown University and SEIU Local 500," signed Oct. 28, 2014, http://www.seiu500.org/files/2014/09/Georgetown-SEIU-Local-500-Collective-Bargaining-Agreement.pdf.

48. Mark Habeeb, interview with Nicholas M. Wertsch, June 19, 2015.

49. Coalition of Academic Labor, "Georgetown University Contract Highlights," Sept. 29, 2014, http://www.seiu500.org/files/2014/09/Georgetown-University-Contract-Highlights.pdf.

50. Ibid.

51. Habeeb interview, June 19, 2015.

52. A. J. Jaeger and M. K. Eagan, "Examining Retention and Contingent Faculty Use in a State System of Public Higher Education," *Educational Policy*, June 13, 2010, https://www.aft.org/sites/default/files/ed_policy_jaeger_0610_2.pdf.

53. Lisa Krim, interview with Nicholas M. Wertsch, Feb. 3, 2015.

54. Lisa Krim, interview with Nicholas M. Wertsch, Apr. 17, 2015.

55. Maureen Tabet, "New Congress Worries Adjuncts," *Hoya*, Dec. 5, 2014, http://www.the hoya.com/new-congress-worries-adjuncts.

chapter 6

Unionizing Adjunct and Tenure-Track Faculty at Notre Dame de Namur University

KIM TOLLEY, MARIANNE DELAPORTE,

AND LORENZO GIACHETTI

Adjunct and tenure-track faculty seldom make common cause and organize together. Researchers have found that tenure-track faculty often prefer to maintain their perceived status in the academic hierarchy and are sometimes loath to align with a labor union, and part-time faculty sometimes have needs and concerns that differ significantly from those of their full-time peers.[1] Nevertheless, in the spring of 2016, adjunct and tenure-line faculty came together to organize at Notre Dame de Namur University (NDNU), a small Catholic institution in the San Francisco Bay Area. Many at the school thought it would be impossible to organize part-time instructors, because previous efforts had failed. Others feared that the unionization of tenure-line professors would stall because of the Supreme Court rulings in *NLRB v. Catholic Bishop of Chicago* (1979) and *NLRB v. Yeshiva University* (1980).[2] Despite these perceived obstacles, NDNU's faculty won the right to unionize within five months and voted to ratify a historic wall-to-wall contract ten months afterward.

This chapter explores the conditions that led the faculty to organize together, analyzes the roles played by contingent and tenure-track faculty in the organizing process, and identifies the specific strategies that led to successful election outcomes. Unionization at NDNU took place in the context of a national movement by the Service Employees International Union (SEIU) to improve the salaries and working conditions of adjunct faculty. This case illustrates the diversity of the institutions where adjuncts have unionized with the SEIU. For instance, unlike at Georgetown University, NDNU did not have an existing Just Employment policy when its faculty began to organize (see chapter 5 in this volume), and SEIU organizers did not initiate unionization on the campus. Throughout the organizing process, NDNU's faculty closely followed developments elsewhere: the failure of SEIU's effort to organize adjuncts at Loyola Marymount University in California, the NLRB's denial of the Tufts University Medical School tenure-track faculty's petition to hold a union election, the unfair labor charge against the University of Southern California for interfering with the adjunct faculty's union vote, and the successful first contract ratifications at a number of San Francisco Bay Area institutions, including Mills College, Dominican University of California, and Saint Mary's College of California.

Working Conditions at NDNU, 2014–2016

The motivations for unionization at NDNU were similar to those that have led employees to organize elsewhere. Twenty-first-century studies of employee attitudes toward unionization suggest that despite a decline in the number of unions in the United States, employees across a wide range of fields still want to have the resources to do their jobs well, earn a living wage, be treated with respect, and have a voice in management decisions.[3] Many faculty members cited low pay as a reason to unionize. As one instructor explained, "I've been a part-timer for 11 years and it's been most difficult the last few years with the change in the economy and the widening gap between the rich and the poor in this country. As a renter in this county, I've seen my family's rent increase over $600/month in the last three years. So now we are being priced out."[4] Full-time faculty members at NDNU were also underpaid: the starting salary for full-time assistant professors was 21 percent lower than that of public high school teachers in the county. From 2014 to 2015, top administrators received large raises, including NDNU's president, whose salary increased 30.6 percent. In contrast, faculty salaries had stagnated for an eight-year period, reaching a point where they were among the lowest in the San Francisco Bay Area. The number of tenure-track faculty had fallen, and the proportion of adjunct faculty working on short-term contracts without health-care or retirement benefits had risen to 75 percent.[5]

For some, it was not about the money. Many faculty deplored the erosion of their participation in decision-making at the university. As one tenured professor put it, "I didn't unionize because of the pay. I did it because shared governance was pretty much gone. They didn't ask us, who are on the ground doing this work with the students, to weigh in even a little."[6] During its accreditation review of the university in 2014–2015, the Western Association of Schools and Colleges Senior College and University Commission noted some of these developments with concern. The association recommended increasing the number of full-time faculty, reducing the faculty's workload, increasing salaries across the board, and clarifying the faculty's role in shared governance.[7]

The school year got off to a rocky start in the fall of 2015. A decline in enrollments caused a budget deficit at NDNU, which operates largely on tuition revenues. This was initially reported as a deficit of $1.2 million out of gross revenues of around $52 million, and the administration immediately scrambled to ensure the university would have enough cash on hand to make ends meet. Rather than roll back administrative costs, university leaders took steps to reduce the funds allocated to instruction. The provost informed faculty that vacant tenure-line positions would go unfilled. The deans in the Schools of Business and Education met with a number of their program directors to give them more bad news: some program directors who worked on 12-month contracts because their programs ran through the summer would be placed on 9-month contracts but still expected to work through the summer on small stipends without the benefit of vacation time; others, including those who managed single programs, were told that they would now be expected to manage two or three consolidated programs without additional compensation. Some program directors learned they would lose their release time units for advising or for program direction but still be required to do the work. They were shocked and alarmed. As one department chair remarked, "These changes may result in some small savings in NDNU's overall budget, but for me, this is a make-or-break salary reduction for my family—I'm barely making ends meet as it is."[8] The university's proposals not only increased faculty workloads and reduced faculty compensation, but also reduced the proportion of the university's budget devoted to instruction, which had already been falling for years. Between 2004 and 2013, NDNU's expenditures for instruction fell from 30 percent of the overall budget to 23 percent, a significant reduction in overall support for teaching.[9]

During the fall semester of 2015, leaders of the faculty senate met several times with NDNU's president and provost to protest the proposals to increase faculty workloads and leave tenure-track positions unfilled. The senate had long been open to all faculty, adjunct and tenure-line. The senate president was a full-time adjunct professor in the School of Business, the vice president was a tenured professor in the School of Education, the secretary was a full-time adjunct professor, and the treasurer was a tenure-track professor. Together this group made up the Faculty Executive Committee (FEC). The FEC reported that the proposed cuts would endanger the quality of academic programs and harm students' learning. Unfortunately, the administrators appeared undeterred by these concerns and seemed determined to move forward with their plans.

In December a small group of concerned full-time faculty and FEC members began to meet during nonwork hours to research the process of organizing, the outcomes of recent efforts to unionize adjunct faculty at other colleges in the San Francisco Bay Area, and the 2014 case of *Pacific Lutheran University*, in which the NLRB published a decision that seemed to open the door for the unionization of full-time faculty in private religious schools. Organizing began in earnest just after the start of the new year.[10]

Some scholars have argued that tenure-track faculty overlook the plight of their contingent peers and sometimes oppose the unionization of part-time faculty, but this did not happen at NDNU. One reason is that all categories of faculty had the opportunity to participate in the senate and on many of the senate's faculty committees. Another reason is that unlike the University of California system, where tenure-track faculty members in high-demand fields can individually negotiate higher-than-average salaries, at NDNU all faculty members were placed on the same salary scale at the point of hire. Both adjunct and tenure-track faculty members had seen their salaries stagnate over the previous 8 years, with the result that they shared a common interest in unionization. The social justice orientation of the Sisters of Notre Dame de Namur, the university's sponsors, also played a role in bringing the faculty together. Although the Supreme Court rulings in *Catholic Bishop* (1979) and *Yeshiva* (1980) had effectively stopped full-time faculty in private religious schools from unionizing for 35 years, the NLRB's 2014 ruling in the case against Pacific Lutheran University raised the possibility of a unified faculty union at NDNU.[11]

The tenured faculty members involved in organizing were well aware of the poor working conditions of adjunct faculty at NDNU. In addition to offering a low rate of pay, NDNU's policies often made it difficult for adjunct faculty to know whether or not they'd actually be able to teach, even if they had signed a contract months in advance. Many wanted a greater assurance of job security. One part-time instructor explained, "As an adjunct, I am looking for job security. I'd like to have an annual contract to reduce my anxiety about whether I'll be working or not." Even those who were assigned courses were not always certain they would receive the full rate of pay. A part-time instructor in the College of Arts and Sciences revealed, "I signed a contract two months ago to teach a course that ended up having only eight students. So two days before the class started, they told me that if I wanted to teach, I'd have to teach it for half the pay as a 'small-group study.'" An adjunct instructor who taught at the graduate level shared a similar story: "I received a contract to teach a class that ended up with only three students enrolled. But the class was required for those students, and so it couldn't be canceled. They asked me to teach it as an independent study. All together, those three students paid around $6,500 in tuition, but for an independent study, NDNU pays the instructor only $150. They may as well have asked me to teach for free."[12] These kinds of problems were not unique to NDNU. As discussed by Adrianna Kezar and Tom DePaola in chapter 2 in this volume, on many campuses part-time faculty have little job security, are let go or are hired at the last minute, and rarely have consistent access to office space, mailboxes, administrative support, or professional development.

Despite the part-time faculty's low salaries and poor working conditions, the greatest challenge to initiating an organizing drive was their lack of participation. Although part-time instructors were members of the senate and regularly received senate information through the NDNU email system, few attended and knew what was going on. Some worked at multiple institutions and spent little time on the campus; others taught while retired or worked full-time at their regular jobs during the day and taught only one or two courses at night. By January 6, the small group of faculty now calling itself the Organizing Committee (OC) had obtained the private contact information of around two dozen faculty members who had expressed interest in unionizing, but only one was a part-time instructor.

The OC knew that it might be difficult to reach part-time faculty, but it was not impossible. Several part-timers had been active participants in the senate during the previous two years and had worked to raise awareness of the low salaries and poor working conditions of adjunct faculty at NDNU. That earlier work provided an important foundation for the rapid unionization of the entire faculty.

The Work of the Part-Time Faculty Task Force, 2014–2015

The groundwork for the successful mobilization of the faculty was laid in January 2014, when Marianne Delaporte, a member of the faculty senate's executive committee, recruited part-time instructor Lorenzo Giachetti to volunteer as a part-time faculty representative to the senate. At the time, he was finishing a dissertation in French literature at Stanford University and supporting himself by teaching at different institutions by day and working in a restaurant by night. Together with other adjunct faculty, Giachetti conducted a survey of NDNU's part-time faculty and presented the results at a faculty senate meeting. Among the many concerns and questions the survey elicited were the low pay, the teaching restrictions imposed by the administration to avoid paying for health care under the Affordable Care Act, and whether or not NDNU's faculty could follow the example of faculty at other Bay Area private institutions that had recently unionized. After hearing the presentation, the senate passed a motion from the floor that Giachetti convene and chair a new Part-Time Faculty Task Force to investigate the issues raised in the survey and present them in more detail the following academic year.[13]

The report produced by the Part-Time Faculty Task Force revealed the plight of adjunct faculty at the university. It showed that during the 2013–2014 academic year, NDNU employed 170 part-time and 65 full-time faculty members. Part-time faculty taught 51 percent of instructional units, but received no health insurance or other benefits, no guaranteed contracts or office space, and the lowest entry-level pay in the Bay Area ($834 per unit). Factoring all levels on the part-time salary scale, the median income for teaching a three-unit course at NDNU equaled $863 per month. The report cited statistics showing that the average NDNU adjunct would need to teach between 30 and 50 courses a year to live and work in the region without being cost burdened.[14]

Many part-time instructors struggled financially as a result of the course reduction policy the university implemented in 2013–2014. While in previous years part-time instructors could teach up to 11 units per semester, in June 2013 the university adopted the policy that new part-time contracts were to be reduced to six or fewer units, but not to exceed eight. This was a preemptive move in response to the Affordable Care Act, undertaken to avoid having to pay health insurance to adjunct faculty teaching more than two classes (6 units) per semester. The task force report demonstrated that according to the final IRS ruling of February 10, 2014, a "reasonable method" for crediting hours of service would still allow part-time contracts up to 11 units without any implications under the Affordable Care Act,[15] yet many adjuncts continued to see their potential workload and income from NDNU slashed by at least one-third. This became a leading point of contention between part-time faculty and the administration during the 2014–2015 academic year, and it revealed a sad irony: part-time faculty members were not fighting to receive health insurance, but for the right to continue working *more* under the same poor conditions.

Although the report on adjunct faculty concluded provocatively with the question, "Can the Part-Time Faculty Unionize?" the document failed to generate the response among part-time faculty that Giachetti had hoped for. Privately, he had been in contact with an SEIU representative over the summer. He had asked the representative to delay delivering union cards until after the report was presented and the part-time faculty stood behind it. The report was sent out to all faculty and staff on September 3, but it generated surprisingly little response from adjuncts. A core of 14 part-time faculty members quietly mobilized, but many spoke of a general fear of retaliation, either from the administration or from the tenured and tenure-track department chairs who assigned part-time instructors to courses.[16]

Giachetti continued to push for change for the remainder of the academic year, but growing commitments to his dissertation and the status of the national job market made it impossible to pursue unionization any further. By the start of the fall 2015 semester, he had left the Bay Area to teach at the University of Washington in Seattle. When he departed NDNU, he had no way of knowing that the groundwork he and other part-time faculty had laid would enable the entire faculty to unionize within a matter of months after the faculty senate meeting on December 17.

Organizing Strategies

Organizing at NDNU proceeded quickly in the spring of 2016 for four reasons: effective use of existing communications networks; collaborative planning among part-time and full-time faculty; self-organizing; and the alignment of organizing goals with the mission of the university.

The plan for organizing was developed at the first OC meeting on January 6, 2016. At that meeting, 8 full-time faculty members—4 from the School of Education, 3 from the School of Business, and 1 from the College of Arts and Sciences—agreed to reach out to all full- and part-time faculty in their respective areas and solicit their private contact information. Two days afterward, in response to an email query, Lorenzo Giachetti provided the OC with the contact information of the 14 part-time faculty members who had previously been active in discussions about adjunct working conditions at NDNU, a group that included a high proportion of faculty from the arts and sciences.

Some of the key leaders of the Organizing Committee emerged from this group.[17]

The OC's networking strategy was highly successful. News of the unionizing effort spread like wildfire. By January 9, the OC had obtained the private contact information of 47 faculty members. By January 14, the OC had recruited 21 members and obtained the contact information of 110 individuals. By January 23, it had obtained the private emails of 157 people, more than half the faculty.[18]

The collaboration of full-time and part-time faculty contributed to the speed with which the faculty organized. Within a few weeks a core strategy group composed of contingent and tenure-line faculty agreed to go public and issue statements about why they were organizing. Once the faculty saw that adjuncts and tenure-track faculty were organizing together, a sense of excitement built among the entire instructional staff, and they quickly signed union cards.

It took time, however, to find a union that would agree to work with a combined group of adjunct and tenure-line faculty. Until late January the faculty had not identified a union to affiliate with. As chair of the OC, Kim Tolley had been in communication with the American Federation of Teachers and the American Association of University Professors Collective Bargaining Congress, but ultimately both unions decided not to work with the faculty of NDNU. Although neither group provided a specific reason in writing, members of the OC believed that these two unions declined because they didn't want to become entangled in a legal defense if the university challenged the full-time faculty's unionization. In contrast, the SEIU provided both resources and staff, and so the OC voted to affiliate with the SEIU.[19] At the time, the SEIU was in the midst of a national movement to unionize adjuncts with its Faculty Forward campaign and was also interested in the idea of unionizing tenure-track faculty in private schools. On December 11, 2015, tenure-track faculty at the Tufts University School of Medicine had filed for a union election to affiliate with SEIU Local 509 in Boston. If successful, that election would have joined more than 70 tenure-line professors at the School of Medicine with unionized part-time colleagues at Tufts and other campuses in the greater Boston area, including Boston University, Northeastern, and Bentley. Tufts University opposed the unionization of its tenure-line medical professors, arguing that they were managerial or supervisory under the National Labor Relations Act of 1935 and the Supreme Court's 1980 ruling in *NLRB v. Yeshiva*.

Notre Dame de Namur University's Organizing Committee debated whether to wait for the NLRB's decision in the Tufts case before proceeding further. Some felt that if the NLRB allowed the Tufts election to go forward, then NDNU's tenure-line and contingent faculty could organize with greater confidence, knowing they stood a good chance of successfully petitioning the NLRB. Others argued against waiting until the outcome of the Tufts decision, pointing out that any delay could seriously harm the momentum of the organizing effort at NDNU.[20]

The part-time and full-time faculty came to agreement on an effective strategy to win union elections. At its third meeting on January 31, the OC members talked with SEIU representatives, signed union cards, and decided to move forward rather than wait for the outcome of the Tufts decision. The committee voted unanimously to adopt the following strategy: if Notre Dame de Namur University opposed the unionization of its tenure-line faculty, the faculty would divide into two groups, and the adjunct faculty would be the first to petition the NLRB for a union election, followed by the tenure-line faculty. That way, if the NLRB ruled against the tenure-line faculty, the adjunct faculty could still unionize fairly quickly. Ultimately, deciding not to wait on the outcome of the Tufts case was the best decision. On April 5, 2016, the NLRB denied the petition of the tenure-track faculty at Tufts to hold a union election. The director for Region 1 of the NLRB ruled that the Tufts School of Medicine tenure-line science professors were managerial because they supervised staff and faculty employees in their labs and had authority in five decision-making categories. Those five areas, which were outlined in the NLRB's previous decision in *Pacific Lutheran University* (2014), were control over academic programs, enrollment management, finances, academic policy, and personnel matters.[21]

Another important strategic decision made by NDNU's Organizing Committee was to self-organize rather than have union organizers come on the campus. Some members of the OC were aware that SEIU organizers had hit roadblocks in southern California. In the fall of 2013, the provost at Loyola Marymount University in Los Angeles had informed the university community that SEIU organizers were interrupting classes to speak with adjunct faculty members. Whether this was true or not, rumors spread that this alleged practice had led some Loyola Marymount faculty to oppose unionization. By organizing themselves, NDNU's faculty hoped to avoid this problem. Although they self-organized, the members of the OC received a great deal of support from the SEIU. Two SEIU organizers advised the OC on strategy and helped the group plan actions and reach out to the public and the local community.[22]

Self-organizing led to a strong sense of community among the faculty. As Richard Moser has pointed out, one of the greatest challenges for faculty unions over the long term is whether faculty, especially contingent faculty, "can create their own vital and democratic unions—ones that do not overly rely on staff resources."[23] By organizing themselves, some of NDNU's OC members believed they could ultimately build a stronger union for the future, one less reliant on outside union staff. Additionally, part-time and full-time faculty developed new collegial bonds and friendships through the work of self-unionizing, and these bonds fostered the development of a community identity and culture for the new faculty union. Partnering with full-time faculty, including department chairs and program directors, helped to alleviate the part-time faculty's fears that unionizing would lead to retaliation and dismissal. This increased sense of safety and solidarity helped unionization proceed swiftly.

Having part-time and full-time faculty plan together provided several benefits in the organizing process. Full-time faculty had extensive experience with the messaging systems and processes of NDNU and had the access and tools to communicate effectively with faculty, students, and staff across the campus. Part-time faculty who worked in professions during the day and taught at night helped the OC develop a fairly extensive network of agencies and community groups, which supported the organizing effort by writing letters to the president and board of trustees. Part-time faculty who taught at multiple institutions had experience with many different kinds of systems and processes, some of which were more effective than those at NDNU. This variety of experience proved invaluable when the OC needed to solicit support from the broader community or make decisions about which messages to use in public relations communications and how to best achieve messaging on the campus.

Throughout the months of organizing, the OC aligned its values and messaging with the social justice mission of the university. Although the Sisters of Notre Dame de Namur no longer teach or serve in any administrative positions, they continue to serve as sponsors to the institution. The role of the sponsoring group is to ensure that the school remains Catholic in identity and mission and remains true to the sponsor's charism, or spiritual orientation. The charism of the Sisters of Notre Dame de Namur is expressed in the "Hallmarks of a Notre Dame de Namur Learning Community," which include an emphasis on community building, social justice, and peace.

Organizing as a Notre Dame de Namur Learning Community

As Nicholas M. Wertsch and Joseph A. McCartin note in chapter 5 of this volume, unionization at NDNU occurred in the context of a national debate over whether Catholic schools should allow their faculty to organize without opposition. A number of Catholic schools opposed unionization on religious grounds. For example, Seattle University, a Jesuit institution, fought the National Labor Relations Board over the right of its part-time faculty to unionize, arguing that the board's certification of the adjuncts' union violated the university's First Amendment right to carry out its faith-based educational mission free from government interference. In the fall of 2016, Seattle University's administration threatened to appeal the NLRB decision all the way to the US Supreme Court.[24] However, the administration at NDNU never opposed unionization on religious grounds, because the university's Catholic social justice orientation supported the unionization of workers.

In previous years NDNU's Sister Dorothy Stang Center for Social Justice and Community Engagement had invited members of Catholic Scholars for Worker Justice to the campus to speak about the rights of workers. Two years before the faculty began to organize, Joe Fahey of Manhattan College had given a talk at the university chapel on the subject of adjunct faculty and Catholic social justice. The audience, which included students, faculty, Sisters of Notre Dame de Namur, and administrators, learned that beginning with Leo XIII's encyclical *Rerum Novarum* in 1891 and continuing through to today's papacy, popes and cardinals had repeatedly addressed the rights of workers to form unions as a basic social teaching of the Catholic Church and even as a basic natural right of free association. Don Carroll, an emeritus member of NDNU's board of trustees, followed up with a roundtable discussion, "The Role of Catholic Universities in Workers' and Faculty Rights." Both Fahey and Carroll were members of the Catholic Scholars for Worker Justice, and in March 2016 the faculty received a statement of support from that organization quoting both NDNU's own *Hallmarks* and the 2004 *Compendium of the Social Doctrine of the Church*, which states that labor unions are "an indispensable element of social life."[25]

The OC also met with four sisters at the Province Center of the Sisters of Notre Dame de Namur, which is housed on the university campus. The goal was to explain why faculty members were unionizing, answer any questions the sisters might have, and ask for their counsel, support, and prayers. The Faculty Executive Committee and the Organizing Committee felt that having the sisters listen and provide guidance was important, since the sisters had always been the moral voice of NDNU.

Having the tacit support of the sisters and the public support of Catholic Scholars for Worker Justice was vital to the unionization effort. Their backing allowed for a shared common language with the surrounding Catholic community and gave moral weight to the faculty's call to unionize.

The Organizing Committee's Two-Pronged Strategy for Affiliating with the SEIU

The OC had hoped to convince the administration to agree to a card check as a means of determining faculty preferences for or against unionizing with the SEIU as a combined union of full-time and part-time faculty. In a card check, a neutral third party counts the number of authorization cards signed by verified employees. By early March, the OC had obtained signed union cards from 92 percent of full-time faculty and approximately 77 percent of part-time faculty. The OC sent a letter to the administration asking the university to "voluntarily recognize this union through a card check and not use student tuition funds or other scarce university resources to oppose the unionization effort. The card-check process will demonstrate that a very strong majority of the entire faculty supports the union."[26]

Although the university did not agree to a card check, it did not oppose the unionization of part-time faculty. In a letter addressed to the full-time faculty, the president wrote: "[I]f SEIU files with the NLRB for an official secret election among a unit of the NDNU part-time [faculty] . . . [and if] . . . the NLRB certifies that in the election a majority of the part-time faculty voted for the union, the university will in good faith treat the union as the contract negotiator for the part-time faculty and will negotiate accordingly under the NLRB law; if the vote is to the contrary, the university will continue our ongoing efforts to be a good employer to our part-time faculty." However, the university was not as open to the unionization of full-time faculty. The president suggested that federal law would prohibit their unionization, and she warned they would "withdraw from their shared governance role" at the university if they unionized.[27]

In response to this letter, the OC developed a two-pronged strategy for part-time and full-time faculty. The two groups would petition the NLRB together with the goal of forming one collective bargaining unit. However, as a backup plan in the event the administration opposed the unionization of full-time faculty, the full-time members would begin amassing documents to support their claim to have no real managerial authority as defined in the National Labor Relations Act. This way, if the university contested the full-time faculty's right to vote in the union election, they could withdraw and petition the NLRB afterward, allowing the part-time faculty to unionize first.

On March 16, the SEIU submitted to the NLRB 140 signed union cards representing 77 percent of the entire faculty. Over the next couple of weeks, the OC decided to move forward with the part-time faculty's petition to the NLRB and to withdraw the full-time faculty's petition for the time being, allowing them more time to collect documents proving they had no real managerial authority as defined in the National Labor Relations Act (NLRA).[28]

The NLRB gave the part-time faculty the right to vote to affiliate with the SEIU. A large majority of the part-time faculty participated. Of the 185 part-timers at NDNU, 159 voted, and when the votes were counted on April 29, 93 percent had voted to unionize.[29]

In mid-April, the full-time faculty resubmitted their petition to hold an election. By that point, they had amassed an enormous collection of documents to support their claim that they were not supervisory or managerial as defined in the NLRA. Ultimately, the administration decided not to enter into litigation over the unionization of the full-time faculty. No administrator ever explained this decision, but the faculty believed it was due to two factors: a desire to avoid drawn-out, costly legal proceedings, and an awareness that the outcome of such proceedings was uncertain, especially in light of the NLRB's ruling in *Pacific Lutheran University*, which granted that institution's full-time adjunct faculty the right to vote to unionize.[30]

Although the administration chose not to litigate against the full-time faculty's right to vote, the university continued to oppose their unionization. Just six days after the NLRB sent out ballots for the full-timers' vote, the president sent the full-time faculty an email titled "Issues Affecting Your Vote." Attached was a letter explaining, "There would need to be profound changes to shared governance in order to accommodate for the labor status of full-time faculty, if that is what the majority votes for." The University of Southern California's provost, Michael Quick, had sent out a similar communication on the eve of the adjunct faculty's vote on that campus. The anxiety and unease sparked by Quick's comments had caused many adjuncts at USC to vote against unionizing, and because of this, the NLRB found USC to have engaged in unfair labor practices.[31] At NDNU, however, most full-time faculty members were undeterred by the language in the president's letter. They believed that they had nothing to lose, because they did not feel that they currently possessed any meaningful shared governance. The vote count on May 25, 2016, revealed that 93 percent participated in the election, and 85 percent voted to affiliate with the SEIU.[32]

Collective Bargaining Outcomes

After the elections, both part-time and full-time faculty joined forces to bargain side by side at the negotiation table. Part-time faculty who taught at multiple institutions had experience with different organizational structures and systems, and that experience enriched faculty discussions about possible changes to NDNU policies in order to strengthen academic quality and improve working conditions. Full-time faculty contributed extensive knowledge of the university's shared governance policies, systems, and procedures.

Although NDNU's faculty had not been able to unionize as a single bargaining unit, they formally agreed to operate as if they were. The results of a bargaining prioritization survey sent out to all part-time and full-time faculty prior to the start of negotiations revealed that the item that received the most votes from both groups was to "create one union contract, uniting full-time and part-time faculty, to build bargaining power for the long-term."[33] The faculty subsequently elected three part-time and three tenure-track members to serve as the bargaining team at the negotiating table, continuing the united front they had maintained throughout the organizing process. Throughout the following year, this team negotiated as a single unit with broad support from the entire faculty, and although the university had initially opposed this approach, the administration's opposition eventually disappeared.

During the negotiations, the faculty bargaining team achieved tentative agreements with the university on increases in salary and benefits and better job security for part-time instructors. Part-time faculty won salary increases ranging from 11.5 percent to 35 percent over a three-year period, with the largest increases going to the lowest-earning faculty. Increases for full-time faculty ranged from 8 percent to 9.5 percent, and the starting salary for an assistant professor on the lowest rung of the salary scale increased 17 percent. Part-time faculty also won the right to compensation for course cancellation, improved access to university resources to support their teaching, and increased job security through a "preferred hiring pool" system based on seniority. They could also teach up to 20 units per semester, and the university agreed to no longer deny courses to part-timers in order to prevent them from becoming eligible for health-care benefits. Full-time faculty won an important protection related to their workload; the final tentative contract agreement barred previous administrative proposals to increase the workload by requiring the full-time faculty to teach five courses per semester instead of four.[34]

Faculty participation in shared governance was also preserved. The tentative agreements guaranteed the continued existence of the standing faculty committees, including rank and tenure, academic standards, curriculum, and faculty development. Portions of the faculty handbook describing shared governance policies and practices were incorporated into the agreements, making them binding and subject to grievance procedures and outside arbitration. Part-time faculty won the right to have elected representatives on all the committees except rank and tenure, along with financial compensation for their committee work. The agreement included the creation of the Joint Labor-Management Committee, with three part-time and three full-time faculty members, which would meet regularly during the academic year to resolve issues related to implementation of the contract, working conditions, and shared governance.[35]

In June 2017, the faculty voted on the proposed final contract, which covered the entire faculty; the ratification vote was conducted as "one single unit: one person—one vote."[36] Although the election occurred during the summer, a large number of faculty members voted; the count on June 27 revealed that 96 percent had voted yes to ratify the wall-to-wall contract, the first of its kind in a Catholic university. The consensus reflected the solidarity among NDNU's faculty. According to Kristen Edwards, a part-time member of the faculty bargaining team, "Despite being certified by the NLRB as two separate bargaining units, we set a priority of winning a single contract covering full-time tenured/tenure track and part-time faculty. The process of working together to support each other's priorities brought together the entire faculty at NDNU and yielded a stronger contract for all of us."[37]

Conclusion

The developments at NDNU challenge long-standing thinking about the lack of shared interests between contingent and tenure-track faculty. Although some scholars have emphasized the different priorities of part-time and tenure-track faculty, the case of unionizing at NDNU illustrates the power and effectiveness of both groups working together.

The Supreme Court decision in *NLRB v. Yeshiva University* made it difficult for full-time faculty in religious schools to unionize, but more recent rulings by the NLRB indicate that unionization is not impossible. Although the

NLRB issued no new ruling because the administration decided not to litigate, NDNU's case suggests that when full-time faculty in a private school can document a lack of real managerial authority, they can attain certification and the right to hold a union election. Today NDNU is no longer the only Catholic institution in which tenure-track faculty have unionized since *Yeshiva*: in the spring of 2017, tenure-track faculty at Saint Martin's University in Washington voted to unionize with SEIU Local 925, following in the footsteps of their adjunct colleagues, who had voted to unionize earlier. Faculty in other private religious schools may soon follow.[38]

Nevertheless, as scholars note elsewhere in this volume, in a shifting political environment, unionization may become more difficult at religiously affiliated colleges and universities. With new appointments to the board by a US president with an anti-labor agenda, the NLRB may reverse earlier decisions or interpret them more narrowly.

In the face of these potential hurdles, it makes more sense than ever for faculty to avoid unionizing in separate silos. As the NDNU case suggests, adjunct and tenure-track faculty can benefit from organizing as a united group. Together, faculty can develop a sustainable, strong union to improve working conditions and strengthen their voice in the governance of their university. As one faculty member explained, "This model supports faculty of all types, the social justice outcomes to which we aspire, and the students whom we serve."[39]

NOTES

1. For the lack of common cause among contingent and tenure-line faculty, see chapter 3 by Timothy Reese Cain in this volume; Christine Maitland, "Temporary Faculty and Collective Bargaining in Higher Education in California," *Journal of Collective Negotiations* 16, no. 3 (1987): 233–57; Gary Rhoades, "Reorganizing the Faculty Workforce for Flexibility: Part-Time Professional Labor," *Journal of Higher Education* 67, no. 6 (1996): 626–59; Rhoades, *Managed Professionals: Unionized Faculty and Restructuring Academic Labor* (Albany: State University of New York Press, 1998). The NLRB has allowed elections for tenure-line faculty in only a handful of private institutions since 1980. See Donna R. Euben and Thomas P. Hustoles, "Collective Bargaining Revised and Revisited" (2001), https://www.aaup.org/issues/collective-bargaining /collective-bargaining-revised-and-revisited-2001.

2. *NLRB v. Yeshiva University*, 444 US 672 (1980); *NLRB v. Catholic Bishop of Chicago*, 440 US 490 (1979), both at https://supreme.justia.com/cases/federal/us.

3. See Richard B. Freeman, "Do Workers Still Want Unions? More than Ever," Economic Policy Institute Briefing Paper 182, Feb. 22, 2007, www.insightweb.it/web/content/do-workers -still-want-unions-more-ever; Seymour Martin Lipset and Noah M. Meltz, *The Paradox of American Unionism: Why Americans Like Unions More than Canadians Do, but Join Much Less* (Ithaca, NY: Cornell University Press, 2004); Richard B. Freeman and Joel Rogers, *What Work-*

ers Want (Ithaca, NY: Cornell University Press, 2006); *California Workforce Survey* (Berkeley: University of California, 2002).

4. This quote is from a set of interviews Kim Tolley conducted during negotiations in the spring of 2017. The names of the faculty members are withheld to preserve their privacy (hereafter cited as Tolley, interviews).

5. Salary information is from Betty Friedman et al., "Faculty Senate Salary and Benefits Committee Report, 2014–15," Notre Dame de Namur University, Faculty Senate Records, (hereafter FSR). Information about NDNU revenues and the pay raises of senior administrators comes from federal form 990 for 2014 and 2015, http://www2.guidestar.org/profile/94-1156646 (accessed Oct. 2, 2016). In 2016–2017, the starting salary for an assistant professor at NDNU was $53,766, according to the "NDNU Full Time Faculty Salary Scale," in *Notre Dame de Namur Employee Handbook*, 64, http://www.ndnu.edu/human-resources/employee-resources (accessed Apr. 24, 2017). The starting salary for a high school teacher with a PhD in the San Mateo Union High School District was $69,794, according to "Certificated Salary Schedule," http://www.smuhsd.org/cms/page_view?piid=&vpid=1226194632318 (accessed Apr. 24, 2017).

6. Tolley, interviews.

7. Western Association of Schools and Colleges Senior College and University Commission, *Report of the WSCUC Team to Notre Dame de Namur University*, 17, 18, 36, 41, http://www.ndnu.edu/about/files/2013/08/NDNU-WSCUC-Team-Report-March-2015.pdf (accessed Apr. 5, 2017).

8. Tolley, interviews.

9. "Faculty Senate Minutes," Dec. 17, 2015, FSR. Percentages of expenditures allocated to instruction were calculated from Notre Dame de Namur University data at the US Department of Education, Institute of Education Sciences, National Center for Education Statistics, nces.ed.gov/ipeds/datacenter (accessed Mar. 15, 2016).

10. "Faculty Senate Agenda," Dec. 17, 2015, FSR; National Labor Relations Board, "Pacific Lutheran University," Case 19-RC-102521 (Dec. 16, 2014), www.nlrb.gov/case/19-RC-102521; Sandra Weese (American Federation of Teachers) email to Kim Tolley, Dec. 7, 2015. Over the phone, Weese provided Tolley with occasional advice on organizing from December 2015 through mid-January 2016.

11. For the need for tenured faculty to be more involved in improving adjunct working conditions, see Donald N. S. Unger, "Academic Apartheid: The Predicament of Part-Time Faculty," *Thought and Action: The NEA Higher Education Journal* 1 (1995): 117–20. For cases where tenured faculty have opposed adjunct unionization, see Gregory M. Saltzman, "Union Organizing and the Law: Part-Time Faculty and Graduate Teaching Assistants," *NEA 2000 Almanac of Higher Education* (2000): 43–55.

12. Tolley, interviews.

13. "Faculty Senate Minutes," Apr. 15, 2014, FSR.

14. Lorenzo Giachetti, Kristen Edwards, and Nelda Lazo-Fuentes, *Faculty Senate Part-Time Faculty Task Force Report on NDNU Part-Time Faculty, 2013/2014 Academic Year*, FSR.

15. Internal Revenue Service, "Shared Responsibility for Employers Regarding Health Coverage" (Feb. 12, 2014), www.federalregister.gov/documents/2014/02/12/2014-03082/shared-responsibility-for-employers-regarding-health-coverage.

16. Giachetti, Edwards, and Lazo-Fuentes, *Faculty Senate Part-Time Faculty Task Force Report*, 25.

17. Lorenzo Giachetti, email to Kim Tolley, Jan. 8, 2016.

18. Kim Tolley, email to NDNU faculty, Jan. 9 and 14, 2016.

19. Tolley, email to NDNU faculty, Jan. 24, 2016.

20. Emma Steiner, "Tufts School of Medicine Tenure[d] and Tenure-Track Faculty File for

Union Elections," *Tufts Daily*, Jan. 29, 2016, https://tuftsdaily.com/news/2016/01/29/tufts
-school-medicine-tenure-tenure-track-faculty-file-union-elections.

21. Tolley, email to NDNU Faculty, Feb. 1, 2016. Morgan, Brown and Joy, LLP, represented
the administration of Tufts University in the NLRB case. See "MBJ Client Victory: NLRB Regional Director Finds Faculty Members to Be Managerial and/or Supervisory under NLRA,"
www.morganbrown.com/news/news.php?id=430 (accessed June 10, 2016).

22. Kevin O'Keeffe, "Provost Hellige Responds to Adjuncts' Unionization Efforts," *Los
Angeles Loyolan*, Nov. 7, 2013, http://www.laloyolan.com/news/provost-hellige-responds-to
-adjuncts-unionization-efforts/article_0cba2e38–47f6–11e3-b922–0019bb30f31a.html; Sydni
Dunn, "Adjunct Unionization Movement Slows in Los Angeles," *Chronicle of Higher Education*
(Mar. 17, 2014), https://chroniclevitae.com/news/388-adjunct-unionization-movement-slows
-in-los-angeles.

23. Richard Moser, "Organizing the New Faculty Majority: The Struggle to Achieve Equality for Contingent Faculty, Revive Our Unions, and Democratize Higher Education," in *Equality for Contingent Faculty: Overcoming the Two-Tier System*, ed. Keith Hoeller (Nashville, TN:
Vanderbilt University Press, 2014), 88.

24. Menachem Wecker, "Can Adjunct Unions Find a Place in Catholic Higher Ed?" *National Catholic Reporter*, Oct. 14, 2016, https://www.ncronline.org/news/justice/can-adjunct
-unions-find-place-catholic-higher-ed.

25. The primary encyclicals addressing workers' rights are Pius XI's *Quadragesimo Anno*
(1931), John XXIII's *Mater et Magistra* (1961), Paul VI's *Gaudium et Spes* (1965), John Paul II's
Centesimus Annus (1991), and Benedict XVI's *Caritas in Veritate* (2009), all at www.vatican.va
/offices//papal_docs_list.html. The 1994 Catechism of the Catholic Church also supports union
rights in article 7.iv, "Economic Activity and Social Justice," www.vatican.va/offices//papal
_docs_list.html (accessed Oct. 26, 2016). See also Don Carroll in "The Role of Catholic Universities in Workers' and Faculty Rights," roundtable discussion, Sister Dorothy Stang Center, Sept.
22, 2014, www.youtube.com/watch?v=Ytjq8RW-Ogo&feature=youtu.be. In his opening remarks, Carroll refers to Joe Fahey's earlier talk at NDNU. For Carroll's views on the unionization of adjuncts, see Gerald J. Beyer and Donald C. Carroll, "Battling Adjunct Unions Fails
Legal and Moral Tests," *National Catholic Reporter*, Apr. 5, 2015, www.ncronline.org/news
/people/battling-adjunct-unions-fails-legal-and-moral-tests. Also see "Hallmarks of a Notre
Dame de Namur Learning Community," http://www.ndnu.edu/about/mission-strategy/hall
marks-of-a-notre-dame-de-namur-learning-community/; Pontifical Council for Justice and
Peace, "Compendium of the Social Doctrine of the Church" (2004), http://www.vatican.va
/roman_curia/pontifical_councils/justpeace/documents/rc_pc_justpeace_doc_20060526
_compendio-dott-soc_en.html, 667.

26. Robert P. Hunter, "The Union Representation Election Process," Mackinac Center for
Public Policy, Aug. 24, 1999, www.mackinac.org/2319; Representatives of NDNU's Faculty
Union Organizing Committee to Judith Greig, Mar. 8, 2016, document in Tolley's possession.

27. Judith Maxwell Greig, email to NDNU Full-Time Faculty Members, Mar. 15, 2016.

28. NLRB, Notre Dame de Namur University, https://www.nlrb.gov/search/all/Notre%20
Dame%20de%20Namur%20University (hereafter NLRB–NDNU), Case 20-RC-172076, "Notice of Hearing in Representation Case" (Mar. 18, 2016).

29. "Stipulated Election Agreement" (Mar. 29, 2016); "Notice of Election" (Apr. 29, 2016);
"Certification of Representative" (May 10, 2016), all NLRB–NDNU; Kim Tolley, email to the
organizing committee, "NDNU Unites Should Email All Faculty ASAP," Apr. 29, 2016.

30. NLRB–NDNU, "Notice of Hearing in Representation Case" (Apr. 14, 2016); "Stipulated
Election Agreement" (Apr. 25, 2016); "Notice of Election" (Apr. 29, 2016); "Certification of
Representative" (June 7, 2016).

31. Judith Maxwell Greig, email to NDNU Full-Time Faculty, May 11, 2016; Rosanna Xia, "USC Violated Labor Rules by Interfering with Union Vote, Federal Report Says," *Los Angeles Times*, Apr. 21, 2016.

32. NLRB–NDNU, "Tally of Ballots" (June 1, 2016) and "Certification of Representative" (June 7, 2016), Case 20-RC-174028. Also see SEIU Local 1021, "Notre Dame de Namur Tenured Faculty Vote to Unionize by 85% in Precedent-Setting Vote," May 31, 2016, http://www.seiu1021.org/2016/05/31/notre-dame-de-namur-tenured-faculty-vote-to-unionize-by-85-in-precedent-setting-vote; Colleen Flaherty, "Notre Dame de Namur Recognizes Tenured Faculty Union," *Inside Higher Ed* (June 1, 2016), https://www.insidehighered.com/quicktakes/2016/06/01/notre-dame-de-namur-recognizes-tenured-faculty-union.

33. "NDNU Faculty Bargaining Survey" (July 1, 2016), document in Tolley's possession.

34. "Collective Bargaining Agreement between Notre Dame de Namur University and Service Employees International Union Local 1021, July 1, 2017, to June 30, 2020" (hereafter NDNU–CBA), available from SEIU Local 1021 upon request.

35. Ibid.

36. Carlos Rivera, "Notre Dame de Namur University Faculty Win Historic, Wall-to-Wall First Contract," SEIU Local 1021, June 30, 2017, http://www.seiu1021.org/2017/06/30/notre-dame-de-namur-faculty-win-historic-wall-to-wall-first-contract. In NDNU–CBA, salary increases for full-time faculty ranged from 8 percent to 17 percent, depending on their placement on the salary scales. Policies and provisions related to faculty participation in shared governance were preserved as part of the collective bargaining agreement, making them binding on the university and enforceable through a union grievance process and binding third-party arbitration.

37. "NDNU Faculty Bargaining Survey." Edwards quoted in "Notre Dame de Namur Faculty Win Historic, Wall-to-Wall First Contract."

38. WA Faculty Forward, "Victory for Tenured/Tenure-Track Faculty and Librarians!" (Apr. 20, 2017), http://wafacultyforward.org.

39. Therese Madden to Kim Tolley, written comment on a draft of this chapter, May 2, 2017.

chapter 7

Unions, Shared Governance, and Historically Black Colleges and Universities

ELIZABETH K. DAVENPORT

Changes in higher education are challenging traditional concepts of faculty governance. Over the past 50 years, the culture, the workforce, and the economic environment have dramatically shifted at American colleges and universities.[1] As a result of these changes, institutions have hired fewer tenure-track faculty members, with the majority of new faculty hires being part-time employees. Today, more than two-thirds of university and college faculty are contingent faculty, making the term "retrenchment"—the elimination of faculty, programs, and jobs—part of the daily lexicon on campuses across the United States.[2]

The effects of economic cutbacks on salaries and the poor working conditions of adjuncts have led many faculty to seek new ways to influence decision-making in institutions of higher education. This search for a new alternative has been fueled by union activists on a number of campuses demanding that college administrations pay a living wage to all faculty.[3] These demands have brought new attention to the role of faculty and staff collective bargaining in academia. As a result of the growth of higher education unionization, collective bargaining rights have been at the center of a national debate in regard to public employees and unions. As higher education faculty's dissatisfaction has grown, the level of unionization among them has increased. In the summer of 2016 at the National Education Association (NEA) representative assembly, I was elected a college and university NEA at-large director due to increased higher education faculty unionization.

On many campuses, a question being contemplated now is whether collective bargaining and unions can coexist with shared governance. "Collective bargaining" is defined as a bilateral process that, with the weight of law, conveys equal power to both unions and administrations to negotiate the terms of employment, which include salary, benefits, and workload.[4] According to the American Federation of Teachers, collective bargaining provides conditions of equality between the administrators and the teaching staff and allows for real negotiations to take place. Contracts negotiated through the collective bargaining process can acknowledge and legitimize shared governance while also conveying power to both faculty and faculty unions. Often the collective bargaining system coexists with a faculty or academic senate that provides faculty with structured involvement in the governance of the institution.[5] "Shared governance" is a foundational concept in American higher education. The principle of shared governance mandates that all college and university employees have a guaranteed voice in decision-making and a role in shaping policy at their college or university.[6] Shared governance is not a simple matter of committee consensus or the faculty engaging with administrators to take on additional work, but it is a multidimensional concept that balances two academic tasks: administrative accountability and faculty and staff participation in planning and decision-making. Shared governance shuns the promotion of individual interests and anchors instead in the collective interests, policies, procedures, ethical standards, and behaviors inherent in the academic profession.[7]

Can shared governance and faculty unions coexist? As a formal concept, shared governance has been part of university culture for nearly two centuries, but in practice it has been the norm for two millennia. In a university, where the nature and substance of the institution is determined by the faculty, the faculty and the university leadership should share the processes of direction-setting and decision-making.[8]

This chapter examines the intersection between faculty unionism and shared governance, with a particular focus on the impact of academic collective bargaining and shared governance on Historically Black Colleges and Universities (HBCUs). I explore the status of shared governance at HBCUs and discuss the potential role of collective bargaining in increasing faculty participation in shared governance and ensuring the longevity of these important institutions.

The question about the relation of collective bargaining and shared governance is complex. According to James T. Minor and William Tierney: "[N]umerous arguments have been put forth that campus governance needs to be revised to meet new challenges. Rethinking admission standards, implementing distance learning, increasing fund-raising, diversifying the faculty, and creating external partnerships are just a few issues that demand timely and informed decisions. For some individuals, these topics create decision-making contexts that stand in contradiction to the tradition of shared governance. To others, shared governance becomes an obstacle to effective decision-making rather than its vehicle."[9]

This issue persists even on my own campus, Florida Agricultural and Mechanical University (FAMU). In 2016, in the midst of a labor struggle (we were at an impasse for the second time in three years), I discussed the concept of shared governance with a colleague. I explained that as a faculty leader, I enthusiastically support shared governance, especially in our institution, an HBCU. I believe that shared governance should and can coexist with collective bargaining. In the state of Florida, unions are constitutionally authorized, and public employees have a constitutional right to collective bargaining.[10] I believe that collective bargaining can and does strengthen shared governance. Therefore, to me, shared governance should be promoted by all segments of the university community and must be discussed and advocated alongside the collective bargaining process when it is available. However, to many faculty, this is debatable.

HBCUs Defined

Historically Black Colleges and Universities were created to give African American citizens equal educational opportunities and were accredited and established before 1964. Today, HBCUs are educational institutions accredited by nationally recognized agencies. In 1965 HBCUs were officially defined by Congress in Title III of the Higher Education Act.[11] The first HBCU, Cheyney University in Pennsylvania, was founded in 1837.[12] Today, there are 105 HBCUs.

Historically Black Colleges and Universities graduate far more than their share of African American professionals. While the HBCUs represent just 4 percent of the nation's institutions of higher learning, they graduate nearly one-quarter of African Americans who earn undergraduate degrees. More than half of all African American professionals are graduates of HBCUs. Nine of the top ten colleges that graduate the most African Americans who go on to earn PhDs are HBCUs. More than 50 percent of the nation's African American public schoolteachers and 70 percent of African American dentists earned degrees at HBCUs. United Negro College Fund members Spelman College and Bennett College produce more than half of the nation's African American women with doctorates in all science fields. Despite these impressive statistics, since the civil rights movement opened the doors of traditionally white colleges and universities to minority students, some policy makers have challenged the necessity of HBCUs, arguing that they serve no purpose in an integrated system of higher education. But they are still relevant.[13]

Twenty-first-century data highlight the ongoing importance of HBCUs. *The Educational Effectiveness of Historically Black Colleges and Universities* (2010) included the following statements about HBCUs:

1. Many distinguished and highly successful Americans have graduated from one of these institutions, including high percentages of African-American congressmen, professors, CEOs, lawyers, and judges. Indeed, during the days of legally mandated segregation, academically talented African-American students desiring university degrees often had few or no options other than HBCUs.

2. According to survey data collected by the National Study for Student Engagement (NSSE), students at historically black colleges and universities ("HBCUs") report higher levels of engagement on some survey dimensions than do their counterparts at non-HBCUs. For example, according to 2004 and 2005 NSSE data from 37 HBCUs, African-American students report more contact with faculty than African-American students at non-HBCUs. Other studies also show that African-American students at HBCUs are more likely to be involved in faculty research projects than are African-American students at non-HBCUs.

3. Generally, HBCUs have less funding and fewer support resources for their students than comparable non-HBCUs.

4. HBCUs have an average graduation rate of 55 percent, which is lower than the 63 percent average graduation rate for non-HBCUs. This may occur, in part, because of HBCUs' generally liberal admission policies and their average student's weaker academic profile. However, for similarly situated students, attendance at an HBCU versus a non-HBCU has no differential effect on an individual African-American student's chances of obtaining a bachelor's degree.

5. HBCUs succeed in educating and graduating disproportionately large numbers of African-American students in part because their admission policies do not create the situation of academic mismatch often found at non-HBCUs. Many African-American students granted preferential admission at elite non-HBCUs, even when they score well compared to

national norms, are competitively disadvantaged in developed ability relative to their school's student body who are admitted without consideration of racial or ethnic preferences. Thus, at some of these institutions, academically well-prepared non-Asian minority students, including African-Americans, have weaker performance and persistence rates than might occur in settings where the competition is in line with their current academic preparation.

6. HBCUs also produce a disproportionately high share of African-American students who receive degrees in science, engineering, technology, or mathematics (the "STEM" fields). Though only about 20 percent of African-American college students attend HBCUs, 40 percent of all African-American engineers received their degrees from an HBCU. The prevalence of academic mismatch, caused by non-HBCUs granting preferential admission to certain minority students as opposed to overt discrimination against African-Americans at non-HBCUs, or African-American students' lack of interest in science, appears to best explain HBCUs' successes in producing African-American STEM graduates.[14]

President George H. W. Bush recognized the unique mission of HBCUs: "At a time when many schools barred their doors to Black Americans, these colleges offered the best, and often the only, opportunity for a higher education."[15] Bush stated that most of those barriers had been brought down by the law, yet HBCUs still represented a vital component of the American higher education system. In 2017, these institutions still fulfill that mission.

Despite a high level of student engagement and accomplishment, HBCUs rank at the bottom of any assessment of faculty participation in shared governance. Faculty governance at HBCUs is generally described as ineffective, slow, weak, empty, and unable to respond promptly in today's rapidly changing higher education environment.[16] Thus, HBCUs face not only a crisis concerning their own survival, but also a crisis concerning shared institutional governance. It is universally believed that to remain viable resources for African American students, HBCUs must examine and clearly define the decision-making role of faculty and address the external and internal challenges that impede success.[17]

Faculty Governance

Effective faculty governance requires a focus on professional academic priorities and the administrative disclosure of all facets of governance. Professors are interested in the quality of their institutions because that directly reflects the faculty's academic abilities. Therefore, the faculty's role will involve attempting to control or, at the very least, participate in the decisions that affect the academic products of their institutions and the faculty's status as professionals. This includes questions of educational policy and administration, such as curriculum development, degree requirements, scholastic standards, evaluation of performance, and academic freedom, since they are central to the educational program and the professional role of the faculty.

A primary goal in establishing the relative roles of administration and faculty should be the creation of an effective system of faculty governance, achieved by the establishment of procedures and divisions of authority that promote the most constructive exercise of the powers and abilities of each party. Faculty governance requires a system of internal representation, such as a faculty senate, or other designation of the traditional areas of authority.[18]

The American Association of University Professors (AAUP) supports the idea of interdependency and mutual support between the administration and faculty, and states that they share primary responsibility for the curriculum, methods of instruction, research, faculty status, and those aspects of student life that relate to the educational process.[19] The AAUP also speaks of the college or university as being a joint enterprise. According to the AAUP, collaborative effort in an academic institution can take a variety of forms. In one structure, the president makes an initial exploration or recommendation with consideration by the faculty occurring at a later stage; in a different form, the faculty makes a first and essentially definitive recommendation, which is subject to the endorsement of the president and the governing board. In another type of governance, student leaders, when responsibly involved in the process, can make a substantive contribution.[20] However, shared governance is a difficult state to achieve because the concept is context specific. As Susan Feiner states, "[Administrators] seem to think shared governance means that they make a decision and then invite us [faculty] to a meeting and tell us the decision, which is *not* shared governance."[21]

In the arena of shared governance, the faculty provides an extremely important voice; however, it is in this area of faculty participation that many HBCUs are lacking.[22] James T. Minor has produced the majority of research related to faculty governance at HBCUs. Minor details the problems at HBCUs in terms of the lack of structure for empowering faculty senates, institution-wide understanding or lack of understanding of shared governance, and a need for a cultural shift that enhances faculty and administrative trust and communication.[23] According to Minor, although many functional elements of HBCUs, such as teaching and learning, are similar to primarily white institutions, the historical foundations, cultural aspects, student population, and racialized climate make HBCUs unique.[24]

Research by Minor indicates that 75 percent of HBCU provosts see shared governance as an important part of their institution's structure; however, 75 percent of HBCU faculty do not think the concept is valued at their institutions.[25] In 2002, Ivory Phillips noted that the structure of academic decision-making at HBCUs has allowed more than a few black colleges to make program decisions without faculty input.[26] Beverly Guy-Sheftall discussed how empowering HBCU faculties could benefit all constituencies. Guy-Sheftall observed that assertive, committed, and engaged faculty members are critical to any college's well-being and continued growth, while passive, disengaged, or fearful faculty members contribute to an institution's stagnation and imperil its future.[27] Marybeth Gasman analyzed the impact of tightened budgets, enrollment shortages, and endowment shrinkage on the leadership approaches of HBCU presidents, noting the role the culture and leadership of HBCUs plays in the faculty's participation in shared governance.[28]

Based on interviews with administrators and faculty, since the 1980s the AAUP has censured eight HBCUs for alleged violations of AAUP policies on academic freedom and shared governance. These institutions are Clark Atlanta University, Stillman College, Benedict College, Virginia State University, Meharry Medical College, Philander Smith College, University of the District of Columbia, and Talladega College.[29]

At my school, FAMU, the effort to establish an environment supportive of shared governance, especially during the Elmira Mangum administration (which ended in 2016), was a continuing disaster, even with a collective bargaining agreement. For example, the president, according to the faculty constitution, should meet and discuss areas of importance to faculty twice a year. In her first year, President Mangum conducted a poorly constructed town meeting concerning FAMU's performance, which was evaluated using the board of governors' performance-based funding model metrics. In the second year of her administration, Mangum simply did not meet with the faculty. According to the constitution, the president should establish councils, committees, and advisory bodies consistent with the effective operation of the university with the advice and consent of the faculty senate. The Mangum administration did not establish these advisory bodies. In fact, there was more exclusion than inclusion. The provost (Marcella David) renamed the dean's council, on which the faculty senate had long-serving representatives, and kicked them off. We never learned the name of this new committee. Requests for consultation by United Faculty of Florida (UFF-FAMU) on issues concerning the terms and conditions of contracts were chiefly ignored, and when they were granted, it appeared that the administration simply didn't get it. Specifically, an April 19, 2016, email request for a presidential consultation, highlighting "flagrant violations of the collective bargaining agreement," was ignored by the administration.[30]

The collective bargaining environment changed with the introduction of a new leader. In September 2016, Mangum agreed to step down as president of FAMU. The FAMU board of trustees approved her separation agreement, and Larry Robinson was approved as the interim president. Despite the union's impasse declaration, Robinson continued to negotiate with faculty, and an agreement was obtained. On February 6, 2017, FAMU faculty ratified the contract 122–0. Therefore, a change of leadership was the impetus to the resolution of the contract dispute. Leadership readiness is a necessary element for HBCU unionization.

Faculty Senates

At most universities, the faculty senate is the supreme legislative body on internal policy, and it advises the president on academic matters and other concerns. It acts in an advisory capacity for major policy changes, such as restructuring, layoffs, economic policy changes, and tenure and promotion, with the senate's recommendations reflecting the consensus of the faculty. Depending on their constitution and bylaws, faculty senates are forums where the elected senators and other faculty members discuss and debate curriculum issues and university concerns. At most universities, routine items are decided by the senate. For the most part, faculty senate deliberations focus on the welfare of the faculty and university operations, and senate members are able to offer their professional expertise.

The faculty senate also serves as a forum for collegial faculty participation in decision-making related to institution-wide academic standards and policies. A collegial academic environment can best be accomplished through senators selected by representatives of the various campus constituencies in accordance with the institution's constitution and tradition. Appropriate matters of concern should be brought before the senate by its members or steering committee, or by the president of the university or representatives.

Matters that may be of concern to the senate include curriculum policy and structure; requirements for degrees and granting of degrees; policies for recruitment, admission, and retention of students; the development, curtailment, discontinuance, or reorganization of academic programs; grading policies; and other matters of traditional concern.[31]

Generally speaking, senates and councils are elected, and they appoint committees that review curricular and tenure and promotion decisions. However, this barely disguises the reality that the president and other administrators have the final authority. Further, when the stakes are high, campus administrators and the board of trustees are fully prepared to overrule a faculty senate decision.[32]

Academic Unions

The unionization of all sectors of the higher education workforce, including tenure-track faculty, graduate student employees, and support staff, is included in academic collective bargaining. Unions are organized groups that use their collective power to voice opinions on issues in the workplace. Workers in a union have the right to impact wages, benefits, work hours, job training, health, safety, and other work-related issues by participating in the collective bargaining process. The Florida Constitution grants all faculty members the right to join a union.[33] Unions provide faculty members with support that ensures they are able to work in a fair and safe environment. In Florida, fairness and respect in the workplace are two of the main reasons workers have organized unions; this is especially true of academic unions. Florida has routinely underfunded higher education and has had to implement more stringent accountability standards.

Nationally, many benefits, such as the minimum wage, social security payments, overtime pay, and the protections of the Americans with Disabilities Act and the Occupational Safety and Health Act, are all enjoyed by Americans as a result of the labor movement.[34] Higher education collective bargaining functions similarly. According to the NEA, there are four basic reasons for faculty to engage in collective bargaining:

1. To achieve greater involvement in the decision-making process and to strengthen shared governance.
2. To clearly define the conditions of employment, including a fair and effective grievance process to resolve disputes.
3. To achieve a negotiated collective agreement that is stable, secure, and

legally binding. The terms will reflect faculty concerns, and the terms cannot be changed without full faculty involvement.

4. To increase legislative advocacy, lobbying, presence, and pressure.[35]

In 2012, more than 430,000 faculty members and graduate students at more than 500 institutions and 1,174 campuses were represented by collective bargaining agreements.[36]

As Timothy Reese Cain discusses in chapter 3 in this volume, a widespread unionization movement erupted on college campuses in the 1960s and 1970s. However, this movement was initially rejected by many faculty and faculty organizations, which believed that unions had no place in academia. In fact, the AAUP, one of the oldest faculty organizations, opposed collective bargaining for the first several decades of its existence. In 1972, when the AAUP supported unionization at its annual meeting, disagreements arose among the participants, and the organization lost 10,000 members.[37]

However, another union, the American Federation of Teachers (AFT), formed in 1916, joined the higher education union movement without controversy. Professors at Howard University in Washington, DC, formed the first AFT higher education local in 1918 and were followed by faculty groups at colleges and universities in New York, Illinois, and California.[38]

The history of faculty union organization has had several waves of mobilization. In the first wave the organizations were more like associations than unions and could not collectively bargain. The second expansion included both faculty and support staff collective bargaining and was fueled by changes in federal and state labor laws during the late 1960s and early 1970s. The third shift in the modern era of union mobilization gained impetus with the ability to collectively bargain. This shift, which occurred in the 1960s, changed the terms of engagement between faculty and administrators and opened up different possibilities for local unions. In 1966, for example, in my home state of Michigan, AFT Local 1650 at Henry Ford Community College led the nation's first college walkout. Union activism was also spurred in New York, and in 1967 public employees were granted the right to choose a collective bargaining agent. This victory was followed by faculty at the Fashion Institute of Technology winning New York's first AFT higher education contract. Other victories followed at the City University of New York (which pioneered the model of a multi-institution merged local), the State University of New York, and the New Jersey state colleges. The fourth wave of union mobilization was the rapid increase in graduate student–employee unionization during the 1990s in response to the increased use of graduate student–employee labor.[39] Today, because university and college faculty are advocating for broader change in educational policy, faculty unions are springing up on campuses across the United States (although the majority of academic unionization has occurred at state institutions rather than at private colleges and universities).

The United Faculty of Florida, an organization in which I am the state president and a local chapter president (UFF-FAMU), represents 20,000 faculty members at all 12 of Florida's public universities, 11 colleges and community colleges, and Saint Leo University, a private college. The UFF also represents 8,000 graduate employees at 4 universities.[40] Three different colleges joined the Florida union movement in the 2015–2016 academic year.[41] The faculties organized to protect their threatened job security and to have a voice in decisions regarding the working and learning conditions on their campuses.[42]

Florida is not the only state where collective bargaining has found a foothold. The NEA represents more than 200,000 higher education faculty, staff, and graduate assistants on public and private campuses.[43] They include educators across the country, from technical and community colleges in Washington state to research universities in the California, Florida, Maine, and Massachusetts systems. Through collective bargaining, unions have developed an impressive list of accomplishments that benefit students, faculty, and staff alike. The NEA's website highlights the following:

- A Western Washington University contract that broke new ground on faculty workload, tying it clearly to the number of students in each class, including online classes;
- A Massachusetts Community College Council contract that provided wage hikes and job protections to its 5,000 part-time faculty members, additional pay to attend campus meetings and training sessions, and greater access to classes for veteran instructors;
- A Klamath Community College contract, its first one ever, that established a grievance process, workload limits, pay raises, and email addresses for adjuncts;
- An Eastern Washington University contract that tied faculty salaries to market rates, an innovative approach that created raises as big as $18,000.[44]

Like the NEA, the AFT now represents more than 200,000 higher education members in all types of institutions, from small community colleges to world-class research universities, across the country.

Unions and HBCUs

More than a third of all nonprofit public and private colleges have faculty unions, but less than one-tenth of HBCUs have faculty unions.[45] Despite a scattering of unionization in various HBCUs, unions for both adjunct and full-time faculty remain scarce at Historically Black Colleges and Universities. Some experts believe that this scarcity is due to the location of the majority of HBCUs in southern states with strict anti-labor laws.[46] Some scholars theorize that unionization is contrary to the culture of these campuses, where faculty are suspicious of outsiders and power is concentrated in the hands of the university president and the rest of the administration.[47]

Most of the HBCUs with unionized faculty members are public institutions in Delaware, Florida, Pennsylvania, and Ohio, where the collective bargaining units were established in the 1970s or 1980s, often as part of a broader unionization of public colleges. An exception is Harris-Stowe State University in St. Louis, where nearly 80 percent of full-time faculty members voted in the fall of 2012 to establish the first faculty collective bargaining unit at any of Missouri's public universities. Contract negotiations between the NEA-affiliated union chapter and the administration in 2013 were contentious. Harris-Stowe professors were severely underpaid in comparison to equivalent institutions; they also had not had a raise in six years. In addition to salary issues, their negotiations centered on academic freedom and student retention. At the time, only 18 percent of the students at Harris-Stowe graduated, meaning 82 percent of their students packed on debt while not obtaining a degree. Additionally, with a student population of approximately 1,300, the administration was bloated, absorbing 75 cents of every dollar spent.[48]

Despite this victory, union activities at HBCUs in the twenty-first century have been sporadic. Faculty at the University of the District of Columbia and Howard University successfully unionized when labor conditions worsened in Washington, DC.[49] In April 2014, Howard University adjuncts voted overwhelmingly to form a union under the auspices of the Service Employees International Union (SEIU), becoming the first part-time faculty members at an HBCU to have a faculty union.[50] Later that same year, adjunct faculty members at the University of the District of Columbia voted 82–25 in favor of affiliating with the SEIU. This union activity is part of an adjunct movement that seeks to address higher education's increased reliance on contingent faculty, a development that has turned what was once a good middle-class profession—college teaching—"into a low wage, no benefit job without any job security."[51] Like in Florida, increased unionization efforts at HBCUs are often responses to autocratic behaviors or, in the case of adjuncts, economic security.

This topic was discussed in 2014 at the annual conference of the National Center for the Study of Collective Bargaining in Higher Education and the Professions. Panelist Derryn Moten, the co-president of Alabama State University's Faculty-Staff Alliance, an AFT affiliate, stated that many faculty members resist faculty unions due to the political interference and neglect that many HBCUs have experienced. Another Alabama State professor stated that many faculty view unions as hostile to their colleagues and as agents of past discrimination against black workers. I was also on that panel, and I argued that unions could unite rather than divide. Unions also can offer HBCU faculty a voice in the operation of their institution.

Conclusion: I Believe in Unions Because We Are Better Together

If we learned anything from the 2016 election cycle, it is that we are *better together*—that when the collective functions effectively, good things happen; when it does not . . . chaos. Every successful individual knows that his or her achievement depends on a community of people working together. On that principle, Hillary Clinton got it right. That is why I am a proponent of shared governance and collective bargaining—both clearly represent an "all minds and hands on deck" philosophy. As Henry Ford once said, "Coming together is a beginning; keeping together is progress; working together is success." We need this at my institution. In the 14 years I have worked at FAMU, we have functioned in separate silos—administration versus faculty.

However, to make FAMU and other HBCUs the best they can be, we—the HBCU faculty and administrators—need to develop and disseminate an entirely new paradigm and practice of collaboration that supersedes the traditional divisions, and replace them with networks of partnerships working together to create academically strong and prosperous institutions able to withstand inner and outer turmoil and fuel our continued success.

Our problems cannot be cured by a few, and it is only through *all* of us being active participants in our fate that we can truly operate through "excellence with caring." It is not they, but we who are the masters of our fate. Our job as educators is to model acceptable behavior for all: students, other faculty, administrators, and the board of trustees. We must realize that to see injustice and not to report it or speak against it only furthers unfairness. For us to see inequality and not attempt to correct it makes us all responsible for the wrongdoing. We are a community, and as its members, we have both rights and responsibilities. Many issues negatively impact the ability of the community to act effectively, such as poor leadership, lack of direction, lack of focus, power plays among different groups, lack of communication, and ineffective planning. It is only by working together that we can cure these problems.

Yes, unions and shared governance can be the foundation of our continued progress.

NOTES

1. On culture, see Association of Governing Boards of Universities and Colleges, *Consequential Board Governance in Public Higher Education Systems* (Washington, DC: Association of Governing Boards, 2016), https://www.agb.org/reports/2016/consequential-board-gover nance-in-public-higher-education-systems; Association of Governing Boards of Universities and Colleges, "Consequential Boards: Adding Value Where It Matters Most," http://agb.org /sites/default/files/legacy/2014_AGB_National_Commission.pdf (accessed July 26, 2017). On the workforce, see Jae Young Seo, "Job Involvement of Part-Time Faculty: Exploring Associations with Distributive Justice, Underemployment, Work Status Congruence, and Empowerment," PhD diss., University of Iowa, 2013, http://ir.uiowa.edu/etd/5057. On the economic environment, see Kristine Anderson Dougherty, Gary Rhoades, and Mark F. Smith, "Bargaining Retrenchment," *NEA 2012 Almanac of Higher Education* (2012), http://www.nea.org/assets /docs/_2012_Almanac_DoughertyRhoadesSmith_final.pdf.

2. For discussion of the macroeconomic forces affecting public higher education funding, see chapter 1 by A. J. Angulo, in this volume. Also see US Department of Treasury with the Department of Education, *The Economics of Higher Education: A Report Prepared by the Department of the Treasury with the Department of Education* (2012), https://archive.org/details /ERIC_ED544780.

3. Association of Governing Boards, *Consequential Board Governance*; Association of Governing Boards of Universities and Colleges, "Consequential Boards."

4. Elizabeth K. Davenport, "Unionization and Shared Governance at Historically Black Colleges and Universities," National Education Association, last modified 2015, https://www .nea.org/home/65416.htm.

5. American Federation of Teachers, "AFT Policy and Collective Bargaining," https://www .aft.org/position/community-schools/aft-policy-and-collective-bargaining (accessed Sept. 18, 2017).

6. Davenport, "Unionization and Shared Governance," 39–54.

7. Ibid.

8. Walter V. Wendler, "Our University: Shared Governance and Collective Bargaining," Higher Education Policy Commentary Paper 94 (Mar. 31, 2011), http://opensiuc.lib.siu.edu/cgi /viewcontent.cgi?article=1095&context=arch_hepc.

9. James T. Minor and William Tierney, "The Danger of Deference: A Case of Polite Governance," *Teachers College Record* 107, no. 1 (2003): 138.

10. Florida Constitution, article 1, section 6.

11. Higher Education Act of 1965, Pub. L. 89–329.

12. Stephanie Gallardo, "Oldest HBCUs in the United States," *HBCU Lifestyle* (Apr. 18, 2013), http://hbculifestyle.com/oldest-hbcus-in-the-united-states.

13. US Commission on Civil Rights, *The Educational Effectiveness of Historically Black Colleges and Universities: Briefing Report* (Mar. 12, 2010), http://www.usccr.gov/pubs/HBCU_web version2.pdf.

14. Ibid., 34.

15. George H. W. Bush, "Remarks on Signing the Executive Order on Historically Black Colleges and Universities," Apr. 28, 1989, http://www.presidency.ucsb.edu/ws/?pid=16979.

16. T. Bernette Wright, "Presidential Leadership: Selecting Competent Leadership at the Nation's Historically Black Colleges and Universities," *Journal of Higher Education Management* 30, no. 1 (2015): 178–89.

17. Minor and Tierney, "Danger of Deference."

18. "Statement on Government of Colleges and Universities," American Association of University Professors, https://www.aaup.org/report/statement-government-colleges-and-universities (accessed July 26, 2017).

19. Ibid.

20. Ibid.

21. Mary Ellen Flannery, "Faculty as Hired Hands: The Erosion of Shared Governance," *NEA Today*, May 26, 2015, www.neatoday.org/2015/05/26/faculty-as-hired-hands-the-erosion-of-shared-governance.

22. James T. Minor, "Decision Making in Historically Black Colleges and Universities: Defining the Governance Context," *Journal of Negro Education* 73, no. 1 (2004): 43.

23. Ibid.

24. James T. Minor, "Discerning Facts about Faculty Governance at HBCUs," *Academe* 91, no. 3 (2005): 34–38.

25. Minor, "Decision Making in Historically Black Colleges," 49.

26. Ivory Paul Phillips, "Shared Governance on Black College Campuses," *Academe* 88, no. 4 (July–Aug. 2002): 53.

27. Beverly Guy-Sheftall, "Shared Governance, Junior Faculty and HBCUs," *Academe* 92, no. 6 (Nov.–Dec. 2006): 33, 30.

28. Marybeth Gasman, "Historically Black Colleges and Universities in a Time of Economic Crisis," *Academe* 95, no. 6 (2009): 26–28.

29. American Association of University Professors, *Clark Atlanta University Report* (2010); *Stillman College Report* (2009); *Benedict College Report* (2005); *Virginia State University Report* (2005); *Meharry Medical College Report* (2005); *Philander Smith College Report* (2004); *University of the District of Columbia Report* (1998); *Talladega College Report* (1986), all www.aaup.org.

30. UFF-FAMU Newsletter, July 2015.

31. "Statement on Government of Colleges and Universities."

32. Ronald C. Brown, "Professors and Unions: The Faculty Senate, an Effective Alternative to Collective Bargaining in Higher Education?" *William and Mary Law Review* 12, nos. 2–3 (1970): 252–332, http://scholarship.law.wm.edu/wmlr/vol12/iss2/3.

33. Florida Constitution, article 1, section 6.

34. "FAQ: How Would a Union Affect Faculty and Staff?" National Education Association, last modified 2015, http://www.nea.org/home/35281.htm.

35. "Organizing and Collective Bargaining," National Education Association, last modified 2015, http//www.nea.org/home/35267.htm.

36. Joe Berry and Michelle Savarese, *Directory of Faculty Contracts and Bargaining Agents in Institutions of Higher Education* (New York: National Center for the Study of Collective Bargaining in Higher Education and the Professions, 2012).

37. Christian K. Anderson, "The Creation of Faculty Senates in American Research Universities," PhD diss., Pennsylvania State University, 2007.

38. "HFCC Local 1650 History," Henry Ford Community College, American Federation of Teachers, Local 1650, last modified 2015, http://www.hfccft1650.org/index2.php?page=history /timeline.html.

39. "Collective Bargaining," American Association of University Professors, https://www .aaup.org/issues/collective-bargaining (accessed July 26, 2017).

40. "FAQ: Collective Bargaining in Higher Education," last modified 2015, http://www.nea .org/home/62147.htm.

41. US Department of Treasury with the Department of Education, *Economics of Higher Education*.

42. "Our History," American Federation of Teachers, www.aft.org/highered/about-higher -education/our-history (accessed July 26, 2017).

43. "Faculty Union Membership Swells in Florida," American Federation of Teachers, Nov. 21, 2016, http://www.aft.org/news/faculty-union-membership-swells-florida.

44. NEA, "Frequently Asked Questions: Collective Bargaining in Higher Education," http:// www.nea.org/home/62147.htm (accessed Sept. 5, 2017).

45. Tony Pecinovsky, "Faculty in Tough Negotiations at Harris-Stowe State U," People's World, Feb. 27, 2014, http://www.peoplesworld.org/article/faculty-in-tough-negotiations-at-har ris-stowe-state-u.

46. Sridhar Sitharaman, "Analysis of Faculty Salaries at Historically Black Colleges and Universities," PhD diss., University of South Carolina, 2008, https://www.airweb.org/Grants AndScholarships/Documents/Grants2008/SitharamanDG2008FinalReport.pdf.

47. US Department of Treasury with the Department of Education, *Economics of Higher Education*.

48. Sitharaman, "Analysis of Faculty Salaries."

49. Ibid.

50. Davenport, "Unionization and Shared Governance," 39–54.

51. Elizabeth Segran, "The Adjunct Revolt: How Poor Professors Are Fighting Back," *Atlantic*, Apr. 28, 2014, http://www.theatlantic.com/business/archive/2014/04/the-adjunct-professor -crisis/361336.

chapter 8

Forming a Union

The Non-Tenure Faculty Coalition, Local 6546 at the University of Illinois, Urbana-Champaign

SHAWN GILMORE

Unions disrupt. This is their fundamental purpose, their promise, and their peril. They disrupt the status quo in the interests of the workers they represent, hoping to better the working conditions, compensation, and lives of those workers. However, these disruptions also make people skeptical of unions, at best viewing them askance, and at worst mobilizing against them. Unions make things uncomfortable, not just for employers, but also for the union members who put themselves at risk when they fight for fair contracts and who ask their skeptical colleagues to come along with them. And they make things uncomfortable for all who rely on the labor that union members do, especially when that labor is about to be withheld.[1]

This is what I was thinking about as we met day after day in our somewhat ramshackle union office in April 2016, planning the first days of what would be the first strike by the Non-Tenure Faculty Coalition, Local 6546, the union that at that point represented just under 500 full-time non-tenure-track faculty members at the University of Illinois, Urbana-Champaign. I was worried not just about whether a strike would have the effect we hoped for—demonstrating our members' commitment to the issues we had been bargaining for over the previous year and a half, and attempting to force the university to settle a collective bargaining agreement with us—but also about the effects of our disruption. We planned to strike, to withhold our labor, including our teaching, grading, advising, and research, and we knew each of those things would have consequences.

Over the previous weeks, our plans had come together. Our strike chair had worked with her committee to generate strategies, prepare a strike manual, and set up for the eventual discussions we were now having. We had entered mediated bargaining but hadn't seen much movement in negotiations. We'd held meetings with our membership, including a vote that authorized the scheme for a potential first strike, at first limited to two days. Following state law, we filed our ten-day notice of intent to strike with the Illinois Educational Labor Relations Board (IELRB) and notified our employer of our potential strike window. We'd signaled to the local media what was on the horizon. And now we were planning the mechanics of the strike, and I was worried.[2]

We planned to close one or more academic buildings, asking our tenure-track faculty and graduate student colleagues to move their classes in solidarity. We planned picket lines, assigned picket captains, made signs, printed flyers with our chants on them, and made solidarity armbands for those who felt compelled to work in struck buildings. We planned speakers for our rallies and food deliveries for those who would be on the picket line all day. We worked on our messaging and materials, knowing that we had to confront the fact that we were most vulnerable to a simple question: "What about the impact on students?" This is what had me most worried. We had an answer: "The best way to benefit our students is to fully support the faculty who teach many of their classes and supervise much of their research, and the only way to fully support those faculty is to settle a fair contract with them." But I worried that this answer wouldn't be enough.

The impact of a strike on our students had been a recurring concern among our members and a cause of much skepticism, especially from those who had no previous union experience. The biggest point of contention in our deliberations about whether to strike revolved around the obligation that we, as faculty, all feel to the educational system, to each of our specific disciplines and interests, and most of all to our students. Now we were on the verge of setting those recurring concerns aside and enacting the very thing that caused much of the tension within our union.

So why were we going on strike?

Forming a Union

The Non-Tenure Faculty Coalition (NTFC) came into being under unusual circumstances, and in some ways is atypical of unions that represent adjunct, contingent, or non-tenure-track faculty at the university and college level. For several decades, a prominent group, the Campus Faculty Association (CFA), populated mostly by tenure-track and tenured faculty, had represented faculty interests on the University of Illinois, Urbana-Champaign (UIUC) campus. Its leadership had, over the years, worked closely with the American Association of University Professors (AAUP), which has a separate local chapter on campus, and several years ago, the CFA began exploring the possibility of forming a faculty union at UIUC. To do so, it had to work not only with the AAUP, but also with the American Federation of Teachers (AFT) and the Illinois Federation of Teachers (IFT), due to an agreement between the AAUP and the AFT about faculty unionization on certain campuses, including UIUC.

So, with the AAUP and the AFT/IFT, the Campus Faculty Association began trying to build a union that would represent faculty at UIUC. At our sister campus, the University of Illinois, Chicago (UIC), both the tenure-track and non-tenure-track faculty unionized around the same time (under the name UIC United Faculty; UICUF), were certified by the IELRB in 2012, and signed their first collective bargaining agreement in 2014 after a successful strike. At the University of Illinois, Springfield (UIS), a union of tenure-track faculty reformed in 2015 (under the name UIS United Faculty; UISUF), retaining their affiliation with the University Professionals of Illinois, Local 4100.[3] At UIUC, after much time and effort, including on-the-ground staff support by the AFT and IFT, it became clear that the campaign to unionize tenure-track and contingent non-tenure-track faculty (NTTF) would have to become two separate campaigns. This was in part due to how NTTF were employed at UIUC before unionization efforts began: nearly all of the nearly 1,000 NTTF at the time were hired on one-year contracts, with no expectation of renewal and no requirement for the university to give cause if a contract was not offered for a subsequent year. They also had a wide range of salaries, with full-time salaries starting at $25,000 or $30,000 at the low end, climbing to just over $200,000 at the top. Further, employment amounts varied widely. Some faculty were employed part-time at only 0.25 or 0.33 of what is called a full-time equivalent (FTE), though NTTF were considered full-time only if they were at or above 0.51 FTE, and only some NTTF were fully employed at 1.00 FTE.

These disparities led to a variety of job types and employment experiences, although they were linked together under the "non-tenure-track faculty" classification. At one end of the spectrum were "funding-contingent" positions, in which salaries relied on grants or directly on the tuition students paid to the employing program or unit. These positions were spread across the research fields, but were also used in units like our Intensive English Institute, whose budget fluctuated wildly from year to year, depending on student demand. This meant that funding-contingent faculty members were sometimes hired by the semester, or had their appointments reduced with little notice, compounding the lack of overall reappointment protections. On the other end were many faculty with stable positions in disciplines like mine, English, or in language studies, business, engineering, mathematics, and cultural studies, among others. These faculty members were often offered one-year contracts and had an understanding that they would be renewed based on performance, but they lacked formal guarantees. These positions seemed satisfying and stable, until problems arose—for example, in the mid-2000s, funding issues in many humanities departments led to what was colloquially called a "purge" during which many NTTF were not rehired. In subsequent years, however, money flowed more freely, and new NTTF were brought in, but by that point those who had been let go had moved elsewhere, taking their talents, expertise, and institutional knowledge with them. Some NTTF made full careers at UIUC, teaching and researching for 20–30 years (or more), surviving funding droughts, cobbling together outside teaching gigs when there weren't enough classes in their department, and reaching the end of their careers with prestigious records. One of these, a faculty member in English, "retired" just as we were moving toward unionization, having taught composition for more than 30 years; there was no fanfare, no reception in his honor, no plaque on the wall. One day in May, not yet having heard if he would be rehired in the fall and worried about whether he had enough saved, he packed up his materials and departed, leaving his teaching career and colleagues behind.

As we advanced our organizing campaign, we heard similar stories from all corners of the campus, and we knew we would have to work to stabilize as many of these positions as possible, while at the same time allowing for the necessary variety of positions that must exist on a campus such as ours. Once the campaign started in earnest, it quickly became clear that our organizing efforts would focus on the most stable population of NTTF, numbering around 500—those considered full-time in the teaching, research, and clinical specializations.

Much of our organizing process was idiosyncratic and tailored to the UIUC campus, which has an unusual diversity of faculty titles and types of employment, so I will not go into additional depth here. Our organizing strategy was developed in consultation with AFT and IFT staff members, who deserve the lion's share of the credit for figuring out *how* to assess, revisit, and discuss the issues of unionization with the many types of faculty involved. In deciding how to construct the campaign, organizers considered how likely it would be to attain a bargaining unit certified by the IELRB, and how long it might take to organize a prospective unit. There is always the chance that in negotiating the composition of a bargaining unit, some changes to the inclusion parameters will occur. The IFT staff handled these nuances, and in the end our bargaining unit was defined much as we thought it would be.

Much of this happened before I became engaged in the process, but as the campaign carried on, I started working on the most pressing part—a card drive, one of the legal methods of forming a union in Illinois. Illinois law allows a bargaining unit to be certified by a demonstration of a majority interest among employees, which requires the signed authorization of 50 percent plus one of those to be included in the potential bargaining unit.[4] The signed cards are collected, and the labor union files a majority interest petition with the IELRB, submitting the signed cards as proof. After much preparation, we launched our card drive, which required individual conversations with every potential member of the bargaining unit, including faculty spread across campus in disparate departments and programs, many with very different ideas about the possibilities and problems of a union for NTTF.

It was through the card drive that I learned the most about our membership, especially the unique perspectives and concerns of NTTF. Working with AFT staff, who brought both their dedication and organizing skills, faculty organizers were in the field every day, signing the most enthusiastic faculty, meeting again and again with faculty new to unions or skeptical of a faculty union at UIUC, and finding that some faculty were not just reluctant to authorize a union, but vowed to oppose one if it formed.

This process introduced me to parts of the UIUC campus I had never seen and faculty perspectives that were new to me. I met veteran teachers in their third or fourth decade of instruction who had to wait until the end of the summer every year to find out if they would be rehired for the fall semester, which started only a few weeks later. I met faculty who did not want to be tied down by multiyear contracts, because they had other employment opportunities in fields like business, engineering, or finance. And I met a swath of faculty who had never thought about forming a union, or who saw unions as primarily for blue-collar workers or, if they were in education, only for K-12 systems.

But the cards came in, sometimes in fits and starts, sometimes all at once. And by May 2014, we had what we thought would be enough to be certified by the IELRB, and we hand-delivered those cards to the board's office in Springfield, Illinois. In July we were certified, still under the name Campus Faculty Association, Local 6546, with IELRB case number 2014-RC-0012-S, which reads in part: "Included: All full-time (i.e., employees who have a 0.51 or greater appointment as a faculty member) nontenure track faculty with respect to educational employees employed at the Urbana-Champaign campus or employed in units located outside Urbana-Champaign which report administratively to the Urbana-Champaign campus. Excluded: All supervisory, managerial, confidential and short-term employees as defined under the IELRA." That refers to the Illinois Educational Labor Relations Act, which also excludes some positions that would typically be considered faculty, including those working in veterinary medicine and law. The certification left a bargaining unit representing most, but not all, of the full-time NTTF at UIUC.

The university immediately appealed our certification, objecting that some titles of faculty in our bargaining unit overlapped with titles held by the faculty at the UIUC University Laboratory High School, who were represented by a separate union affiliated with the National Education Association and the Illinois Education Association. The university's challenges lasted for nearly a year, until the Illinois Supreme Court declined to take up the last appeal in May 2015.[5]

We had begun negotiating our first collective bargaining agreement in October 2014. Even before then, our drive to unionize had changed some of the employment conditions for NTTF at UIUC. Just before we concluded our card drive (and just after a prominent faculty union strike at our sister campus, UIC), our provost raised the salary floor for most full-time NTTF to $40,000. In addition, the university took steps to make more NTTF fully employed, attempting to ensure that fewer NTTF were employed at only two-thirds or three-quarters FTE, and that many fewer were employed below the full-time threshold. Finally, two policy documents, called *Provost Communications*, were issued, which attempted to better define and address issues of promotion and advancement for NTTF. Though only indirectly related to our unionization, most of these changes would not have happened had we not highlighted the systemic issues affecting the employment of NTTF at UIUC. And, though we welcomed many of these administrative changes, they did not address some of our chief concerns and didn't carry the weight of a collective bargaining agreement.

Highlighting Our Members' Demands

We entered bargaining hopeful that we could surface our members' key demands and settle contract language that would address them in some way. When we surveyed our members, they identified a wide range of issues around the employment of NTTF at UIUC, some of which I noted above. But the two primary concerns centered on the contingent nature of our employment and our lack of shared governance. Non-tenure-track faculty expressed concern over UIUC's one-year contracts and how those contracts were or were not renewed. They were also concerned about the limited roles that NTTF played in their respective departments and units. They wanted to have a voice in the governance of those departments and in the development of policies affecting their employment, including evaluation and promotion methods. Unlike some unions, our primary concerns were not economic, though we also hoped to make clear that NTTF needed to be included in salary programs when they were announced for faculty across campus, and we hoped to raise the salary floor in a systematic fashion.

The process of bargaining, however, obscured and threatened to deny any contract language that would address these concerns. The reasons for this are somewhat unclear to me, even now, and though I will not attempt to summarize the very long back-and-forth of bargaining, two factors stand out. First, the university's bargaining team resisted considering the specific concerns that we brought to the table, instead giving us what they called a "comprehensive" proposal (without any economic issues included) nearly five months into bargaining. The university had given a nearly identical boilerplate proposal to the faculty union at UIC during its first contract negotiations and to the faculty union at UIS during its ongoing negotiations, despite these two unions' very different sets of concerns. This proposal shifted negotiations to the university's terms and successfully buried much of what we had hoped to achieve until very late in the bargaining process. Second, as I later learned, the channels of communication between the university's bargaining team and the key administrators who could approve changes in policy or funding were quite weak. This meant that we were bargaining against a team that had little discretion to agree to any of our proposals, and that our primary concerns, even if understood by the university's team, didn't make their way back up the chain. As a result, negotiations ultimately lasted for 19 months, with more than 100 hours at the bargaining table and in mediated bargaining.

As bargaining proceeded, so did the building of our union. We ratified a constitution that established an executive council (composed of elected officers and committee chairs) and a stewards council, which would be the backbone of the union, with representatives divided among the colleges and schools of the university. We also held officer elections, in which I was elected as our union's first president and which filled our other six executive council positions. This allowed us to continue working on and expanding our organizing and member mobilization, which continues to occupy much of our time throughout the year. The non-tenure-track population at UIUC turns over between 15 percent and 25 percent each year, which means 100 or so new NTTF come to our campus every fall, each of whom needs an introduction to the union and typically several conversations before we ask if they want to join by signing a membership card. At UIUC, as elsewhere in Illinois, all bargaining unit members receive the full protections of our collective bargaining agreement and are obligated to pay dues, but only card-signed members vote on the direction the union takes, including voting in elections, on dues structures, and at general membership meetings.

Throughout, we had to connect the building of a union with our bargaining efforts. We did so with a variety of strategies: rallies at key administrative buildings, "work-ins" that involved many of our faculty doing their work in public spaces to demonstrate what that work looks like, silently protesting the board of trustees (which ultimately signs our collective bargaining agreements), inviting our members to observe and participate in the bargaining process, and stressing the diversity of our membership and their concerns. We varied our approach during a year and a half of bargaining, but throughout we made sure that our members were well aware of the negotiations taking place on their behalf and that they had a hand in shaping how we operated as a union.

Along the way, we found our voice and identity as a union, not just as a bargaining unit. Our members wanted a clear, distinct identity, and after looking at dozens of options we settled on a new name, the Non-Tenure Faculty Coalition, which seemed to best capture the distinct shape of our union and distinguish us from other faculty groups. We also picked a slogan that encapsulated our main arguments about why we needed a fair contract: "Education First." This became our rallying cry and part of our public image, which we worked to establish over our first couple of years—clarifying who we were, why we unionized, and what we were fighting for. Further, we joined the UIUC Campus Labor Coalition, which unites the twenty-odd labor unions on campus, as well as Champaign County's AFL-CIO Central Labor Council. We also helped form a coalition with the faculty unions on the other two University of Illinois campuses: UICUF at Chicago and UISUF at Springfield. This coalition was spurred by an IFT program designed to jump-start union initiatives that might otherwise be difficult to establish, like linking the union leaderships and efforts on three different campuses.

And yet, despite all of that, bargaining was stalled, and mediated bargaining apparently would not get us contract language on our core issues without more pressure. So, our executive council put to our membership a simple question: Will you authorize a strike? They did.

Going on Strike, Twice

Initially, the NTFC membership authorized a two-day labor withholding and selective building picket, to take place on April 19–20, 2016, in the hope that those actions would be enough to pressure the administration to move forward with bargaining. Since we were nearing the end of a semester, there was a good deal of concern that an open-ended strike would not give us a way out should the semester close before we could settle a contract. Our members made clear that they were concerned about the amount of strength we could demonstrate, since we were not a large union like the Graduate Employees' Organization (GEO) at UIUC, which struck in 2009 and is about five times our size.[6] Further, there was concern over the impact on students, classes, and research that a work withholding would entail. I shared these worries as well, because I would have to cancel my own classes and notify my students that I would be unavailable for any academic labor while I was on strike.

But the vote to authorize a strike was overwhelming, so we began implementing the plans we had been laying out all month. There was a flurry of work and meetings, notifying the personnel of buildings we planned to close, meeting with the union leadership of our local AFSCME (American Federation of State, County, and Municipal Employees), SEIU (Service Employees International Union), GEO, and CFA chapters to solicit solidarity support, establishing a strike fund for donations—our union still had no budget of its own—reaching out to local- and state-level politicians, and working with campus officials, including the police, to make clear what we were planning to do.

The two days of our first strike were an amazing display of solidarity, with full building closures and pickets bordering our campus's central quadrangle and prominent bus routes, both of which are trafficked by students and administrators alike. We staged a midday rally each day with a variety of speakers, and an end-of-day rally wrapped up our activities to drive home the importance of why we were out on picket lines. Importantly, we also deployed a messaging campaign aimed at undergraduates, which featured a union representative or solidarity partner at every picket line to hand out flyers and answer questions.

Our strike was the first that many of our undergraduates had experienced, and though not all of those on campus were directly impacted by canceled classes and closed labs, many were. Students had questions, and we positioned ourselves as those best qualified to answer. They expressed frustrations, and we made it clear that we had considered the impact of our strike and wouldn't have chosen to take such a dramatic step without good reasons, which we were happy to provide. Along the way, we made ourselves available to the media, to student groups like the student senate, and to anyone else who expressed concerns. And from the university administrators . . . we heard nothing. Their main tactic seemed to be to rely on the promise of the next mediated bargaining session, scheduled for later that week, presenting it as the only obvious remedy. They offered no additional bargaining sessions, and they claimed nothing else could be done, despite our repeated requests and complete availability. So, I was still worried. My concern was no longer about our messaging or the impact on students, but I had come to realize something about unions: it was hard to know which tactics might work to add pressure in the right ways. Our members met again about what to do once it was apparent that a two-day strike had no direct impact on bargaining.[7]

We asked the membership to vote again, this time on an open-ended strike. What followed was the most contentious discussion we had had as a union. We waited hours to vote until all our members' concerns were raised. But the issues were stark—the university had not acceded to our main demands, which we felt we had made abundantly clear, and without an open-ended strike, we would lose our ability to put enough pressure on bargaining. In the end, the vote was again overwhelmingly in favor.

When we returned to the picket lines the next day, April 28, we doubled down on our previous plans, with more flyers, more conversations, more closed buildings, and more pickets and rallies. Journalism classes sent their students to cover the strike and conduct interviews. Student groups expressed their solidarity, and other unions kept up their support. Bargaining continued sporadically, and I split my time between the bargaining room and the picket line. Finally, some progress was made, but one of our primary issues— the one-year contracts—still wasn't being addressed by the university's team. On the second day of our open-ended strike, I came back from bargaining to speak at a campus May Day rally (the holiday was observed on the Friday before May 1). I could tell the crowd and the picketing union members on the sidewalks in front of me, "This is working. We're moving things at the table. But we have to keep it up—only pressure out here will move things in there."

And it was true. I was suddenly a lot less worried, though one more tense day brought new concerns.

Settling a Contract and Sustaining a Union

We started our last day of mediated bargaining on a rainy Saturday, April 30, in the basement of a building called the Illinois Fire Service Institute, in rooms set up for seminars and training sessions. These were the rooms we'd been in over and over for the previous year and a half, and both sides knew that if that day's bargaining didn't settle a contract, NTFC members would be back on the picket lines on Monday, and a few days later, classes would end for the semester, grades would be due, and we might hit a wall with how far our members were willing to go.

We went back and forth all day, finally getting a full economic proposal from the university's team, finally discussing possible solutions to our issues with the one-year contract cycle, and finally working with administrators with the authority to make decisions about changes in policy and able to offer new, binding contract language. The day was not without some peril—we worked on what our mediator referred to as a "supposal" system, where each side could *suppose* a scenario of linked proposals and make minor alterations without exchanging each item in writing.[8] This meant that by early evening, we had hashed out much of a final collective bargaining agreement, but we had not agreed to specific language; if we didn't finish the final pieces and get tentative agreements from both sides, the day's work would evaporate, and our side didn't expect we'd be back in the room on Sunday.

In the end, our lead negotiator and I made the last deals with the university's lead negotiator and an associate provost, and we arrived at a solution to our members' chief demand. We had wanted to solve the one-year contract problem I described above, but didn't want to disrupt the multiyear contracts that were already in place for a few of our members. So we agreed to a long-term contract provision that would kick in after NTTF were successfully re-hired into their sixth year of employment—at that point, they would be offered that year plus a guarantee for the subsequent year. This way, NTTF who planned to make a career at UIUC could have increased security even in uncertain times. In addition, those job offers would come earlier in the cycle, so that NTTF could have a better sense of whether they would be offered a new contract. We signed a side letter, or memorandum of agreement, requiring departments and units to clarify the role of NTTF in their governance structures and to create clear evaluation systems for them.[9]

Additionally, we secured eligibility for campus salary programs, raises to the base salary for NTTF that would start in the fall of 2017 ($43,000) and the fall of 2018 ($45,000). We also secured the reinstatement of retroactive salary increases that had been suspended when we formed the union. This set of frozen merit raises had been a contentious issue because the university claimed it had to suspend step raises because they were now part of the required subjects of bargaining. These raises, however, had been announced before we entered bargaining, which we believed meant they should have been implemented for the many bargaining unit members whose salaries would have increased. We filed an unfair labor practice charge on behalf of our membership, which we ultimately lost. Some bargaining unit members held the union responsible for the salary freeze, which created a good deal of animosity. To everyone's relief, that salary program was reinstated fully and protected via our collected bargaining agreement.

In short, we signed a tentative agreement for a contract that satisfied our members' key concerns, which the bargaining team brought to the membership the next day. Members voted to suspend our open-ended strike and to hold a vote on the collective bargaining agreement, which was settled on May 5, 2016. Though the contract didn't cover every issue it might have, the membership voted nearly unanimously in favor. Ultimately, we signed a five-year contract, in effect from August 2014 to August 2019, with provisions that were only possible because of the pressure we applied to the bargaining table by our actions outside the bargaining room.

But that's certainly not the end of our union's story. We have much to do, including implementing many of the new provisions of our collective bargaining agreement. We now have, for example, a clear grievance structure, through which we have pursued multiple grievances on behalf of our members. We also are still at work on the final steps that will fully establish our union—implementing a dues structure and creating a stewards council. Perhaps equally important, we will work to maintain our relationships with the other unions on campus, in our community, across the state, and across the nation. Our strikes brought in speakers from the IFT, AFT, and AAUP, and we relied on our solidarity partners at all steps to picket with us, to rally with us, and to work with our members to show what union strength looks like.

And we'll continue to build the Non-Tenure Faculty Coalition, Local 6546, defending our members, addressing issues that didn't make it into our first collective bargaining agreement, and staying strong *because* we are made of our members and their commitments. I'm no longer worried, since this is our story, and we are a union, in solidarity.

NOTES

1. Studies of union disruption abound. For example, see Christine M. Wickens, "The Organizational Impact of University Labor Unions," *Higher Education* 56 (Nov. 2008): 545–64, doi:10.1007/s10734–008–9110-z; Maureen Amos, Victor H. Day, and Elizabeth Power, "Student Reactions to a Faculty Strike," *Canadian Journal of Higher Education* 23 (1993): 86–103; Gordon B. Arnold, *The Politics of Faculty Unionization: The Experience of Three New England Universities* (Westport, CT: Bergin and Garvey, 2000); Julian Barling and Jill Milligan, "Some Psychological Consequences of Striking: A Six Month, Longitudinal Study," *Journal of Occupational Behaviour* 8 (Apr. 1987): 127–37.

2. I should make clear at this point that my reflections here are from my perspective alone. I have chosen to use the titles of union officers, committee chairs, and staff throughout rather than individual names, as I am not attempting to represent their sense of these events. It is not my intent to minimize their impact, since these individuals have made and continue to make our union what it is.

3. For developments at the University of Illinois, Chicago, see Walter Benn Michaels and Scott McFarland, "From One Bargaining Unit to One Faculty," Nov.–Dec. 2015, https://www
.aaup.org/article/one-bargaining-unit-one-faculty#.WGuz5hQ4lz8. For developments at the University of Illinois, Springfield, see UIS, Office of Human Resources, "FAQ: Petition to Organize a Bargaining Unit," https://www.uis.edu/humanresources/labor/faq-petition-to-organize-a
-bargaining-unit-4 (accessed Jan. 3, 2017).

4. For Illinois laws regarding unionization and collective bargaining, see Illinois Educational Labor Relations Board, "Frequently Asked Questions," https://www.illinois.gov/elrb/Pages
/faq.aspx; and "Joint Committee on Administrative Rules: Administrative Code," http://www
.ilga.gov/commission/jcar/admincode/080/08001110000800R.html (both accessed Jan. 28, 2017).

5. News Bureau, Illinois, "Illinois Supreme Court Denies U. of I. Appeal," June 4, 2015, http://news.illinois.edu/ii/15/0604/IL_supreme_court.html.

6. See Peter Campbell, "University of Illinois Caves after Two-Day Grad Strike," *Labor-Notes*, Nov. 18, 2009, http://www.labornotes.org/2009/11/university-illinois-caves-after-two-day
-grad-strike; "Grad Employees Strike at UIUC," Socialist Worker, Nov. 16, 2009, https://socialist worker.org/2009/11/16/grad-employees-strike-uiuc.

7. For some media coverage, see Christina De Angelo, "NTFC Strike Information for GEO Members: The Strike Has Been Called!" http://www.uigeo.org/geo-activism-archives/ntfc-strike
-info (accessed Jan. 28, 2017); Julie Wurth, "Nontenure-Track Faculty Union: 2-Day UI Strike Starts Tuesday," *News-Gazette*, Apr. 18, 2016, http://www.news-gazette.com/news/local/2016
–04–18/nontenure-track-faculty-union-2-day-ui-strike-starts-tuesday.html; Randi Weingarten, "Solidarity with Striking NTFC Local 6546," Chicago Teachers Union blog, Apr. 19, 2016, http://www.ctunet.com/blog/solidarity-strike-ntfc-local-6546-university-illinois; John K. Wilson, "Non-Tenure-Track Faculty at U of Illinois Strike," *Academe*, Apr. 19, 2016, https://acade meblog.org/2016/04/19/non-tenure-track-faculty-at-u-of-illinois-strike; Daily Illini Editorial Board, "Editorial: Non-Tenure Faculty Strike Exemplifies Peaceful Protest," *Daily Illini*, May 12, 2016, http://dailyillini.com/opinions/2016/05/12/editorial-non-tenure-faculty-strike-exempli fies-peaceful-protest.

8. For the use of "supposals" in collective bargaining, see Larry W. Hunter and Robert B. McKersie, "Can 'Mutual Gains' Training Change Labor-Management Relationships?" *Negotiation Journal* 8, no. 3 (1975): 319–30; Joel Cutcher-Gershenfeld, "Interest-Based Bargaining," in *The Oxford Handbook of Conflict Management in Organizations*, ed. William K. Roche, Paul Teague, and Alexander J. S. Colvin (Oxford: Oxford University Press, 2014), 150–67.

9. For a discussion of side letters, see William L. Sharp, *Winning at Collective Bargaining: Strategies Everyone Can Live With* (New York: Rowman and Littlefield, 2003), 79, 164.

chapter 9

Wall to Wall

Industrial Unionism at
the City University of New York, 1972–2017

LUKE ELLIOTT-NEGRI

Union density in the United States has been on the decline since its peak in the 1950s, one factor leading to the end of what Paul Krugman, following Goldin and Margo, has called the "Great Compression."[1] But soon after private-sector union density began to decline, public-sector union organizing surged. The Professional Staff Congress (PSC), the union representing full- and part-time faculty, professional staff, and graduate student–workers across some two dozen urban campuses of the City University of New York (CUNY), was chartered as an American Federation of Teachers local during this era of upsurge, through the merger of two previously existing unions. In 2015–2016, national public-sector density was 35.7 percent, compared to 6.7 percent in the private sector. In New York City, the most unionized of all major US cities, 17.8 percent of the private sector was unionized, and the public sector had a stunning 69.6 percent density.[2] Some 25,000 of the roughly 901,000 unionized New Yorkers are PSC members.

The PSC is rare among higher education unions in the country. Several chapters in this book discuss bargaining units composed of both full- and part-time faculty. But the PSC's additional inclusion of professional staff and graduate student–workers creates an unusually broad industrial model of higher education unionism. Table 9.1 provides an overview of the segments of the CUNY workforce represented by the PSC; it describes pay and workload parity, job security, and governance access, using tenured faculty as the standard. This chapter explores both the benefits and the tensions that this expansive bargaining unit produces. Under what conditions have contingent workers gained from their formal connection with tenured faculty through

TABLE 9.1.
Key Professional Staff Congress Constituencies, City University of New York

	Pay parity	Workload parity	Governance access	Job security
Tenure-line faculty	yes	mixed	yes	yes
• community colleges	yes	no	yes	yes
• senior colleges	standard	standard	yes	yes
Higher education officers (professional staff)	mixed	—	mixed	yes
• HEOs, HEAs, HEas	yes	—	mixed	yes
• assistants to HEOs	no	—	no	yes
College laboratory technicians	no	—	no	yes
• adjunct CLTs	no	—	no	no
Non-tenure-track faculty	no	no	mixed	mixed
• adjunct faculty	no	no	mixed	mixed
• lecturers (full-time)	no	no	mixed	yes
Nonteaching adjuncts	no	—	mixed	no
Graduate assistants	no	no	mixed	mixed

Source: Luke Elliott-Negri developed this chart based on participant observation and interviews, and then vetted it with the PSC's executive director.

Note: CLT = college laboratory technician, HEA = higher education associate, HEa = higher education assistant, HEO = higher education officer.

the PSC? In what ways has this broad organizational model facilitated or hindered part-timers' access to benefits generally and to university governance specifically?

To approach these questions, I draw on both the labor sociology and social movements literatures. There has been a long debate over the trade-offs between occupational and industrial models of unionism. For much of the twentieth century, industrial unions like the PSC—in which workers from multiple occupations join a single organization—seemed to be the most powerful vehicles for workers. But with the erosion of union power in the private sector since the 1970s and the more recent assaults on public-sector unions, some scholars and practitioners have begun to look to the occupation unions of the nineteenth and early twentieth centuries as models for contemporary organizing efforts.[3]

James Jasper identified an extension dilemma that organizers face: "The further you reach out to expand your team or alliance, the more diverse it will be and the less unified—in goals, resources, skills and contacts. You gain breadth but you lose depth. A more focused identity may concentrate enthusiasm for your cause, but generate less power to pursue it."[4] This analysis centers the dilemmas and trade-offs that players experience as they interact strategically with both allies and targets. At several points in the PSC's history, adjuncts have contemplated leaving to build their own occupational union—and at one point they tried. But adjuncts have most often sought to build power within their current industrial union. Each path involves trade-offs.

I begin with a history of the union, going back to its founding in 1972. For decades, adjuncts were largely disenfranchised, but when a new coalition of members took over the union in 2000, part-timers were an important part of the effort. That year was a turning point for adjunct enfranchisement in the PSC, and the next section explores the gains made during this phase. I then turn to the current situation for adjuncts in the PSC and explore the barriers to expanded adjunct organization—which are clearer in the 2010s, now that the dust has settled from the takeover of 2000. I conclude with two brief sections that together address the question: What lessons do several decades of adjunct unionism at CUNY provide for new organizing efforts today, especially in the context of a Trump presidency and Supreme Court (SCOTUS)?

The PSC before the New Caucus: 1972–2000

The Professional Staff Congress formed in 1972 with the merger of two groups—the Legislative Conference (LC) and the United Federation of College Teachers (UFCT).[5] The LC had formed in the late 1930s, an organization of full-time faculty, but not initially a union. The UFCT was chartered as an independent local in 1963, having previously been a project of the United Federation of Teachers, New York City's union for public school educators. In the years leading up to the merger, the two unions competed for members at CUNY. The LC had long been composed of full-time faculty, but the UFCT organized more broadly—among adjuncts, lecturers, and other professionals in the system who were not the focus of the LC. The use of adjunct faculty was already significant in the 1960s, but it was no doubt fueled by CUNY's move to open admissions, beginning with the class of 1970.[6] According to PSC historian and former treasurer Irwin Yellowitz, even in this era, part-time faculty were more than a third of faculty and staff at CUNY, so the UFCT had a meaningful base.[7]

New York state's passage of the Taylor Law in 1967,[8] which continues to govern public-sector unions, was the beginning of the end of this competition. The LC sought two bargaining units, one for full-timers and one for part-timers. The UFCT, on the other hand, sought a unified bargaining unit, excluding only college laboratory technicians (CLTs, who typically manage research laboratories).[9] The Public Employment Relations Board (PERB)—the body formed to administer the Taylor Law—ultimately ruled that there were two distinct units. The LC won the right to represent the first unit, composed of full-timers, in a runoff election. Meanwhile the UFCT won in the second unit, among part-time workers.

Several years later, for reasons that were at once financial and political, the two unions decided to merge, forming the Professional Staff Congress. A caucus from the LC camp won internal union elections (in large part thanks to the slightly less than two-to-one ratio of full- to part-time faculty) and thus led negotiations with CUNY management.[10] The first PSC contract was signed in 1973—after a strike authorization vote by the full membership—and contained elements of both previous contracts. Though certificates of continuous employment for CUNY lecturers (in essence, contractual tenure) survived the journey from the UFCT to the PSC, a key provision for adjuncts did not. Under the UFCT's contract, adjuncts had a preferential hiring system (tantamount to a seniority list, based on the initial date of hire), but under the new PSC contract, this system was abandoned. To this day, adjuncts have not managed to recover this vital provision.[11]

The loss of seniority was significant enough, but through the '90s, the PSC leadership took active steps to make adjunct organizing difficult. In the words of adjunct activist Marcia Newfield, "We had to beg [the president] for membership cards. He would give us two or three or five at a time, whatever. It was not an easy task . . . [just] to get a membership card."[12] Even signing up a few new members involved a fight. But the problems for adjuncts who tried to organize went much deeper than this.

Section 208.3(a) of the Taylor Law allows unions to receive agency fees from nonmembers covered by the collective bargaining agreement. This means that the union collects dues from its members and a comparable agency fee from nonmembers. However, until the 2000s, the PSC leadership refused to collect this fee from adjuncts in the bargaining unit. Newfield recounted: "I asked [one leader], 'Why didn't you?' She said, 'Well, we didn't want to put more burden on the graduate students [and adjuncts].'"[13] Leadership had its public logic, but this exceptional behavior was clearly strategic. Adjuncts were poorly paid relative to full-timers, and they were represented by a union leadership that sought actively to dissuade them from joining. Leaders' decision not to collect agency fees ensured that adjuncts would not build power within the PSC or with respect to CUNY.

The social movements literature has long discussed the "free-rider" collective action problem: Why should rational individuals spend time or money on a collective action project, when they stand to benefit from it even if they are not involved?[14] Notwithstanding valid cultural critiques of rational actor models,[15] the free-rider problem is readily apparent in the union world. So-called right-to-work states do not allow unions to negotiate contracts in which all workers are compelled to fund the union even if they elect not to be members. In free bargaining states, however, such fees are legal—nonmembers who are covered by a collective bargaining agreement can be compelled to pay an agency fee to cover the costs of collective bargaining. While some scholars and activists have criticized the effects of this kind of clause from the left,[16] it certainly overcomes the free-rider problem. Indeed the US Supreme Court defended this logic for public-sector unions in the *Abood* decision of 1977—a precedent that is unlikely to survive the Trump SCOTUS.[17]

The exceptional decision of the PSC leadership not to collect agency fees suggests yet another key theoretical point. Clever players can sometimes overcome social patterns or structural barriers to organization (like the free-rider problem) by *creating* their own structures (like agency shop contracts). Yet even then, such structures must be *enforced*, which again involves the decision-making of key organizational players. This history of the PSC reveals agency in what otherwise might be called "structure." Structures exist, but they generally have origins in the decisions of specific agents. And most structures require active, thoughtful enforcement by players who benefit in a host of ways from enforcing them—or, in this case, failing to enforce them.

It was under this system of disenfranchisement that a group of adjuncts in the 1980s sought to decertify the PSC as the bargaining agent for part-time faculty in the CUNY system. This group chose one horn of the extension dilemma. Though there was theoretically more power in one industrial union, part-timers were so excluded from governance that a separate union seemed like the only option. In theory this new unit might have then participated in joint bargaining with the remaining members of the PSC, another approach to the extension dilemma. But this option was not necessary: PERB granted the vote, but the effort failed. The CUNY part-timers remained PSC members. However, the brief campaign appeared to have consequences. Until 1986, CUNY adjuncts were without health insurance. According to activists at the time, Chancellor Joseph Murphy (and not the PSC!) brought this issue to the bargaining table. But it is likely that the decertification effort encouraged the PSC leadership to take health insurance more seriously. However, unlike for other members, the 1986 deal that PSC ultimately struck financed adjuncts' insurance directly from the union's welfare fund, which was designed only to provide *supplemental* health benefits. This model presented a problem decades later, as the number of adjuncts grew and health insurance costs skyrocketed.

By the 1990s, a new movement was afoot in the PSC. Starting in the first year of the decade, a slate of progressive full-time faculty took over the PSC campus leadership at LaGuardia Community College. In 1993, Steve London (who would become the PSC vice president in 2000) was elected to be the chapter chair at Brooklyn College. The action soon spread to the Borough of Manhattan Community College, where another group of insurgent faculty took over. By 1995 these groups had joined forces with a network called CUNY Concerned Faculty (active since the '80s), and together they founded the New Caucus, a CUNY-wide effort to take over the union.[18]

From the outset, adjuncts were part of the New Caucus. But erasing the historical and cultural tensions within the PSC was not easy. Again, Newfield: "We [adjuncts] met up with the New Caucus to try to ally. At some point we felt dissed and formed our own [organization]. We didn't go away from them, but didn't [stay close]."[19] The New Caucus placed parity for adjuncts on the agenda from day one, and indeed Alberta Grossman, an adjunct from the Borough of Manhattan Community College, helped to draft the New Caucus platform. But as Newfield signaled, some adjuncts did not feel fully incorporated. Organizations like CUNY Adjuncts Unite, of which Newfield was a part, straddled being inside and outside of the New Caucus.

The New Caucus ran a union-wide slate in 1997, but fell short. In 2000, however, it prevailed. Barbara Bowen became the fourth president in the PSC's history. And whatever tensions between full- and part-time workers, this victory was a new opening for CUNY adjuncts.

Adjunct Enfranchisement: 2000–2010

The New Caucus victory in the spring of 2000 was a sea change for adjuncts. Tensions notwithstanding, the new leadership made moves for and with adjuncts on two key fronts: internal union restructuring and contract bargaining.

Adjunct enfranchisement was fundamental. Shortly before the New Caucus victory, part-time activists led by Alex Vitale—then a graduate student and today the PSC vice president for senior colleges—and others had launched a petition drive for a referendum on the PSC leadership's refusal to collect agency fees. They used vehicles like the Doctoral Students' Council of the CUNY Graduate Center and its affiliate organization, the Adjunct Project, to facilitate this work. But the new leadership was committed to making the change without a referendum. "In [February] 2001, for the first time in the union's history, agency fees were implemented to include all part-time non-members of the PSC (including adjuncts, graduate assistants, continuing education teachers and hourlies)."[20] It is hard to overstate the importance of this change. Organizing adjuncts to build power through the PSC went from incredibly difficult to conceivable. Activist Vincent Tirelli reported: "Some would say, 'Oh I don't want to pay them anything,' but all of us who were active knew it was in our best interest."[21] Conversations convincing adjuncts to sign a union card became substantially easier. In addition, the new leadership reformed dues from a flat rate to a percentage of salaries, which greatly benefited lower-paid workers. Further, in a largely symbolic gesture, full-time members paid 1.05 percent of their salary, while part-timers paid just 1 percent.

Adjunct activists from the early 2000s reported bringing thousands of the approximately 7,500 total adjuncts covered by the collective bargaining agreement into the union. The new leadership invested money in what is today called the part-time liaison program. Susan DiRamo, a long-time activist, said: "[First Vice President Steve London] wanted me to work as a union organizer. And I said, no I'll only do it half-time. I like teaching."[22] So the union brought on a second member organizer, Diane Menna. Together they worked to capitalize on the new enforcement of the agency fee. Today, the part-time liaison program has one member organizer on each CUNY campus, who is paid the equivalent of the salary for one course.

Bowen and London recalled that when they were elected, they found hundreds of adjunct grievances backlogged with just one adjunct grievance counselor working a few hours a week. The new vice president for part-time workers began to respond to them more vigorously, and "adjuncts were also appointed to the Grievance Policy Committee, which is a powerful committee that decides if grievances will be taken to arbitration," according to London.[23] Today there is an adjunct grievance counselor in the office Monday through Friday. Still far short of the grievance counselor on every campus that full-time faculty enjoy, this change at least provided adjuncts with a reasonable channel through which to enforce the provisions of the contract that applied to them.

Two other changes mattered a great deal. The new PSC leadership began to build an internal organizing department; none had existed before. Organizers today are each responsible for several of the CUNY campuses, working with both full- and part-time members of the unit on parochial and union-wide issues. In addition, in the early 2000s, Marcia Newfield opened up the adjunct committee of the delegate assembly—commonly known as the First Friday Committee—to any adjunct interested in organizing. To this day, First Friday is the main CUNY-wide adjunct organizing body inside the PSC, notwithstanding other and sometimes competing formations. DiRamo, Menna, and others who worked closely with the New Caucus chose a very different path than those who sought to decertify in 1986. In fact, Tirelli, who had helped to spearhead the decertification effort, pivoted to join the insurgency. Adjunct activists in the 1990s and 2000s chose the other horn of the extension dilemma. Under newly elected leaders, they saw the opportunity to build power inside the union for part-timers, in coalition with full-time faculty.

The internal changes to PSC governance and the more equitable distribution of resources provided the foundation for new adjunct organizing. CUNY adjuncts still have not seen anything close to parity, but they have made gains, particularly in the first contract, which covered 2000–2002. Alex Vitale, part of the group that launched the agency fee referendum, also helped to lead a campaign for a paid adjunct office hour, which began in the '90s but became a reality in the first contract negotiated by the New Caucus. He characterized the campaign development in the following way:

> [There] was a lot of discussion about what to focus on. There was a lot of difficulty even agreeing that we needed to focus. The grievances were so many, and all of them totally legitimate grievances and serious issues, that it made it very hard to focus in strategically and say, well, this is the linchpin issue. There wasn't—it was clear there was no one linchpin issue. You've got different types of adjuncts, you've got 18 different campuses, different beefs at different places. You've got a lot of bad actors. The union was a bad actor, CUNY was a bad actor, department chairs were bad actors sometimes. But I kept making the point that we're never going to make any real progress until we develop one or two really specific campaigns and carry them out. Then we will build some strength, build our momentum, build our notoriety, and then we can move on to the next one.[24]

Vitale and his fellow organizers attempted to finesse the extension dilemma: they used and built organizations outside of the PSC (the Doctoral Students' Council, the Adjunct Project, and CUNY Adjuncts Unite), but they also attempted to influence the union, rather than build an alternative to it, as some had tried in 1986. This inside-outside approach netted gains. In bargaining, PSC leadership leveraged management's demand for over-scale full-timer pay to win the office hour. Beginning "September 1st, 2002, adjuncts assigned to teach six or more contact hours at the same college will be paid at 100 percent of their teaching rate for one additional hour per week in order to engage in professional assignments related to . . . academic responsibilities."[25]

The office hour provision was designed to reward financially and symbolically those adjuncts who teach two or more courses. In the same contract, the bargaining team negotiated a host of equity increases for lecturers, graduate assistants, and other workers not at parity with full-time faculty. The PSC also made an effort to win job security for adjuncts who until then had been appointed on a semester basis: "After six consecutive semesters (exclusive of the Summer) in the same department, an adjunct shall be entitled to year-long appointments."[26] However, this has had a limited effect since colleges can cancel an adjunct's course due to low enrollment without penalty.

The subsequent two contracts also provided some gains for adjuncts. In the 2002–2007 contract, the bargaining team negotiated a disproportionate raise for adjuncts on their top salary step. The logic was to steer money toward long-serving adjuncts. But of course, while benefiting some members, this raise did nothing to curb CUNY's deep financial incentive to hire new adjuncts. If anything, the raise increased it. In addition, nonteaching adjuncts—who work in libraries, in writing centers, and directly for faculty and staff as research assistants and teaching assistants—received paid sick leave.

Perhaps the most creative and structurally important gain in the 2002–2007 contract was the creation of 100 "dedicated" full-time lecturer lines (98 of which were ultimately used). Under the PSC contract, lecturers—there are currently fewer than 1,000 total—are teachers who have the job security that many adjuncts seek. They are compensated more highly than adjuncts, though not as highly as tenure-line faculty, and unlike tenure-line faculty they do not have a research requirement. The second New Caucus–negotiated agreement created 100 lecturer positions, which were *dedicated* to long-serving adjuncts. Colloquially, these are known as "conversion" lines, but in reality that language is aspirational. Departments across the CUNY system were given the option to convert long-serving adjuncts to the lecturer title, but they were not required to do so.

For adjuncts who have managed to get a conversion line, the change in status has been fundamental. Some PSC activists report that lecturers have become central to governance and to departmental operations where they were once marginal. One activist told the story of an adjunct who always sat in the outer ring of chairs during job talks. After getting a lecturer line, he quite literally had a seat at the table. Linda Coull converted in 2007: "I'm on a number of committees [now], including admissions, grade appeal, commencement, and disability studies. . . . It changes your status, doing the committee work. You meet more people, show up to more meetings." She also reported, "It's a good thing for my own life, because I don't want to go job hunting at my age."[27] Before becoming a lecturer, Coull worked two or three jobs in the CUNY system, traveling around the city daily. Now "I don't need to worry about whether or not I'll have classes, [and] I've been paying in to [the teacher retirement system] since I got a lecturer line. When I was an adjunct, I wasn't making enough money to think about retiring." For those who have been able to transition, the results are significant. Michael Batson, an adjunct who has been active in the PSC since the mid-2000s reported: "I would say that the conversion lines might be the answer to cracking the two-tier system."[28]

The bargaining team for the 2007–2010 contract negotiated another 100 dedicated lecturer lines (93 of which were ultimately used, constituting a second cohort of "converted" adjuncts), in addition to forming a modest adjunct professional development fund, and closing a loophole under which adjuncts who served on substitute lines lost their accrued benefits when they returned to adjunct status. These conversions are as close to a structural intervention in the long-running adjunctification of CUNY as the PSC has yet been able to muster.

By all accounts, the dedicated lines have been a success. The PSC executive director, Debbie Bell, reported that "81 percent [of the first cohort] were still employed at CUNY as of 2013. Seventy-three were lecturers with certificates of continuous employment [contractual tenure], and 6 were [in professor titles]. . . . As of fall 2015, 91 percent [of the second cohort] were still employed . . . at CUNY: 88 as lecturers with certificates of continuous employment and 7 in professor titles."[29] But the broader bargaining unit data are sobering. Figure 9.1 captures the proportions of adjunct, lecturer, and tenure-track faculty in the teaching workforce from 2000 to 2015.

After a small spike (less than 1 percent) between 2005 and 2010, the proportion of lecturers returned to previous levels and remained steady over time, notwithstanding the negotiation of dedicated lines. It is important to note that the percentage of annual instruction delivered by full-time faculty actually increased marginally over a few years (from 48.1 percent in 2010 to 48.6 percent in 2014).[30] This divergence from figure 9.1 is likely explained by the fact that full-time faculty and lecturers have a much higher teaching load

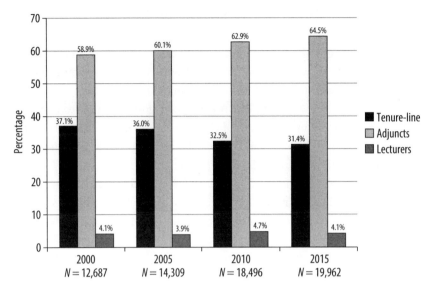

Figure 9.1. Professional Staff Congress at CUNY, Teaching Staff Composition, 2000–2015. Source: This figure is based on publicly available data generated by CUNY management. I have included "instructors" in the category "lecturers" and have excluded "distinguished lecturers," who have an entirely different status. All substitute and visiting lines are excluded from these data. Graduate assistants—who sometimes conduct research and sometimes teach—are also excluded. Finally, these numbers include library and counseling faculty, who do not, technically speaking, teach. Raw data can be found at http://www2.cuny.edu/about/administration/offices/hr/hris/#1445531936648-a1b11c09-4c88.

than do adjuncts, most of whom do not reach the contractual maximum of 15 credit hours per semester. It matters that the new lecturers were pulled from a pool of long-serving adjuncts, but the fact remains that the CUNY labor force is structurally similar to that of previous years.

The Years without a Contract: 2010–2016

The 1982 Triborough Amendment to New York's Taylor Law stipulates that expired contracts are still enforceable until a new union contract is signed.[31] This protection has led to a culture in many public-sector unions of allowing long stretches without a new contract, and then negotiating retroactive pay and provisions. In this context, the Professional Staff Congress went without a contract from 2010 to 2016.

Though CUNY is a city institution, state funding for four-year colleges increased dramatically as a result of the 1975 fiscal crisis in New York City.[32]

Hence the PSC is one of a small number of unions that bargains with both the New York City mayor and the New York state governor, in addition to local management. Signing a new contract was nearly impossible under Mayor Michael Bloomberg, who refused to offer raises to municipal unions; so when Mayor Bill de Blasio replaced him in 2013, many unions settled contracts.[33] But Governor Andrew Cuomo had previously negotiated punitive contracts with several state unions, and he used CUNY as a bargaining chip in his battle with the mayor, rather than working to settle a strong retroactive agreement with workers in the system, full- or part-time.[34]

During this phase without a contract, the PSC was able to make one important move for adjuncts. In 1986, as noted above, adjuncts had gained access to health insurance but only through the union's welfare fund with a fixed contribution from CUNY. "Unfortunately, as CUNY expanded its reliance on adjuncts and healthcare costs increased, CUNY's flat rate of funding covered less and less of the cost of adjuncts' health insurance."[35] According to Steve London, "Barbara [Bowen] and I [expended enormous political capital to keep] the AHI program cobbled together for over a decade, with continuing equity payments [including $30 million in retroactive contract money in 2006] until it was impossible to do any longer."[36] In 2011, the welfare fund, at the behest of PSC leadership, announced that the model would no longer work. The union spent the next two years attempting to shift adjuncts' insurance to the city plan, with increased contributions from CUNY. Finally, under Mayor de Blasio, this transfer happened, protecting both adjuncts' health insurance and the welfare fund.[37]

However, the full contract—which in 2014 had already been expired for four years—was far from settled. One key sticking point for the PSC was that city and state unions typically bargain based on a pattern with other public-sector unions, and state workers received a 4 percent pay increase for 2010.[38] De Blasio was relatively sympathetic to the PSC, but Cuomo did not want to supply this 4 percent increase, not to mention increases for the intervening years—which by PSC calculations should have totaled 20 percent.[39] Finally, in the fall of 2015, with some 50 PSC activists—both full- and part-timers—committing civil disobedience in front of CUNY Central, management offered a 6 percent package over five years. The bargaining team rejected this offer, demanding a 14 percent package.[40]

Shortly thereafter, the PSC leadership announced that the union would hold a strike authorization vote for the second time in the union's history. The vote was a lightning rod for much of the membership. On the campus where

I am elected chairperson—the CUNY Graduate Center, a unique senior college dedicated exclusively to granting PhDs and master's degrees—we signed up hundreds of new members over the course of the 10-day vote, and the turnout included a significant majority of our members. The Graduate Center went from a small elected leadership team to five active committees doing an array of work, with a primary focus on part-time workers, both adjuncts and graduate assistants. Other chapters experienced similar energy, and although the vote was more of a negotiating tactic than the beginning of a strike effort, it caused many members to reflect seriously on their union.

Finally, in the summer of 2016, the two sides settled a contract based on a 10.41 percent package, matching the pattern of other city unions, but without the 4 percent increase that state unions had received in 2010. Many adjuncts, however, were unsatisfied. They ratified the contract at a lower rate (86 percent) than the overall membership (92 percent) did.[41] The across-the-board percentage raises meant that adjuncts and full-timers alike received 10.41 percent salary increases, widening the already existing pay inequality between full- and part-time faculty.[42]

Notwithstanding the inequity of these raises, a job security gain in the 2016 contract was notable. Adjuncts who teach six credit hours (two courses) for ten consecutive semesters automatically become eligible for three-year appointments, establishing due process protections for that group. President Bowen and Vice President London of the PSC both reported publicly and in interviews that though CUNY viewed this as a noneconomic item, it was a hard-fought provision. No doubt CUNY had little interest in limiting its flexibility to deploy the massive contingent labor force at will. Somewhere between 1,000 and 2,000 of CUNY's approximately 10,500 teaching adjuncts are eligible for the new provision.[43] Unlike the one-year contracts from the 2000–2002 contract, management will have an obligation to compensate or find other work for adjuncts who have a course pulled at the last minute due to low enrollment.[44] Some 45 years later, this is as close as the adjuncts have been able to get to the system of job protection that disappeared from the UFCT when it merged to form the PSC in 1972. Limited though the provision is, adjunct activist Michael Batson said: "I see [these three-year contracts] as a bridge."[45]

We can think here of adjuncts getting a package of gains and losses as a result of activist leaders choosing one horn of the extension dilemma. The dues base of the PSC is drawn largely from well-compensated full-time faculty and professional staff, and these resources bolstered a campaign against all three of the "bosses" on the other side of the bargaining table. Protests, civil disobedience, and lobbying activities were coordinated with vigor by activist members, but also by staff and consultants. Adjuncts benefited from the strength of this effort. On the other hand, adjuncts were just one constituency among many, and the contract that was finally signed in 2016 was of far greater financial benefit to the full-time faculty. As the extension dilemma suggests, working in coalition provides more power but can result in submerged or displaced goals. Unlike previous contracts, the bargaining team did not negotiate pay equity increases for adjuncts, making the outcome bittersweet for many part-time workers.

Organizing under Trump: 2017 and Beyond

The election of Donald Trump to the highest political office in the United States should change the strategic calculations of any serious union organizer, especially in the public sector. The death of Supreme Court justice Antonin Scalia in 2016 left SCOTUS divided 4–4 over *Friedrichs v. the California Teachers Association*.[46] If he had not passed away, public-sector unions nationwide would likely have lost the ability to negotiate agency fees. Under Trump, the court will likely eliminate agency fee shops. Public-sector unions, no matter the type of workers they cover, must be prepared.

This reality has especially serious implications for industrial model unions like the Professional Staff Congress. CUNY adjuncts have made gains through their union especially since new leaders came to power in 2000. However, neither independently organized adjuncts nor the union of which they are a part have been able to change fundamentally the structure of the CUNY labor force. It is important to note that thousands of tenure lines have been added at CUNY in the twenty-first century; however, enrollment increases have negated the effect of this growth. Adjuncts are still increasing as a proportion of the teaching staff, while tenured faculty are decreasing proportionally (though, as already mentioned, there has been a marginal increase in the percentage of annual instruction delivered by full-time faculty; see figure 9.1 and discussion above). Moreover, a starting CUNY adjunct in 2016 makes less than $3,200 per course, and even at the top of the pay scale, adjuncts make less than $5,300.[47] These are paltry wages, especially by New York City standards, even for adjuncts who teach the maximum number of courses allowed under the contract. Compare this to adjuncts at Rutgers University, across the river in New Jersey, who make a minimum of $5,052 per three-credit course.[48] If agency fees are made illegal, many CUNY adjuncts will likely choose not to pay dues. Of course the committed activists will stay members, and the PSC will continue to bargain for adjuncts. But the vast inequities between full- and part-time faculty, combined with a loss of agency fees, could change the PSC—and CUNY—permanently.

Conclusion

What has worked for CUNY adjuncts in the PSC, and what have been the barriers to more substantial changes to the structure of the instructional labor force? What lessons are there in this analysis, and how do they apply under a Trump presidency?

The biggest barrier to adjunct gains under the PSC contract is management opposition—from New York City, New York state, and CUNY administrators alike. The CUNY system broadly has experienced a decades-long decline in per-student funding. In the words of PSC president Bowen: "More than half of the workforce . . . is systematically, radically underpaid. . . . The other [issue], and it relates to money too, is that the management, accepting conditions of scarcity and having failed to challenge them successfully over all these years, has adopted just-in-time production, where it suits them very well to have what they would call a flexible workforce and what I would call a workforce without any job security."[49] The state and city together have chosen to defund CUNY over the decades, which makes CUNY management's reliance on contingent labor practical and necessary.

Yet the PSC has made decisions over the years in response to these antagonistic forces, and these decisions matter. The New Caucus came to power in 2000 with support from adjuncts, but it has always been led by full-time faculty. Its primary electoral base was and is full-time workers, and, in part because of the difficulties associated with organizing contingent workers, efforts to support adjuncts did not necessarily fuel reelection prospects. This was not a problem in 2003, when the New Caucus went unchallenged. But in 2006, it faced opposition from a group of full-timers who were politically to the caucus's right. The group decried the leftist politics of the New Caucus, and according to Steve London (who was PSC vice president in this era), they ran "an anti-adjunct dog whistle campaign." He reported that CUNY managers refused to sign the 2002–2007 contract until the results of the election were counted, hoping that they could finalize the agreement under new PSC leadership. Clearly, management had a preference in the race. President Barbara Bowen received 3,201 votes (54.6 percent) to the challenger's 2,654 (45.4 percent). London received 53.6 percent of the votes for his seat. While the margin was not razor thin, the race was close.[50] This outcome may well have encouraged the New Caucus to consolidate power in its full-time base, rather than double down on expanding organizing among adjuncts.

Adjuncts, of course, face their own specific barriers to organizing. While both the First Friday Committee and the part-time liaison program have expanded adjunct participation in the PSC, they have not developed the political force necessary to make adjuncts an integral part of the union's governance and strategy. Michael Batson rightly noted that the composition of the adjunct workforce is quite varied, and he suggested that there are four main types: "[There is the] classic adjunct—people [who] have a full-time career out there. . . . The second one would be this kind of new group of [secondary] school teachers who are coming in here and teaching, and I don't think that's the same as that classic [group]. . . . The third would be the core adjuncts, like myself, who are trying to carve a living out of this. And then there's a fourth, [where] this is a part-time job amongst other part-time jobs."[51]

We could add to this graduate assistants, but we could also simplify this typology into a binary—there are part-timers who have full-time work elsewhere and part-timers for whom the job is an integral part of earning their living. It is the latter group that is the subject of most discussions of the multitier system in higher education and that it is essential to organize. But that work is notoriously difficult—sometimes even *finding* an adjunct who does not have her own office and who moves among campuses and jobs to earn a living is hard.[52] But as the office hour gain from 2002 suggests, organizing adjuncts to make meaningful gains inside an industrial union model is possible. However, as Vitale noted, "There was a lot of difficulty even agreeing that we needed to focus." To this day, adjunct formations like the First Friday Committee vacillate between providing an opportunity to vent about adjunct working conditions and providing an opportunity to organize. If adjuncts in the PSC are to survive a Trump presidency and the SCOTUS rulings that it will bring, they will need to be focused on turning the organizations they have—First Friday and the part-time liaison project—into broader and stronger formations that can provide a vehicle for adjuncts to make far more substantial gains through the bargaining process.

Throughout the history of the PSC, adjuncts have sometimes imagined that life would be easier if they just chose the other horn of the extension dilemma—and built their own occupational union. In 1986, under oppressive organizational conditions, some attempted to make this happen. Starting in 2000, adjuncts more fully chose the other horn and began to make gains by engaging with their union. After 17 years, adjuncts have made a host of notable gains geared especially toward long-serving adjuncts at the top of the pay scale. And yet the structure of the CUNY labor force and the conditions that adjuncts face are more like those from the '90s than what many have hoped for.

Yet the barriers faced by PSC adjuncts are no reason to long for occupational unionism. In fact, if the PSC—and indeed all public-sector unions— are going to survive a Trump SCOTUS, they will need maximum internal organization and maximum political leverage at the local and state levels. For the PSC, this means that full-timers must understand why organizing adjuncts is central to preserving the tenure system, which continues to erode, and adjuncts must address the extension dilemma, along the inside-outside lines that the adjunct office hour campaign suggested. Notwithstanding the potential goal displacement associated with coalition work, full-timers and part-timers alike must build the political force of their union to resist Trump and to fight for a fully funded system of higher education. Failure to do this will mean a continued loss of power for both constituencies. But if the two groups build their combined power, mutual solidarity, and a union that is equipped to tackle and win broad political fights, there is hope.

NOTES

1. Paul Krugman, "Introducing This Blog," *New York Times*, Sept. 18, 2007, http://krugman .blogs.nytimes.com/2007/09/18/introducing-this-blog/?_r=0; Claudia Goldin and Robert Margo, "The Great Compression: The Wage Structure in the United States at Mid-Century," *Quarterly Journal of Economics* 107, no. 1 (Feb. 1992): 1–34.

2. Ruth Milkman and Stephanie Luce, "The State of the Unions 2015: A Profile of Organized Labor in New York City, New York State, and the United States," policy report funded by the Joseph S. Murphy Institute, Sept. 2015, http://media.wix.com/ugd/90d188_91d7cdc3f7574 0909eef83a22cee9cdb.pdf.

3. See Ruth Milkman, *LA Story* (New York: Russell Sage Foundation, 2006); Dorothy Sue Cobble, "Organizing the Post-Industrial Work Force: Lessons from the History of 20th Century Waitress Unionism," *Industrial and Labor Relations Review* 44, no. 3 (1991): 419–36.

4. James Jasper, *Getting Your Way* (Chicago, IL: University of Chicago Press, 2006), 127.

5. *Methodological note.* I am indebted to Irwin Yellowitz's organizational history of the PSC, *25 Years of Progress*, 1997, http://www.psc-cuny.org/sites/default/files/25%20Years%20of%20 Progress%20by%20Irwin%20Yellowitz.pdf; and to Vincent Tirelli, "The Invisible Faculty Fight Back: Contingent Academic Labor and the Political Economy of the Corporate University," PhD diss., City University of New York, 2007, for my understanding of the early PSC. The data for the bulk of the chapter are based on three years of participant observation as a rank-and-file member, elected alternate delegate, and elected chapter chair of the PSC at the CUNY Graduate

Center; nine interviews with key organizational informants; the personal archives of two informants; and past issues of the PSC newspaper, the *Clarion*. All quotes in the piece that are not attributed otherwise come from interviews I conducted.

6. Michael Fabricant and Stephen Brier, *Austerity Blues* (Baltimore, MD: Johns Hopkins University Press, 2016), 83.

7. Yellowitz, *25 Years of Progress*.

8. W. B. Gould, "The New York Taylor Law: A Preliminary Assessment," *Labor Law Journal* 18, no. 6 (1967): 323.

9. See Yellowitz's theory in *25 Years of Progress*, 5, about why the union excluded CLTs.

10. M. A. Farber, "City U's Merged Union Set to Act for 15,000 on Staff," *New York Times*, Apr. 16, 1972, http://cdha.cuny.edu/items/show/3172.

11. Tirelli, "Invisible Faculty Fight Back," documents this history well.

12. Marcia Newfield, interview with author, 2016.

13. Ibid.

14. Mancur Olson, *The Logic of Collective Action* (Cambridge, MA: Harvard University Press, 1965).

15. For an effort to integrate cultural and rational actor approaches, see James Jasper and Jan Willem Duyvendak, *Players and Arenas: The Interactive Dynamics of Protest* (Amsterdam, Netherlands: Amsterdam University Press, 2015).

16. See, for example, Stanley Aronowitz, *False Promises: The Shaping of American Working Class Consciousness* (1973; repr., Durham, NC: Duke University Press, 1992), 217–18.

17. *Abood v. Detroit Board of Education*, 431 US 209 (1977); C. M. Rehmus and B. A. Kerner, "The Agency Shop after *Abood*: No Free Ride, but What's the Fare?" *Industrial and Labor Relations Review* 34, no. 1 (1980): 90–100; Moshe Z. Marvit, "Labor Opponents Already Have the Next 'Friedrichs' SCOTUS Case Ready to Go under Trump," *In These Times*, Jan. 4, 2017, http://inthesetimes.com/working/entry/19776/will_trumps_supreme_court_reverse_fair _share_fees_unions_foes_hope_so.

18. Based on interviews with John Hyland and Steve London in 2016.

19. Newfield interview, 2016.

20. Diana Rosato, "Current PSC Dues/Fee Structure and History," PSC-CUNY, http://www .psc-cuny.org/current-psc-duesfee-structure-and-history (accessed Dec. 20, 2016).

21. Vincent Tirelli, interview with author, 2016.

22. Susan DiRamo, interview with author, 2016.

23. Steve London, interview with author, 2016.

24. Alex Vitale, interview with author, 2016.

25. See PSC-CUNY, 2000–2002 contract summary, http://archive.psc-cuny.org/documents .htm.

26. Ibid.

27. Linda Coull, interview with author, 2016.

28. Michael Batson, interview with author, 2016.

29. Debbie Bell, correspondence with author, 2016.

30. See CUNY's publicly available performance management process reports, https://cuny .edu/about/administration/offices/ira/ir/data-book/current/accountability/PMP_University _Data_Book_2015_final_20150806_v2.pdf (accessed Dec. 21, 2016).

31. J. E. Freeman and P. Kolozi, "Between a Rock and a Hard Place: Public Sector Unions and New York's Triborough Amendment," *Thought and Action* 32, no. 1 (2016): 109–20.

32. Fabricant and Brier, *Austerity Blues*, 88.

33. Steven Greenhouse, "For de Blasio, Contract Talks Offer Problem," *New York Times*, Nov. 11, 2013, http://www.nytimes.com/2013/11/12/nyregion/union-demands-leave-de-blasio -in-a-quandary.html; Sally Goldenberg, "De Blasio Bases 'Real Budget' on UFT Pattern," *Polit-*

ico, May 8, 2014, http://www.politico.com/states/new-york/city-hall/story/2014/05/de-blasio
-bases-real-budget-on-uft-pattern-012833.

34. See press release from governor's office: "Governor Andrew Cuomo Announces Five
Year Labor Agreement with Civil Service Employees Association," June 22, 2011, https://www
.governor.ny.gov/news/governor-andrew-cuomo-announces-five-year-labor-agreement-civil
-service-employees-association; Vivian Yee, "Cuomo Faces Loud Backlash over Push to Cut
State's CUNY Funding," *New York Times*, Mar. 24, 2016, https://www.nytimes.com/2016/03/25
/nyregion/after-moving-to-cut-cuny-funding-cuomo-faces-loud-backlash.html.

35. "Timeline: Adjunct Health Insurance," PSC-CUNY, http://www.psc-cuny.org/issues
/timeline-adjunct-health-insurance (accessed Dec. 20, 2016).

36. London interview, 2016.

37. "Timeline: Adjunct Health Insurance."

38. Glenn Kissak, "Cuomo, Wall Street and Class Struggle at CUNY," *Socialism and Democracy* 30, no. 3 (2016): 12–36.

39. Barbara Bowen, "PSC Makes Salary Proposal," PSC-CUNY, May 20, 2015, http://www
.psc-cuny.org/psc-makes-salary-proposal.

40. See "Members Organize for a Strike Authorization Vote," PSC-CUNY, Dec. 17, 2015,
http://www.psc-cuny.org/contract-campaign-mass-meeting.

41. Barbara Bowen, "Contract Ratified by a 94% 'Yes' Vote," PSC-CUNY, Aug. 4, 2016, http://
www.psc-cuny.org/contract-ratified-94-yes-vote.

42. Mathematically, uniform percentage increases exacerbate preexisting inequality. For
example, if person A makes $100 and person B makes $1,000, the difference between their
earnings is $900. If both people are given a 10 percent raise, then person A makes $110, person
B makes $1,100, and the difference between their earnings is now $990.

43. See "Contract FAQs: Adjunct Multi-Year Appointments," PSC-CUNY, Sept. 28, 2016,
http://www.psc-cuny.org/ContractFAQs#multi-year.

44. See the PSC-CUNY 2010–2017 contract memorandum of agreement for the exact language, http://www.psc-cuny.org/sites/default/files/MOA_2010–2017.pdf (accessed Jan. 12, 2017).

45. Batson interview, 2016.

46. Chris Maisano, "The Road to *Friedrichs*," *Jacobin*, Jan. 11, 2016, https://www.jacobin
mag.com/2016/01/friedrichs-public-sector-unions-abood-right-to-work.

47. PSC-CUNY salary schedule, http://www.psc-cuny.org/sites/default/files/Teaching&Non
TeachingAdjunctSchedule.pdf (accessed Jan. 12, 2017).

48. See the collective bargaining agreement for members of the Part-Time Lecturer Faculty
Chapter, Rutgers Council of AAUP Chapters, AAUP-AFT, http://www.rutgersaaup.org/sites
/default/files/images/PTL_Final_Draft.pdf (accessed Dec. 20, 2016).

49. Barbara Bowen, interview with author, 2016.

50. PSC-CUNY 2006 election results, http://archive.psc-cuny.org/PDF/April06results.pdf
(accessed Jan. 12, 2017).

51. Batson interview, 2016.

52. Vincent Tirelli, "Adjuncts and More Adjuncts: Labor Segmentation and the Transformation of Higher Education," *Social Text* 51 (2007): 75–91.

chapter 10

California State University, East Bay

Alignment of Contingent and Tenure-Track Faculty Interests and Goals

KIM GERON AND GRETCHEN M. REEVY

California State University, East Bay (CSUEB), is one of 23 campuses in the California State University system, the nation's largest public four-year university system, serving 475,000 students. Faculty in the CSU system forged a state-wide collective bargaining unit in 1983 called the California Faculty Association (CFA). The bargaining unit was decided by a vote of the faculty in an election between two competing faculty associations. The CFA from its inception was composed of both tenure-line faculty (tenured and tenure-track) and contingent faculty (known as lecturers in the CSU system). While lecturers have had basic union protections since the CFA was founded, lecturers' rights and working conditions have improved with successive contract negotiations. Additionally, lecturers' activism and involvement in CFA leadership have increased since the CFA negotiated its first contract in 1983; however, the largest gains came in the late 1990s and forward, as lecturers became better organized within the CFA and sought a greater voice.[1] At the local level, the CFA East Bay chapter has worked to be inclusive of all faculty both in the chapter and in campus governance.

This chapter is a case study of how lecturers and tenure-line faculty work together in a higher education faculty union to address the needs and concerns of union members and nonmembers. We provide a brief description of the models of unionization of higher education faculty in the United States, an analysis of the factors that enabled the CFA to win a successful reopener contract in 2016, and a discussion of local efforts to strengthen tenure-line faculty's and lecturers' rights and equity at CSUEB in the CFA chapter and in the university senate.

Models of Unionization of Higher Education Faculty in the United States

Laws in the United States allow for various types of unionization of higher education faculty. One model involves tenure-line and contingent faculty in the same bargaining unit, such as at our university, the CSU, and other public universities, including the City University of New York's Professional Staff Congress and the State University of New York's United University Professions, which were both organized in the early 1970s, and the University of Oregon, which was organized in 2012.[2] In a second model, tenure-line and contingent faculty are represented by the same union but with separate bargaining units, such as at the University of San Francisco (California Federation of Teachers/American Federation of Teachers) and Long Beach City College (Community College Association/California Teachers Association). Rutgers University faculty have a joint union affiliated with both the American Association of University Professors and the American Federation of Teachers, which represents full-time faculty (tenured and nontenured), graduate assistants, teaching assistants, and others under one contract, with part-time lecturers, postdoctoral associates, winter-summer instructors, and Educational Opportunity Fund counselors each having separate contracts.[3]

At some universities, tenure-line and contingent faculty are both unionized but represented by different unions. For example, in California, part-time faculty at the College of the Canyons, North Orange County Community College, and Citrus College are represented by the California Federation of Teachers while the tenure-line faculty are represented by the Community College Association and the California Teachers Association. There are also growing numbers of campuses where contingent faculty are unionized, but tenure-line faculty are not, such as the University of California where the contingent faculty are represented by the California Federation of Teachers, but the tenure-line faculty do not collectively bargain over wages and working conditions. Also, in recent years contingent faculty at many private institutions, such as Tufts University and American University, have been organized by the Service Employees International Union.

The factors that determine the unionization style of a particular university are many. Of course, the desires of the faculty partially determine the model. Many of the original public university faculty bargaining units that formed in the 1970s began as tenure-line only. As noted by Timothy Reese Cain in chapter 3 in this volume, although contingent faculty have participated in faculty unions since the early twentieth century, their proportion of the overall professoriat was smaller in the 1960s and 1970s than it is today. Later, as the numbers of contingent faculty grew, they organized more frequently to be represented by a union. Throughout this period there was competition between unions over which could best represent faculty, sometimes leading to different bargaining units and different unions representing faculty on the same campuses. Other factors include the federal and state laws that determine bargaining units. In the case of our university, the California Public Employment Relations Board determined that tenure-track and non-tenure-track faculty belong in the same bargaining unit because the two groups of CSU faculty share a "community of interests" and "perform functionally related services or work toward established common goals."[4]

We believe this style of union works well for us. We acknowledge that our union model is not perfect. Many lecturer faculty desire all of the rights and responsibilities (and the higher pay) afforded tenure-line faculty. Some tenure-line faculty state that the CFA is "only for lecturers." However, joining together in one bargaining unit gives us the power of numbers (26,000 faculty). We argue that the two groups of faculty work best together when there is greater equity between the groups. The CFA's successful contract win in 2016 illustrates the power of effective collaboration among contingent and tenure-line faculty.

How the CFA Won a Successful Reopener Contract in 2016

A number of factors laid the groundwork for the successful reopener contract that CFA secured in April 2016. The contract is referred to as a "reopener" because a number of terms had been settled previously, and in that settlement a clause allowed for some issues to be revisited prior to the expiration of the contract. In this section we describe the immediate context of the struggle and provide a brief history of the developments that led to success.

The tentative agreement for the reopener contract occurred a few days before a five-day CSU system-wide strike was scheduled to occur. The settlement meant that all CSU faculty would receive a 10.5 percent general salary increase given out in three increments between June 30, 2016, and July 1, 2017, and some faculty would receive an additional 2.65 percent increase during fiscal year 2017–2018. This was far more than the salary increase the university offered initially, which was 2 percent for each of 2015–2016 and 2016–2017, the remaining two years of a three-year contract (2014–2017). (Salary and other provisions for the first year of the contract, some of which is described below, had been settled in the previous year, and aspects of this settlement, we argue, likely helped lead to the successful win in 2016.)

During October 2015, 94 percent of CFA members who voted in a strike ballot indicated that they were ready for concerted job actions, which could include a strike, should contract negotiations over salary fail.[5] This high rate of endorsement of a strike occurred partly because CSU faculty were frustrated and angry. Many had not received a significant salary increase in close to a decade; the majority had not received *any* salary increase, even a cost-of-living increase, for most years of the previous decade or longer. A salary analysis conducted by the CFA revealed additional facts that further angered the faculty: the average salary for CSU faculty in the fall of 2014 would have been $63,000 if all faculty were full-time (the majority are not), and half of CSU faculty would have had a salary of $55,000 per year or less.[6] These wages were unlivable for most faculty in California, many of whom made their homes in some of the most expensive areas in the United States and many of whom were also paying on student loans accrued while attending doctoral or master's degree programs. In contrast, the salaries of campus presidents grew by 36 percent between 2004 and 2014. Additionally, faculty were concerned about the erosion of tenure-line positions and had seen increases in their workload. Between 2004 and 2014, the number of full-time equivalent students served by the CSU increased by 24 percent, the number of managers increased by 19.2 percent, the number of temporary faculty (mostly lecturers) increased by 46.4 percent, and the number of tenure-line faculty decreased by 3 percent.[7]

If the strike had occurred, it would have been the largest strike in higher education in the history of the United States. Some of the faculty had been involved in a one-day strike on 2 of the 23 campuses in 2011, but in all likelihood, most faculty had never been involved in a strike. In the spring of 2016 CFA representatives on campuses were regularly receiving emails and calls from faculty who were uncertain about what the strike would actually look like and feel like to them, how students might be impacted, how their relationships with administrators or with other faculty might be affected, whether they would lose pay, and other concerns. Yet overall, despite these feelings of discomfort, uncertainty, and risk, faculty were ready to strike, and many were directly involved in the preparations for the strike; they were moving full steam ahead. Then, on Friday, April 8, five days before the strike was scheduled to start, faculty received an email from the CFA stating the strike had been called off—the CFA and the CSU had reached a tentative agreement.

Laying the Groundwork for Solidarity between Two Faculty Groups

We believe that some events that helped lead to the successful win occurred many years prior to the settlement—as far back as the 1990s—and they involved the elevation and empowerment of lecturers. As Elizabeth Hoffman and John Hess noted in their history of the unionization of CSU faculty, in the early CFA in the 1980s, tenure-line faculty dominated leadership positions.[8] Issues that would concern only lecturers were not addressed; Hoffman and Hess described lecturers as "marginalized" within the union. They stated that the change toward more solidarity in the union occurred when a tenure-line faculty member, Susan Meisenhelder, who had been a lecturer, was elected as CFA president in the late 1990s. Additionally, for the first time, a lecturer, Jane Kerlinger, was elected as CFA vice president. Furthermore, the newly hired CFA general manager, like Meisenhelder and Kerlinger, saw the value in meeting the needs of both groups of faculty, tenure-line and lecturer, in order to create a stronger union. An additional factor was that a "fair share" agency fee bill had been passed by the California legislature. This state law requires that an employee pay for the representational costs of the union for handling grievances and for other union services when the employee refuses dues-paying membership in the union.[9] The revenues generated from agency fees gave the CFA more resources than it had previously. These multiple factors created a climate in which the two faculty groups could work together for the optimal benefit of all faculty and the students they taught.

Changes in working conditions and benefits for lecturers, which occurred during the Meisenhelder-Kerlinger years or after, empowered lecturers in tangible ways and decreased inequities between the two faculty groups, thereby making solidarity with tenure-line faculty more likely. For instance, during the Meisenhelder-Kerlinger years, the CFA bargained health benefits for all lecturers with at least a 40 percent time base and a one-semester appointment. In the 2002 contract, the CFA bargained language that gave incumbent lecturers preference for work over people who were not incumbents (i.e., newly hired lecturers). Contract language also allowed longer-serving lecturers preference for additional work, which meant that part-time lecturers could sometimes work up to full-time appointments and entitlements for future work. Coupled with some earlier provisions for lecturers—such as bargained language that required that when lecturers are rehired they must receive the same or higher salary as in the past and that lecturers who have been evaluated in a department must receive "careful consideration" for future work in that department—this meant that lecturers in the CSU have working conditions that are superior to those of most non-tenure-track faculty in the United States.[10]

By 2016, many more lecturers had come to hold leadership positions within the CFA, allowing them to stand up for their interests (whether those interests apply to lecturers only or are shared with tenure-line faculty) and leading to frequent interactions between lecturer and tenure-line leaders, which increased solidarity between the two groups. Of the 25 positions on the CFA board of directors in 2016, 4 were specifically designated for lecturers, and most of the other 21 positions could be held by either a temporary or tenure-line faculty member. Another leadership structure within the CFA, the general assembly, was composed of three to five representatives from each campus. One of these representatives from each campus was the lecturer representative to the assembly (a position that could only be filled by a lecturer), and the other positions, which could be held by any CFA member, were most often held by tenure-line faculty but were also frequently held by lecturers or other temporary faculty. Additionally, a state-wide lecturers council existed within the CFA, which included each campus's lecturer representative and other lecturer activists. The council typically met four times a year—two meetings when the general assembly met in the fall and spring and two other meetings of longer duration.

Negotiations over the collective bargaining agreement that was settled in April 2016 went on for two years. In the summer and fall of 2014, the CFA bargaining team, which included tenure-line faculty, lecturers, representatives from other faculty groups included in the bargaining unit (a counselor and a librarian), and attorneys, considered coming to agreement over changes to the contract, including salary for the first year only, while reserving the right to reopen the contract in the following two years over two issues only: salary and benefits for faculty who teach in extended education. As described earlier, the salary issue was a highly contentious one between the CFA and CSU. In the summer and fall of 2014, CSU offered a 3 percent salary pool for the 2014–2015 academic year, and the union was ready to recommend this settlement to its members. The salary pool offer meant that CSU would spend a specific amount of money on faculty pay raises: the equivalent of a 3 percent salary increase for all faculty. CSU was allowing the CFA to decide how that money would be distributed among faculty: as a 3 percent general salary increase or in any other way that the union chose.

The CFA pushed for an unequal distribution of this pay such that, in general, those with lower pay or those who had been stagnant in their pay for longer periods of time would receive higher increases than those with higher pay or more recent salary increases. This meant that some faculty, lecturers in particular, received high percentage salary increases. In the rare cases of lecturers who had received very low pay, some received up to 30 percent salary increases (but usually still ended up with significantly lower salaries after that pay increase than most tenure-line faculty). Many long-time faculty, both lecturer and tenure-line, received 4.6 percent increases, and the remainder of the faculty, many of whom were full professors, received 1.6 percent salary increases. The CFA secured an additional and relatively small pool of money (beyond the 3 percent) called "equity pay," from which some tenure-line faculty benefited. This salary pool was designed to address a salary issue of concern among tenure-line faculty: inversion, where more recently hired tenure-line faculty were earning more than more experienced faculty. As the chair of the CFA bargaining team, Kevin Wehr, reported, this overall increase in pay was well under what the faculty deserved, but served as "triage" to "stop the bleeding."[11] This settlement of the first year of the contract may have helped to bring the two faculty groups together, although this interpretation depends on one's perspective. This settlement did create greater pay equity among the faculty by "bringing up the bottom," possibly helping lecturers to feel more solidarity with tenure-line faculty.

We believe that all of these developments, from the 1990s through 2014, helped to lay the groundwork for the solidarity that was necessary to win a successful contract in 2016. We theorize that partly because of the empowerment of lecturers over the years, they felt less marginalized and were more likely to support faculty issues from which they might not directly benefit, such as higher wages for newly hired tenure-line faculty or increased protection of tenure itself. Some tenure-line faculty received 4.6 percent increases and/or equity pay (which was usually fairly small, but which could have a significant psychological effect), and this likely helped these people to feel a sense of solidarity with other faculty, including lecturers. However, some faculty, particularly some full professors who had received the smallest pay increases, were disappointed or angry about their very low percentage increases, and they channeled their anger toward securing better terms.

Additional Factors That Led to the Win in 2016

The salary settlement described above was ratified in November 2014. In May 2015, the CFA decided to reopen the salary article of the contract, as expected. A few months prior to this, the CFA had begun to tap into its resources and utilize strategies that had been effective in the past: holding frequent activities for faculty, which would keep the fight in their minds and keep them working together; seeking the support of allies, including students, other labor unions, politicians, and the public; and creating newsworthy events and keeping in contact with the media, so that the fight was continually publicized. The CFA highlighted the low salaries of its faculty by publishing four papers over a few months, called the Race to the Bottom series. These four papers were helpful in the CFA's general strategy to create solidarity among faculty and to enlist many allies in the fight for higher salaries for CSU faculty. The Race to the Bottom papers were as follows: "CSU's 10-Year Failure to Fund Its Core Mission," describing CSU faculty salary data over 10 years, and comparing CSU faculty salaries to those of other university faculty and other public workers; "Salary, Staffing Priorities, and the CSU's 1%," comparing the salaries of faculty to those of administrators, changes in these salaries over time, and changes in the numbers of faculty and administrator positions over time; "Losing Ground and Losing Faith," presenting CSU faculty stories about the effects of low salaries and inferior working conditions on their quality of life and that of their families; and "The Price Students Pay," explaining how low faculty salaries and inferior working conditions (such as contingency) affect the faculty's ability to teach the diverse students of CSU.[12]

Once the contract was reopened, the CFA bargaining team presented its case to the CSU, including the information from the Race to the Bottom papers. As CFA bargaining team chair Wehr reported in an article he wrote for CFA's magazine, *California Faculty*, in the first bargaining session, in the summer of 2015, the CSU claimed that faculty salaries were fine, presenting salary data which were very different from the CFA's data; bargaining team members called the CSU salary data "dishonest."[13]

Although the Race to the Bottom papers did not appear to have much effect on the members of the CSU bargaining team, they did serve to further agitate the faculty and to recruit allies. The union called for a strike authorization vote of its members in October 2015. As described earlier, CFA members voted overwhelmingly for job actions, including a strike, if needed. The

CFA made sure that the media publicized the results, and the strike vote made the news throughout California. At the same time, CFA leadership was planning a march and rally that would occur at the November California State University board of trustees meeting in Long Beach. The union had organized successful marches and rallies at board of trustees' meetings in previous years. The purposes of the march and rally were to get the faculty riled up and ready for further job actions (including a strike), if needed; to further communication and interaction with potential allies, including students, other labor union leaders, and legislators; and to show management that CFA members and allies were united and powerful. The November 17 rally was successful, involving more than 1,000 CSU faculty, students, labor allies, and others and receiving media attention throughout California. Labor allies included some California legislators who spoke at the rally and an AFL-CIO leader. By then, the CFA had created its slogan for the struggle: "Fight for Five."[14]

The university's management still did not budge on its 2 percent offer. The California Higher Education Employer-Employee Relations Act (HEERA) requires that a particular process take place before faculty can take job actions, including striking.[15] A next step was "fact-finding," in which an impartial party hears the cases presented by the two sides and issues a nonbinding report, typically favoring one side over the other. Fact-finding began soon after the November 17 rally and lasted through the following March.

As the fact-finder was doing her work, CFA leadership arranged for its Fight for Five campaign to continue on the many fronts mentioned above: the CFA worked to make sure that faculty, both tenure-line and lecturer, were in solidarity and ready to strike if needed; it communicated with allies in the legislature, asking them to put pressure on the CSU chancellor and board of trustees to settle a fair salary for faculty; it also communicated with the community, enlisting support. For instance, in December 2015, the CFA arranged for leaders of national education or labor organizations, including the California Teachers Association, the American Association of University Professors, and the Service Employees International Union, to send letters to the chancellor, asking him to settle the faculty contract. The union leadership also encouraged CFA members to wear Fight for Five buttons and stickers to campus and wear red when they returned to work in January to show solidarity with one another and to communicate to the administration and others that they were strong and united.

In January 2016, CFA leaders contacted central labor councils up and down the state, asking for "strike sanctions" from the other unions. Agreeing to strike sanctions would mean that the leaders of other unions would ask their members to avoid crossing the picket lines of CSU faculty. The unions that were sanctioning the strike could also support the strike in other ways, such as withholding deliveries to CSU campuses or not engaging in repairs or other contracted work on campuses. In the following months, the CFA gained strike sanctions from all the local labor councils in the state, including nearly all the unions in California. The CFA was extremely active on many fronts in February. The union began to instruct faculty about how to talk with students about the strike. For instance, faculty wrote articles for the student newspapers, explaining the salary stagnation and how faculty working conditions affect student learning conditions. The union worked with CFA student interns and the campus-based chapters of Students for Quality Education, a studentorganization focused on improving higher education in the CSU, to communicate with fellow students about the strike in person and through social media. The CFA also organized faculty through direct contact with them in numerous ways, such as speaking at department meetings, hall walking, and frequent emails. By February, more than 30 legislators had sent letters to the chancellor about reaching agreement to prevent a strike. By the end of the month the California Democratic Party had endorsed the Fight for Five. Probably most dramatically in February, the CFA announced the April strike dates. This announcement made it into news media throughout the state.[16]

In March the fact-finder's report was finally issued, and it supported the faculty position. In the two weeks before the scheduled strike, the CFA stepped up the pressure. The union launched an email campaign to the governor. Faculty and students marched in Sacramento and held a rally on the steps of the state capitol. That same day, Eliseo Medina, a representative of one of our three national affiliates, the Service Employees International Union, who was a former secretary treasurer of the union and farm workers organizer, met with the governor's labor liaison to update him and encourage him to help settle the dispute as quickly as possible.

The mounting pressure from inside and outside the CSU, the militant determination of CFA faculty to strike, and CSU students' support of their faculty finally brought the university's chancellor directly into the bargaining process, and soon afterward a settlement was reached. The economic advances agreed to by the CSU were important for low-paid faculty who had gone many years without a significant raise. More important, the contract victory was a testament to the years of organizing among lecturers and tenure-line faculty in the CFA, which laid the foundation for strong unified action.

Lecturers and Tenure-Line Faculty Working Together

Lecturers and tenure-line faculty often work together in faculty governance throughout the CSU, including at CSUEB where we both work. Here we are referring to governance at each level of the university: in disciplinary departments, at the college level, and in the campus-wide academic senate and its committees and subcommittees. However, a number of factors operate as potential obstacles to building inclusive and effective faculty governance on campus.

One issue is that tenure-line faculty are paid and/or receive service credit for campus service, including participation in governance, but lecturer faculty only rarely receive payment or service credit for campus service. This limits the participation of many lecturers who cannot afford to do unpaid work in the costly East Bay region of the San Francisco Bay Area. For instance, many must work at multiple campuses to earn a living, or perhaps, if they work only at CSUEB, they opt to teach as much as they are allowed, incurring very heavy teaching loads, since all classroom teaching is paid work. Governance work among lecturers may effectively be restricted to those who are relatively well-off financially. Also, lecturers do not have a presence in faculty governance that is proportionate to their numbers or full-time equivalent status. In the academic senate there are currently 42 seats dedicated to tenure-line faculty and 4 seats dedicated to lecturers. Tenure-line faculty on campus number between 325 and 350, and lecturers number 400–500 currently.[17] Additionally, the representation of lecturers at the department and college levels is uneven across campus. In some departments lecturers are encouraged to attend departmental faculty meetings and may vote whereas in other departments lecturers' attendance is not encouraged and they have no voting rights.

Another inequity that threatens solidarity between tenure-line and lecturer faculty is that lecturers are not recognized for their years of service at CSUEB; this can make lecturers feel that they are not acknowledged as part of the CSUEB community. Tenure-line faculty are recognized in campus-wide ceremonies for career accomplishments, particularly tenure and promotion. Additionally, tenured faculty can become emeritus faculty after 12 years of service on the campus whereas lecturers are not eligible for emeritus status regardless of years of service or excellence of their contributions in any area—

teaching, publishing, other professional work, or service to the university. At no point in lecturers' careers are they thanked or acknowledged by the university for the body of work produced at CSUEB.

Other inequities involve professional development and advancement. Lecturers in many departments often find it very difficult to receive campus funding for travel to conferences to present papers and participate in the profession, as is provided to tenure-line faculty. This often makes it financially unfeasible to attend professional activities and limits lecturers' ability to fully participate as members of the professoriat. Also, when a department is hiring on the tenure track and an incumbent, qualified long-term lecturer applies for the job, most often the lecturer is not hired. At present, the practice in the CSU has been to recruit nationally and internationally for tenure-line positions. Incumbent, qualified lecturers with the appropriate area of expertise are therefore competing with individuals who have placed themselves on the national or international job market. In some cases the incumbent lecturers have research/professional records that are similar to other applicants' records, but in other cases incumbent lecturers have been teaching much too much to be able to accrue a professional record that stands out to a hiring committee. Certainly, a number of factors, some legitimate and others that may reflect a lack of understanding about what individuals can achieve while working in lecturer positions, affect these hiring decisions. The end result is that long-term lecturers are still in relatively low-paid positions with tenuous job security and limited recognition for their work. The CFA is aware of this issue and is currently discussing possible remedies.

Despite these differences between the two groups of faculty in rights, opportunities, pay, acknowledgment, and responsibilities, they work together in faculty governance for the good of the university. Lecturer seats on the academic senate are always filled, and in our opinion the lecturer senators participate in meetings—they speak up—at equal rates to tenure-line senators. (We have each served many terms in the academic senate.)

Lecturer senators represent the university as a whole and additionally represent their fellow lecturer faculty, often bringing forth initiatives that are of particular interest to lecturers; they are visible and vocal on issues that impact lecturers, and their presence has kept issues of concern to lecturers front and center in the senate. At CSUEB a committee exists within the academic senate with a charge to address lecturers' issues. A subcommittee of the Faculty Affairs Committee, the Subcommittee on Lecturers became a "regular" subcommittee in 2003 (it had sometimes existed as an ad hoc committee prior to that). It is charged with "review and recommendations of changes to current policies and procedures relating to lecturers, and recommendation of new policies and procedures relating to lecturers."[18] The subcommittee is composed of three lecturers, three tenure-line faculty, and a nonvoting presidential appointee, who in recent years has been the associate provost.

Since 2003, the lecturer and tenure-line members have worked together and successfully created or favorably revised three policies that affected working conditions for lecturers in the following ways: improving the office hour policy for lecturers, clarifying that lecturer senators count as part of the quorum of the senate, and clarifying the language in the senate bylaws that determines how lecturers are elected to the academic senate. The committee also has worked on several other documents, most of which have been approved by the senate but were not approved by the university president and therefore did not become policy, for instance, emeritus status for lecturers and an improved policy for salary increases (called "range elevation") for lecturers. Additionally, in 2006 the subcommittee worked to increase the number of lecturer seats on the academic senate from two to four; this initiative, which involved support from two other committees and the full academic senate, and was put to a vote of the CSUEB tenure-line faculty, was successful. Several CSUEB lecturers have served on this subcommittee and/or have served multiple times on the academic senate over the years, including Suzanne Busch, Margaret Harris, Felix Herndon, Mark Karplus, Jeffrey Newcomb, Andrew Pasquinelli, Vibha Puri, Gretchen Reevy, Wendy Sarvasy, Michael Schutz, and Valerie Smith. Jair Fory is notable as being the first athletic coach to serve as a lecturer representative to the academic senate.

Over the past 10 or so years some lecturers have begun to serve in senate positions that have typically been held only by tenure-line faculty. Most recently, the senate elected a lecturer as senate chair for the first time in the history of CSUEB. Veteran lecturer Mark Karplus was elected senate chair for 2016–2017. Karplus, who has worked for 22 years as a lecturer at CSUEB, has served in various roles in the academic senate for many years, beginning as a lecturer representative to the senate and more recently serving as the senate's secretary (2013–2016). Since 2007 three lecturers have served one or more terms on the executive committee of the academic senate: Mark Karplus, Jeffrey Newcomb, and Gretchen Reevy. These are probably the only times that lecturers have served on the executive committee in the history of CSUEB.

Because of the institutional inequities in faculty governance, CFA activists have pushed and continue to push for changes in the senate to be more inclusive of lecturers' voices. While the CFA respects the unique role of the senate to address curriculum and other faculty affairs and that the senate is the center of campus shared governance efforts with the local administration, CFA members who are active on the senate and in faculty governance have supported the efforts of lecturers to achieve equity and fairness on the campus.

On the CFA chapter level, we have developed ways to support the input and leadership of lecturers in campus chapter activities. Lecturers have grown to have influence in lecturer affairs, holding regular meetings for lecturers on campus, including a popular unemployment insurance workshop led by CSUEB lecturer Vibha Puri. Several lecturers sit on the CFA executive board and hold chapter offices. The CFA tenure-line and lecturer faculty work together on common issues, such as faculty rights, political and contract campaigns and other campus-wide areas of concern. Through these joint efforts the distinctions between permanent and contingent faculty are minimized as are other distinctions, such as between librarian faculty, counselor faculty, athletic coaches, and classroom instructors.

The ability of all faculty to work together on our campus has added to the success of many campaigns. Most notably, we held a one-day strike of all faculty on November 17, 2011, at CSUEB and CSU Dominguez Hills; the two campuses shut down their classrooms and most other services directed by faculty. The 2011 strike was also an example of faculty-student solidarity: students at CSUEB held an overnight vigil on campus before the strike. They joined with their faculty on the picket lines and did not cross the lines to attend classes. Students were educated about the history of union picket lines and why not to cross them. This 2011 strike achieved the desired result of bringing the university back to the bargaining table with the CFA.

Conclusions

In sum, tenure-line and lecturer faculty work together in both the union and campus governance at CSUEB and on the other CSU campuses. The issue of whether faculty unions should include both contingent and tenure-line faculty is a complex one, but we believe that, at least in our system, working together is the most effective and most satisfying route. We believe that our ability to work together is made more likely because our two groups of faculty share more commonalities due to greater equity than is observed in other university systems. In general, the CFA has worked to reduce the inequities between the groups of faculty in recent years, which may have been a proximate factor that contributed to the 2016 union win.

ACKNOWLEDGMENTS

We acknowledge Mark Karplus and Lil Taiz for their assistance with our fact-checking and for providing comments on a draft of this chapter.

NOTES

1. Elizabeth Hoffman and John Hess, "Organizing for Equality within the Two-Tier System: The Experience of the California Faculty Association," in *Equality for Contingent Faculty: Overcoming the Two-Tier System*, ed. Keith Hoeller (Nashville, TN: Vanderbilt University Press, 2014), 9–27.

2. Irwin Yellowitz, *25 Years of Progress* (New York: PSC-CUNY, 1997), http://cdha.cuny .edu/files/original/1997_PSC_25YearsofProgress.pdf; United University Professions, "Historical Overview of UUP," http://uupinfo.org/history/index.php (accessed Feb. 15, 2017).

3. AAUP-AFT Rutgers, http://www.rutgersaaup.org (accessed Feb. 15, 2017).

4. State of California, article 6, "Unit Determinations," section 3579(a)(1), https://leginfo. legislature.ca.gov/faces/codes_displayText.xhtml?lawCode=GOV&division=4.&title=1.&part =&chapter=12.&article=6; Hoffman and Hess, "Organizing for Equality," 12.

5. California Faculty Association, "Strike Vote 2015: Members Vote 'Yes' to Strike," CFA Headlines, Nov. 4, 2015, http://www.calfac.org/headlines/cfa-headlines-november-4-2015.

6. California Faculty Association, "Race to the Bottom: CSU's 10-Year Failure to Fund Its Core Mission," 2015, http://www.calfac.org/race-to-the-bottom.

7. California Faculty Association, "Race to the Bottom: Salary, Staffing Priorities, and the CSU's 1%," 2015, http://www.calfac.org/race-to-the-bottom.

8. Hoffman and Hess, "Organizing for Equality," 16–17.

9. University of California, San Diego, Human Resources, "Agency Fees/Union Dues: FAQ," http://blink.ucsd.edu/HR/labor/unions/fees/FAQ.html (accessed Feb. 15, 2017).

10. California Faculty Association, "Collective Bargaining Agreement (Contract), 2014–2017," http://www.calfac.org/resource/collective-bargaining-agreement-contract-2014–2017# appointment (accessed Feb. 15, 2017).

11. Kevin Wehr, "The Fight for Five: The Faculty Take a Stand for Respect, Fair Pay and the Future of Feaching in the CSU," *California Faculty: The Magazine of the California Faculty Association* (Fall 2015): 3–7, http://www.calfac.org/item/fight-five.

12. All four papers are available at California Faculty Association, http://www.calfac.org /race-to-the-bottom (accessed July 28, 2016).

13. Wehr, "Fight for Five."

14. California Faculty Association, "Faculty Challenge CSU Trustees to Resolve the Difficult Conflict between Teaching Excellence and Earning a Living," CFA Headlines, Sept. 16, 2015, http://www.calfac.org/headlines/cfa-headlines-september-16-2015.

15. HEERA is the state law that governs employee-employer relations in public higher education in California. See State of California, Public Employment Relations Board, "HEERA," https://www.perb.ca.gov/laws/heera.aspx (accessed Feb. 15, 2017).

16. See California Faculty Association, "CFA Strike Announcement in the News," http:// www.calfac.org/post/cfa-strike-announcement-news (accessed Feb. 15, 2017).

17. California State University, East Bay, "IPEDS Employees," 2016, http://www.csueastbay .edu/ir/files/html/University.Employees.8–1.html.

18. California State University, East Bay, Academic Senate, "Faculty Affairs: Subcommittee on Lecturers," 2016, http://www.csueastbay.edu/faculty/senate/committees/fac/fac-sub-lecturers .html.

Reflections on the Possibilities and Limitations of Collective Bargaining

KIM TOLLEY AND KRISTEN EDWARDS

Adjunct instructors are members of the "academic precariat," a growing class of faculty who often work with no job security, no benefits, and low wages. As scholars have shown, the proportion of faculty off the tenure track has been rising for nearly half a century. This trend reflects the growing inequality in our society, in which many employment sectors are divided between a large precariat and a small, highly paid elite. The shift in higher education is particularly troubling, because research suggests that an overreliance on poorly paid and unsupported part-time faculty hurts student retention and achievement.[1]

Can unionization improve the working conditions of contingent faculty and stop the increasing reliance on part-time gig labor? In this concluding chapter we explore the possibilities and limitations of collective bargaining by analyzing collective bargaining agreements ratified between 2010 and 2016 at 35 colleges and universities (see appendix table 1). As some of the authors in this volume point out, it may become more difficult in the future for adjunct faculty to unionize with new appointments to the National Labor Relations Board and the passage of anti-union legislation under a Republican White House and Congress. With this possibility in mind, we also discuss alternative ways that faculty and concerned citizens can help to roll back the growing exploitation of adjunct faculty in higher education.[2]

Improvements to Salary, Benefits, and Working Conditions

Collective bargaining is the process by which unions negotiate contracts with employers to determine their working conditions and terms of employment.

Once faculty members have voted to form a union, they collectively select their priorities for bargaining and elect a bargaining committee to negotiate on their behalf.[3]

Unionization may not be able to solve all the problems in higher education, but collective bargaining can improve the salary, benefits, and working conditions of contingent faculty. Twenty-first-century studies of national data have concluded that unionized faculty members have higher rates of pay than nonunion faculty.[4] The ratified contracts bear this out, with adjunct faculty winning salary increases at every institution, as shown in appendix table 1. For instance, at Rutgers University, where adjuncts are in a union affiliated with the American Federation of Teachers (AFT) and the American Association of University Professors (AAUP), instructors with 12 semesters of teaching experience at the university gained a 5 percent pay raise, plus increases of around 2 percent over the remaining two years of the contract. At Point Park University in Pennsylvania, adjunct faculty affiliated with the United Steelworkers gained a 23 percent pay increase and payment for last-minute class cancellations. At Hamline University in Minnesota, adjuncts affiliated with the Service Employees International Union (SEIU) also won pay raises—most received a 15 percent increase in the first year and then saw their base pay increase by 20 percent the second year. Other SEIU-affiliated adjunct unions also enjoyed large increases: at Washington University in St. Louis, adjuncts won a 26 percent increase over the subsequent four years; Boston University adjuncts won pay raises between 29 percent and 68 percent over the three-year period covered by their contract; in California, Mills College adjuncts gained a wage scale that rewards seniority, with raises ranging from 1.75 percent to 60 percent.[5]

Adjunct faculty members also increased their benefits at the majority of the institutions in our sample. Most (89 percent) of the contracts include provisions allowing part-time faculty to receive health insurance. For example, at Northeastern University, adjuncts who work 30 hours or more per week won health insurance plans, and part-time faculty gained the right to participate in the university's basic retirement plan after two years of service. At New York University, where adjunct faculty voted in 2002 to affiliate with the United Auto Workers, adjuncts ratified a collective bargaining agreement in 2010 that allows those teaching at least 84 contact hours or providing at least 150 hours of individualized instruction during an academic year (fall, spring, summer) to apply for the same health-care coverage that is available to the university's full-time faculty. Lecturers in the California State University system who teach at least half-time for four consecutive quarters or three consecutive semesters are entitled to benefits through the California Public Employees' Retirement System, receive health-care benefits, and participate in the university's voluntary retirement program.[6]

Almost all (97 percent) of the collective bargaining agreements in our sample provided increased job security for contingent faculty. Job security is very important to adjunct instructors, who often do not know from one period to the next whether they'll be rehired to teach. The University of Illinois, Urbana-Champaign, agreed to offer multiyear contracts "whenever appropriate" to adjunct faculty. At Florida Agricultural and Mechanical University, instructors and lecturers may receive "two- to five-year fixed multi-year appointments." George Washington University agreed that part-time faculty in their second consecutive academic year of teaching would be reappointed to courses they had previously taught and denied reappointment only under limited, specified circumstances. Tufts University agreed that "normally, the university will appoint a part-time faculty member to a term of one year" and also agreed to a system whereby part-time instructors could gain multiyear contracts. Adjuncts at most institutions also won the right to some form of compensation when their classes are canceled. For instance, at Georgetown University, an adjunct faculty member appointed to teach a standard course will be paid $300 if the course is canceled within 21 calendar days of when the first class is scheduled to begin.[7]

Adjuncts have also gained increased access to professional development through collective bargaining. Most (94 percent) of the contracts we examined guarantee professional development benefits in union contracts. Some link faculty development funds to improving teaching, while others award these funds for independent scholarly research or creative activity. At Montgomery Community College in Maryland, part-time faculty members are now eligible for a maximum professional development benefit of $600 each (with a $50,000 cap on the maximum benefits payable by the college). At Howard University, faculty members are now eligible for a maximum benefit of $700 per employee. Adjuncts at other institutions won similar benefits, including increased access to free or discounted tuition for professional training. Part-time faculty at Notre Dame de Namur University won the right to apply for the rank of senior lecturer after teaching 60 semester units, and once they have reached that rank, they can apply for sabbatical.[8]

At most institutions (83 percent), adjunct faculty members have won increased resources to support their teaching and advising of students. In addition to contractually guaranteed access to email, photocopying, space in which to prepare for classes and meet with students, and administrative support services, at some institutions faculty have gained reimbursement for authorized field trips and classroom expenses. For instance, for every month they teach, part-time adjuncts at Antioch College in Ohio gained a $25 transportation allowance, and full-time adjuncts gained an $80 transportation allowance; additionally, full-time and "core" adjunct faculty gained a $500 one-time allowance and an annual $250 allowance to set up and maintain a home office. At the Maryland Institute College of Art, adjuncts are now guaranteed access to instructional resources as well as credit union membership, bookstore discounts, a discounted gym membership, and other benefits.[9]

Adjunct faculty members have also gained the right to academic freedom. Academic freedom allows college and university faculty to research topics of their choice, to challenge conventional thinking in classroom discussions, and to publish controversial papers. This empowers faculty to advance knowledge through research and creative activity and to teach students to think independently. Most institutions of higher education have formal policies ensuring academic freedom, and most of the regional accreditation organizations require institutions to protect it. Additionally, numerous professional organizations and national academic organizations, such as the AAUP, the Association of American Colleges and Universities, the American Council on Education, and the Association of Governing Boards, have issued policy statements about the importance of preserving academic freedom in higher education.[10] In reality though, tenured faculty have the greatest academic freedom, because they enjoy the greatest protection from arbitrary dismissal. Ensuring academic freedom protection for contingent faculty is therefore an important goal in collective bargaining. Adjuncts at 83 percent of the institutions we sampled gained this right through collective bargaining. For example, at the College of Saint Rose, adjuncts gained the right to academic freedom through a collective bargaining agreement that includes a policy statement explicitly based on the AAUP's "1940 Statement of Principles on Academic Freedom and Tenure."[11]

Limitations of Collective Bargaining

Despite noteworthy gains, some goals remain elusive. The agreements in union contracts vary from school to school. At many colleges and universities, adjunct instructors have won health-care benefits, but at some they have not. To some extent, this variation occurs because of the different bargaining priorities of the faculty at each school, but it also occurs because of the nature of the negotiation process, which usually involves some compromise on both sides. As a result, union negotiators typically achieve some—but not all—of the contract agreements their members desire.[12] Among the 35 collective bargaining agreements in our sample, we identified three areas in which collective bargaining has failed to achieve meaningful gains: attaining true parity in salary and benefits with tenure-line faculty, obtaining meaningful participation in shared governance, and halting the increasing overreliance on part-time instructors in higher education.

Part-time adjuncts have yet to achieve parity in salary and benefits with tenure-line faculty. This is true even in institutions where adjuncts have been unionized for years. The SEIU's Faculty Forward campaign aims to establish "a national standard of $15,000 per course—total compensation including both salary and benefits," an aspirational goal that, if achieved, would provide pro rata parity with associate professors in many colleges and universities. There have been some significant salary increases on campuses where adjuncts have ratified first contracts. At Tufts University, adjuncts gained a minimum pay of $7,300 per course; at Mills College, adjuncts on multiyear contracts gained a pay of $8,500 in the third year; at Dominican University of California, adjuncts who have completed 3 years of a multiyear contract gained pay tied to 80 percent of the salary of a tenure-track associate professor. Nevertheless, though such gains are impressive, they still fall short of providing adjunct faculty with true parity in salary and benefits with tenure-line faculty. Even in large public systems that have been unionized for years, improvements have come slowly. As Kim Geron and Gretchen M. Reevy show in chapter 10 in this volume, in the California State University (CSU) system, contingent faculty's rights and working conditions have improved with successive contract negotiations, with the largest gains achieved in the late 1990s, around 15 years after the union was established. According to Luke Elliott-Negri in chapter 9 in this volume, contingent faculty have seen similar developments in the Professional Staff Congress at the City University of New York (CUNY). In both CSU and CUNY, the greatest obstacle to improving adjuncts' salary has been the intransigence of management. To move forward in negotiations, both unions had to put more pressure on management by rallying their members to go on strike. Other contract improvements in long-standing unions suggest that serious gains in parity with tenure-line faculty can only happen with this level of concerted effort and solidarity among all categories of faculty.[13]

The second area in which collective bargaining has not yet produced widespread gains for adjunct faculty is shared governance. Shared governance in higher education is commonly defined as joint effort and shared responsibility for decision-making among the faculty, administration, and boards of trustees. According to the AAUP, "Faculty should have primary responsibility for such fundamental areas as curriculum subject matter and methods of instruction, research, faculty status, and those aspects of student life which relate to the educational process." The Association of Governing Boards of Universities and Colleges emphasizes the ultimate authority of boards of trustees but also recognizes the faculty's role in shared governance: "Boards should recognize that academic tradition, especially the status accorded faculty because of their central role in teaching and generating new knowledge, creates the need for deliberation and participation of faculty and other key constituents in decision making."[14] As Elizabeth K. Davenport points out in chapter 7 in this volume, shared governance has been the norm in universities for nearly two centuries. But adjunct instructors—who represent the largest segment of the faculty—rarely participate in institutional decision-making on American campuses. Acknowledging the problem, in 2013 the AAUP issued a report calling for departments and faculty senates to make sure that contingent faculty can vote in their meetings and elections and hold offices, just as tenure-line faculty do. Several large unions have issued resolutions supporting the rights of contingent faculty to participate in shared governance, including the National Education Association and the American Federation of Teachers.[15]

Although some research indicates that unionization can strengthen faculty participation in shared governance, this outcome is not always achieved. A 2001 research study by Christine Maitland and Gary Rhoades, which analyzed 294 collective bargaining agreements covering all categories of faculty, including those on the tenure track, revealed that just over a third mentioned governance issues and 92 referred to faculty senates. Based on the contracts analyzed in their study, the authors concluded that when collective bargaining pays attention to issues of shared governance, union contracts can protect and strengthen existing governance structures, producing campuses where unions and faculty senates mutually support each other.[16] Nevertheless, few of the collective bargaining agreements in our sample even mention shared governance. Most agreements provide for a "labor-management committee" that meets one or more times per year to discuss matters of interest to adjunct faculty, but this sort of arrangement does not ensure that adjunct faculty are well integrated into the existing shared governance structures in which tenure-track faculty participate. For instance, one university's tentative agreement states that the goal of labor-management meetings is "to discuss matters of general interest to the Adjunct Faculty Members or the University" and "shall not be used for negotiations or to discuss pending grievances."[17] This is a far cry from ensuring that adjunct faculty members have meaningful input into the academic decisions of their own departments and institutions. Some contracts state that adjunct faculty are welcome to attend department and university meetings and events if they wish, but this sort of language does not really ensure the participation of adjunct faculty in shared governance. Many adjuncts cannot afford to spend unpaid time on campus. Even with the provision of remuneration, such contract language does not provide adjuncts with the right to communicate their concerns to the board of trustees or vote on issues of importance, nor does it give adjuncts the ability to run for election to the assemblies and committees on which full-time faculty serve.

Only 23 percent of the collective bargaining agreements we examined include provisions to ensure adjunct faculty's participation in shared governance. Of these, some have explicit statements to provide contractual support to existing governance structures, as in Antioch University's agreement with SEIU Local 925: "The Parties recognize the University's long record of shared governance through which the faculty historically have provided recommendations to administrators and the Chancellor on matters of academic policy. The Parties support the principle of shared governance and the Antioch University Seattle's faculty governance structures, including the Faculty Leadership Team and the Faculty Assembly." Similarly, the agreement between Mills College and SEIU Local 1021 upholds the college's current policy, which allows eligible part-time faculty to vote on issues of importance to faculty, based on whether they have taught at least three course credits for at least three years. At Saint Mary's College of California, adjuncts gained the right to submit an annual report to the board of trustees, attend all open sessions at faculty forums, and receive additional compensation for any assigned service to governance committees. At Lesley University, adjunct faculty in each school and college gained the right to elect one faculty member each "to participate as full members of the University Council." At the University of Illinois, Urbana-Champaign (UIUC), a "side letter agreement" states that within two years, all colleges, departments, schools, and units will amend their bylaws to address participation "by bargaining unit members in shared governance and faculty governance." At Notre Dame de Namur University, the collective bargaining agreement increases part-time faculty participation in shared governance by requiring that part-time representatives be elected and compensated to serve on faculty committees that advise the administration on curriculum, standards, and professional development.[18]

The lack of traction in shared governance provisions in most collective bargaining agreements may be due to two factors: the scope of bargaining and the priorities of the bargaining unit. Under the National Labor Relations Act, the scope of bargaining is defined in a way that requires both parties to negotiate over "mandatory subjects": issues that directly impact wages, hours, or working conditions. In contrast, parties are not required by law to bargain over "permissive subjects" that fall outside the realm of mandatory issues. This means that at the bargaining table management may refuse to even discuss permissive issues that involve questions of academic policy, such as faculty participation in shared governance. Even in cases where management agrees to bargain over shared governance, a majority of the adjunct faculty of the bargaining unit would have to prioritize shared governance provisions for the final ratified contract to include them. As Shawn Gilmore explains in chapter 8 in this volume, it took a strike at UIUC to attain agreements on some of the bargaining unit's top priorities, including a side letter ensuring adjunct faculty participation in shared governance. Not all bargaining units are willing to take such a strong stand to achieve their top priorities. Moreover, at every contract negotiation, union members leave some items on the bargaining table when they finally vote to ratify a contract, and often salaries and benefits are prioritized over other important issues. Researchers have found that for such reasons, unions generally negotiate less favorable outcomes for permissive than for mandatory issues.[19]

The third area where collective bargaining appears to have limited efficacy is in reducing the overreliance on part-time, contingent faculty in higher education. Research indicates that most part-time instructors would prefer to work full-time. A 2010 national survey conducted by the AFT found that this was particularly true of younger instructors. A 2015 study based on survey data from 4,000 part-time instructors at around 300 colleges and universities found that 73 percent of part-time instructors want to have a full-time position but are not able to find one.[20] Based on this, one might expect that unionization would increase the number of full-time and tenure-track positions, but this has not happened. In a 1997 study of 183 higher education union contracts, researchers found that although administrators across the country were increasingly replacing full-time faculty with part-timers, most contracts failed to limit the number of temporary adjunct faculty hired.[21] As several authors point out elsewhere in this volume, in CUNY the unionization of adjunct faculty has had no impact on the proportion of part-time faculty teaching in the system, and although faculty members in the CSU system have been unionized since 1983, the number of tenure-line faculty in that system has actually decreased by 3 percent since the early 2000s.[22]

None of the 35 contracts we examined includes any agreements by management to increase the proportion of full-time and tenure-line positions. Only one has a provision about the proportion of the faculty. The collective bargaining agreement between the Pennsylvania state colleges and universities and the Association of Pennsylvania State College and University Faculties (APSCUF) states, "The full-time equivalent (FTE) of temporary and regular part-time faculty members at any University shall not exceed twenty-five percent (25 percent) of the full-time equivalent (FTE) of all faculty members employed at that University as of October 31 of the previous year. A university and local APSCUF may, by written local agreement, exceed the limit provided herein."[23]

It is possible that the lack of collective bargaining agreements addressing the issue of creating more full-time positions stems not only from management being opposed to the increased costs of hiring full-time faculty, but also from part-time instructors who want to keep their current jobs and see this as a threat. Some critics of adjunct unions have argued that increasing the proportion of full-time positions in the professoriat is against the interests of many part-time instructors, because any increase in full-time positions diminishes the amount of part-time work available.[24] Given the different priorities among adjuncts, improving full-time employment opportunities for contingent faculty will require not only sustained activism and effort at the bargaining table, but also the cooperation of all categories of part-time faculty, from those who are teaching at multiple institutions to support themselves to the retirees and working professionals who just want to teach the occasional course on the side.

Looking to the Future: Political Advocacy at the National and Local Levels

While collective bargaining can improve many aspects of adjunct faculty's day-to-day working conditions, political advocacy on the national level holds promise to change the long-term outlook for the entire professoriat. To this end, some of the nation's largest unions have joined forces to issue recommendations for the reauthorization of the Higher Education Act (HEA). The HEA governs the administration of federal student aid programs; the law was passed and signed into law under President Lyndon B. Johnson in 1965. Every five years, the act must be reapproved or reauthorized by Congress. The NEA, the AFT, and the American Association of University Professors Collective Bargaining Congress have recommended that the next reauthorized HEA "[p]rovide incentives for investment in instruction and student support services that lead to greater student success, including incentives for institutions that make progress in reversing harmful employment trends among faculty and that transition from a majority contingent instructional workforce to a well- supported, predominantly full-time and tenure-track faculty."[25]

Another important goal is to reform the accrediting agencies. What are they doing about the increasing exploitation of contingent faculty in higher education? Not much, according to a report by the American Association of University Professors. Regional accrediting bodies oversee the educational integrity of colleges and universities in the United States. According to the US Department of Education, their goal is to "ensure that education provided by the institutions of higher education meets acceptable levels of quality." Their influence is important, because accreditation is required for access to federal funds, including student aid. But as the AAUP report points out, though all of the accrediting organizations direct colleges and universities to assure educational quality and enhance instructional effectiveness, they have been largely mute on the increasing reliance on adjunct faculty.[26] Most accreditors have taken no official position, and the wording in most accreditation documents is vague. The New England Commission requires the institution to define the roles of adjuncts and ensure that the composition of the faculty "is periodically reviewed." The Southern Commission directs the institution to be "judicious" in its use of part-time instructors because the "achievement of the institution's mission . . . will require a critical mass of permanent, full-time, qualified faculty to provide direction and oversight of the academic programs." The Western Senior College and University Commission simply asks the institution to show "that it employs a faculty with substantial and continuing commitment to the institution" and "employ[s] at least one full-time faculty member for each graduate program offered." None of these organizations provides specific guidelines or benchmarks describing the optimal composition of the faculty or the level of resources and support that adjunct instructors need to provide students a high-quality education. The Higher Learning

Commission, which accredits postsecondary institutions in the North Central region, has no written guidelines that would preclude a faculty composed entirely of part-time employees.[27] Given the lack of attention from the accrediting organizations and the financial incentive for colleges and universities to hire faculty at the cheapest rates possible, it is not surprising that adjunct faculty have unionized in increasing numbers over the years.

Current accreditation standards require colleges and universities to demonstrate that they provide some form of faculty development and attend to faculty recruitment, workload, evaluation, and incentives, but they rarely require institutions to demonstrate that they include contingent faculty in such provisions. Accreditors should develop stronger standards regarding the employment of part-time faculty in colleges and universities, and they should penalize institutions that exploit such faculty. Accrediting team members should receive training that includes information about the changing faculty workforce, its impact on institutional quality and student outcomes, and best practices for supporting contingent as well as tenure-line faculty. During the accreditation process, visiting teams should focus on meeting with all groups of faculty. Since adjuncts represent the majority on most campuses, they should have a significant voice and receive substantial attention in the accreditation process.[28]

In recognition of the important role played by accreditation in improving academic quality, the American Federation of Teachers has called on institutions and accreditation agencies to develop more rigorous standards with regard to the "working conditions and compensation of contingent instructors in higher education as well as with regard to the percentage of faculty that are full-time, tenure track." The AFT has developed rigorous accreditation standards that the accreditation agencies could use in evaluating the employment of part-time faculty, full-time non-tenure-track faculty, and graduate student employees in colleges and universities.[29]

Regardless of the success or failure of the reforms proposed on the national level, individuals at the local level can also take steps to enact reforms at their own institutions. The changed political environment under a Republican federal government may well pose serious challenges for those trying to pass new legislation favorable to unions. New appointments to the National Labor Relations Board may also make it more difficult for adjunct faculty to organize. Nevertheless, as Nicholas M. Wertsch and Joseph A. McCartin argue in chapter 5 in this volume, faculty and students can make a difference by working to implement just and equitable employment policies at their own colleges and universities. Although many institutions claim to advance social justice or develop democratic communities, few have acted on their own principles when it comes to giving adjunct faculty a living wage and a real voice in decision-making. Everyone who cares about the quality of education at American colleges and universities should demand they do so.[30]

All tenure-track faculty should work to transform their departments into places where contingent faculty members are respected and treated as professional equals. As Adrianna Kezar and Tom DePaola point out in chapter 2 in this volume, it is critical to acknowledge and support the contingent faculty's role in creating an effective learning environment for students. Department chairs should advocate for equity in salary and benefits for contingent faculty. Chairs should ensure that those faculty have the resources they need to provide students an excellent education, and they should invite adjuncts to attend meetings and participate in professional development activities. Faculty senates and other faculty governance bodies should revise their bylaws to encourage the participation of adjunct faculty members and allow them to vote on issues that affect the academic quality of their institution.

At institutions where unionization is possible, tenure-track faculty should support the unionization efforts of adjunct faculty. As Kim Tolley, Marianne Delaporte, and Lorenzo Giachetti explain in chapter 6 in this volume, even when they suffer from low salaries and poor working conditions, adjunct faculty are sometimes reluctant to participate in discussions about organizing because they fear retaliation, not only from the administration but also from tenure-track faculty who serve as program directors and department chairs.

Strengthening adjunct faculty strengthens the professoriat as a whole. Since the founding of the nation, the purpose of American colleges and universities has been to provide the most empowering education to students, one that promotes flexible, creative, analytical thinking and the capacity for understanding and problem solving. This purpose will never be realized with a professoriat composed predominantly of instructors who often work without the protection of academic freedom, no role in shared governance, no job security, no benefits, low wages, and no real hope of ever finding a full-time position. It is essential to prevent colleges and universities from slipping into a corporate culture in which they forget their historic purpose and focus primarily on the bottom line. Because collective bargaining can improve the working conditions of adjunct faculty, unionization is an important means to this end.

NOTES

1. In this volume, see chapter 1 by A. J. Angulo and chapter 3 by Timothy Reese Cain for the increasing proportion of adjunct faculty, and see chapter 2 by Adrianna Kezar and Tom DePaola for how the poor working conditions of adjunct faculty harm students. For the term "academic precariat," see Kwame Anthony Appiah, "The Ethicist," *New York Times Magazine,* Jan. 1, 2017, 19.

2. The sample of 35 collective bargaining agreements discussed in this chapter was retrieved on February 12, 2017, through an online search. See appendix table 1 for the list of institutions and the details. See chapter 4 by Gregory Saltzman and chapter 5 by Nicholas M. Wertsch and Joseph McCartin, both in this volume, for the possible negative impact of antiunion legislation and NLRB appointments under a Republican White House and Congress.

3. Harry Katz, Thomas Kochan, and Alexander Colvin, *An Introduction to Collective Bargaining and Industrial Relations* (New York: McGraw-Hill, 2007); Gary Chaison, *The New Collective Bargaining* (New York: Springer Science and Business Media, 2012).

4. Stephen G. Katsinas, Johnson A. Ogun, and Nathaniel J. Bray, "Monetary Compensation of Full-Time Faculty at American Public Regional Universities: The Impact of Geography and the Existence of Collective Bargaining," paper presented at the 43rd Annual National Conference of the National Center for the Study of Collective Bargaining in Higher Education and the Professions, New York, Apr. 3, 2016, http://www.chronicle.com/items/biz/pdf/2016-4-3%20 Compensation%20of%20FT%20faculty%20at%20Regional%20Universities-Katsinas%20 Ogun%20and%20Bray.pdf; Stephen G. Katsinas and David E. Hardy, "An Assessment of the Impact of Collective Bargaining on Faculty Compensation at Community Colleges," *Journal of Collective Bargaining in the Academy* (Nov. 16, 2012), http://thekeep.eiu.edu/cgi/viewcontent .cgi?article=1187&context=jcba. Also see Peggy Christidis, Karen Stann, and Luona Lin, "How Does Collective Bargaining Affect Faculty Salaries? News from APA's Center for Workforce Studies," *Monitor on Psychology* 46, no. 9 (Oct. 2015), www.apa.org/monitor/2015/10/data point.aspx.

5. Colleen Flaherty, "Big Gains for Adjuncts," *Inside Higher Ed*, Jan. 15, 2016, https://www .insidehighered.com/news/2016/01/15/does-new-crop-first-adjunct-union-contracts-include -meaningful-gains; "SEIU Contract Highlights: The Union Difference," http://seiufacultyforward .org/seiu-contract-highlights-the-union-difference (accessed July 26, 2017); "Mills' Adjunct Professors Win First Ever Contract; Includes Best in the Nation Job Protections," SEIU, Mar. 21, 2016, http://www.seiu1021.org/2016/03/21/mills-adjunct-professors-win-first-ever-contract -includes-best-in-the-nation-job-protections.

6. Article 32, California Faculty Association, "Collective Bargaining Agreement (Contract), 2014–2017," http://www.calfac.org/resource/collective-bargaining-agreement-contract-2014 –2017#benefits (accessed Feb. 13, 2016); "Collective Bargaining Agreement between Northeastern University and Service Employees International Union Local 509, CTW" (Mar. 2016, 25, http://www.northeastern.edu/part-timeinfo/FINAL-CBA-03022016.pdf; "Collective Bargaining Agreement between New York University and International Union, UAW, AFL-CIO and Local 7902: Adjuncts Come Together, UAW, September 1, 2010–August 31, 2016," 35–36, https://www.nyu.edu/content/dam/nyu/hr/documents/unioncontracts/adjunct.pdf.

7. Article 10, "Agreement by and between the Board of Trustees of the University of Illinois and Non-Tenure Faculty Coalition Local #6546/AFT/IFT/AAUP Non-Tenure Track Faculty, Effective August 16, 2014, through August 15, 2019," http://www.local6546.org/wp-content /uploads/2016/05/NTFC_Contract_2014_2019_signed.pdf; "Approval of Collective Bargaining Agreements, Florida Agricultural and Mechanical University Board of Trustees Action Item, Governance Committee, November 9, 2016," 13, http://www.famu.edu/BOT/Collective

%20Bargaining%20Agreements.pdf; article 5, "Collective Bargaining Agreement between the George Washington University and Service Employees International Union, Local 500, CTW, August 9, 2014–June 30, 2016," 5–6, https://facultyaffairs.gwu.edu/sites/facultyaffairs.gwu.edu/files/2014–16%20CBA.PDF; "Tufts University Part-Time Lecturers Union Contract: Collective Bargaining Agreement between Service Employees International Union Local 509 and Tufts University, October 27, 2014, through June 30, 2017," 12, http://tuftsfacultyforward.org/part-time-lecturers-contract; article 19, "Collective Bargaining Agreement between Georgetown University and Service Employees International Union, Local 500, CTW, October 2014–June 2017," 18, http://www.seiu500.org/files/2014/09/Georgetown-SEIU-Local-500-Collective-Bargaining-Agreement.pdf.http://www.seiu500.org/files/2014/09/Georgetown-SEIU-Local-500-Collective-Bargaining-Agreement.pdf

8. "Agreement between Montgomery Community College and Service Employees International Union, Local 500, CTW, from July 1, 2014, through June 30, 2017," 11, http://cms.montgomerycollege.edu/edu/department.aspx?id=16505; "Collective Bargaining Agreement by and between Howard University and Service Employees International Union, Local 500," July 2015, 13, http://www.seiu500.org/files/2016/09/HU-and-SEIU-Local-500-Collective-Bargaining-Agreement.pdf.

9. "Collective Bargaining Agreement by and between Antioch College and SEIU Local 925, May 1, 2016–June 30, 2019," 12–13, http://www.seiu925.org/files/2016/07/Antioch-University-May-1-2016-through-June-30-2019.pdf; "Collective Bargaining Agreement between the Maryland Institute College of Art and Service Employees International Union, Local 500, CTW, August 31, 2015–June 30, 2018," 13, 25–26, https://www.mica.edu/Documents/Provost/CBA%20signed%20%2010.8.15.pdf.

10. Matthew W. Finkin and Robert C. Post, *For the Common Good: Principles of American Academic Freedom* (New Haven, CT: Yale University Press, 2009); J. Peter Byrne, "Academic Freedom of Part-Time Faculty," *Journal of College and University Law* 27 (2001): 583–93. Also see American Association of University Professors, "1940 Statement of Principles on Academic Freedom and Tenure," https://www.aaup.org/report/1940-statement-principles-academic-freedom-and-tenure; Association of American Colleges and Universities, "Academic Freedom and Educational Responsibility," Jan. 6, 2006, www.aacu.org/about/statements/academic-freedom; Association of Governing Boards of Universities and Colleges, "Statement on Board Responsibility for Institutional Governance," Mar. 26, 2010, agb.org/statements/2010/agb-statement-on-institutional-governance; American Council on Education, "Statement on Academic Rights and Responsibilities," June 23, 2005, www.acenet.edu/news-room/Pages/Statement-on-Academic-Rights-and-Responsibilities.aspx.

11. Article 13, "Contract between SEIU Local 200 United and the College of Saint Rose, April 14, 2016–December 14, 2018," 9. Copy in author's possession. Despite this provision, the AAUP placed the College of Saint Rose on its list of censured institutions for violating principles of academic freedom and tenure on June 18, 2016. See AAUP, "Professors Group Adds Saint Rose to Censure List," https://www.aaup.org/content/professors-group-adds-saint-rose-censure-list.

12. Researchers have identified numerous factors that influence collective bargaining outcomes, including power relationships, commitment to the bargaining process, and the nature of the subject being negotiated. Terry L. Leap and David W. Grigsby, "A Conceptualization of Collective Bargaining Power," *ILR Review* 39 (June 2016): 202–13; Robert E. Livernash, "The Relation of Power to the Structure and Process of Collective Bargaining," *Journal of Law and Economics* 6 (Oct. 1963): 10–40; Harry H. Wellington and Ralph K. Winter Jr., "The Limits of Collective Bargaining in Public Employment," *Yale Law Journal* 78 (June 1969): 1107–27.

13. SEIU, "Faculty Forward: Uniting to Transform Higher Education," http://seiufacultyforward.org/about-us (accessed Oct. 11, 2016). According to the AAUP, the average associate professor salary for all categories of institution combined was $77,192 in 2015–2016. AAUP,

"Survey Report Table 1: Average Salary and Average Compensation, by Category, Affiliation, and Academic Rank, 2015–16 (Dollars)," www.aaup.org/sites/default/files/SurveyReportTables MA16.pdf.

14. AAUP, "Statement on Government of Colleges and Universities," 1966, https://www .aaup.org/report/statement-government-colleges-and-universities; AGB, "Statement on Board Responsibility for Institutional Governance," 2010, http://agb.org/sites/default/files/agb-state ments/statement_2010_institutional_governance.pdf.

15. AAUP, "New Report on Contingent Faculty and Governance," Jan. 2013, https://www .aaup.org/news/new-report-contingent-faculty-and-governance#.WHQB-xQ4lz8; National Education Association, "Resolution F-14: Contingent Faculty and Professional Staff Protection," in *2014–2015 NEA Resolutions*, 67, www.nea.org/assets/docs/nea-resolutions-2014-15.pdf; American Federation of Teachers, "Shared Governance in Colleges and Universities: A Statement by the Higher Education Program and Policy Council," https://portfolio.du.edu/download Item/139191 (accessed Jan. 9, 2017).

16. Christine Maitland and Gary Rhoades, "Unions and Faculty Governance," *NEA 2001 Almanac of Higher Education* (2001): 27–33, http://www.nea.org/assets/img/PubAlmanac/ALM _01_03.pdf.

17. "Draft Copy of the Entire Collective Bargaining Agreement," 10, http://bentleyadjuncts .org/wp-content/uploads/2016/07/Bentley-Final-Tentative-Agreement.pdf (accessed Feb. 12, 2017).

18. Article 3, "Collective Bargaining Agreement by and between Antioch College and SEIU Local 925, May 1, 2016–June 30, 2019," 1, http://www.seiu925.org/files/2016/07/Antioch-Uni versity-May-1-2016-through-June-30-2019.pdf; "Collective Bargaining Agreement between Mills College and the Service Employees International Union Local 2021, March 18, 2016, through June 30, 2019," 21–22, copy in author's possession; article 17, "SMC Adjunct Union Contract," http://smc-union.squarespace.com/smc-pledges (accessed July 26, 2017); article 19, "Adjunct Faculty Union Contract Effective July 1, 2015: Collective Bargaining Agreement: Lesley University and Service Employees International Union Local 509," 23, https://www.lesley .edu/sites/default/files/2017-05/Adjunct-Faculty-Union-Contract-2015.pdf; "Agreement by and between the Board of Trustees of the University of Illinois and Non-Tenure Faculty Coalition Local #6546 AFT/IFT/AAUP; Non-Tenure Track Faculty, Effective August 16, 2014, through August 15, 2019," 20, www.local6546.org/wp-content/uploads/2016/05/NTFC_Contract_2014 _2019_signed.pdf.

19. Michael Evan Gold, *An Introduction to Labor Law* (Ithaca, NY: Cornell University Press), 39–48; John Thomas Delaney and Donna Sockell, "The Mandatory-Permissive Distinction and Collective Bargaining Outcomes," *ILR Review* 42 (July 1989): 566–83.

20. American Federation of Teachers, "A National Survey of Part-Time/Adjunct Faculty," *American Academic* 2 (Mar. 2010), http://www.aft.org/sites/default/files/aa_partimefaculty 0310.pdf; M. Kevin Eagan Jr., Audrey J. Jaeger, and Ashley Grantham, "Supporting the Academic Majority: Policies and Practices Related to Part-Time Faculty's Job Satisfaction," *Journal of Higher Education* 86 (May–June 2015): 448–83. The AFT study found that although 40 percent were satisfied with part-time work, 60 percent of those below the age of 50 wanted full-time positions.

21. Gary Rhoades and Rachel Hendrickson, "Re(con)figuring the Professional Workforce," *NEA 1997 Almanac of Higher Education* (1997): 63–73, http://www.nea.org/assets/img/Pub Almanac/ALM_97_06.pdf.

22. Luke Elliott-Negri, chapter 9, in this volume; California Faculty Association, "Race to the Bottom: Salary, Staffing Priorities, and the CSU's 1%," http://www.calfac.org/sites/main/files /file-attachments/race_to_the_bottom-_salary_staffing_and_the_csus_1.pdf (accessed Nov. 10, 2016).

23. "Agreement between Association of Pennsylvania State College and University Faculties (APSCUF) and the Pennsylvania State System of Higher Education (State System), July 1, 2015, to June 30, 2018," 23, http://www.passhe.edu/inside/hr/syshr/bargaining_agreements /apscuf_agr.pdf.http://www.passhe.edu/inside/hr/syshr/bargaining_agreements/apscuf_agr .pdf

24. Jason Brennan and Phillip Magness argue that attempts to improve the working conditions and pay of adjunct faculty will result in "unpleasant trade-offs": once adjuncts unionize and win the right to higher pay and benefits, institutions can realistically provide such improvements to only a small portion of current adjuncts, and the rest could lose their jobs through restructuring. See Brennan and Magness, "Estimating the Cost of Justice for Adjuncts: A Case Study in University Business Ethics," *Journal of Business Ethics* 133 (Jan. 2016): 1–14. Also see Colleen Flaherty, "The Cost of Being Decent to Adjuncts," *Inside Higher Ed*, Mar. 17, 2016, https://www.insidehighered.com/news/2016/03/17/paper-argues-adjuncts-push-better-pay -and-working-conditions-prohibitively-expensive.

25. US Congress, Senate, Committee on Labor and Public Welfare, Subcommittee on Education, *Higher Education Act of 1965: Hearings, Eighty-Ninth Congress, First Session* (Washington DC: US Government Printing Office, 1965), vols. 4 and 53; AAUP, AFT, and NEA, "Recommendations from AAUP, AFT, and NEA for the Reauthorization of the Higher Education Act," https://www.aaup.org/sites/default/files/Joint%20AAUP_AFT_NEA_HEA%20recs.pdf (accessed Jan. 17, 2017).

26. AAUP Committee on Contingent Faculty and the Profession, "Looking the Other Way? Accreditation Standards and Part-Time Faculty," https://www.aaup.org/report/looking-other -way-accreditation-standards-and-part-time-faculty (accessed Dec. 15, 2016); US Department of Education, "Accreditation in the United States," https://www2.ed.gov/admins/finaid/accred /index.html?exp=5 (accessed Jan. 8, 2017).

27. Commission on Institutions of Higher Education, New England Association of Schools and Colleges, "Standards for Accreditation," July 1, 2016, 18, https://cihe.neasc.org/standards -policies/standards-accreditation/standards-effective-july-1-2016; Southern Association of Colleges and Schools, Commission on Colleges, *Resource Manual for the Principles of Accreditation: Foundations for Quality Enhancement* (2012), 24, http://www.sacscoc.org/pdf/Resource%20 Manual.pdf; Western Senior Commission, *Handbook of Accreditation 2013, Revised*, 20, https:// www.wascsenior.org/content/2013-handbook-accreditation; Higher Learning Commission, "Criteria for Accreditation," http://policy.hlcommission.org (accessed Jan. 7, 2017).

28. See Adrianna Kezar, Daniel Maxey, and Judith Eaton, "An Examination of the Changing Faculty: Ensuring Institutional Quality and Achieving Desired Student Learning Outcomes," paper presented July 11, 2013, to the Council for Higher Education Accreditation, https://www .chea.org/userfiles/Occasional%20Papers/Examination_Changing_Faculty_2013.pdf.

29. AFT, "Accreditation Standards for Academic Staffing," http://www.aft.org/position /academic-staffing/accreditation-standards-academic-staffing (accessed Jan. 21, 2017).

30. For liberal ideals in college and university mission statements, see David Franklin Ayers, "Neoliberal Ideology in Community College Mission Statements: A Critical Discourse Analysis," *Review of Higher Education* 28, no. 4 (2005): 527–49; Ira Harkavy, "The Role of Universities in Advancing Citizenship and Social Justice in the 21st Century," *Education, Citizenship and Social Justice* 1, no. 1 (2006): 5–37.

appendix

APPENDIX TABLE 1.

Improvements to Contingent Faculty's Salary, Benefits, and Working Conditions: Evidence from Contracts Ratified between 2010 and 2016 (N = 35)

Institution	Salary	Benefits	Job security	Professional development	Intellectual property	Academic freedom	Resources and support	Shared governance
American U. (SEIU)	✓	✓	✓	✓	✓	✓	✓	
Antioch U. (SEIU)	✓	✓	✓	✓		✓	✓	✓
Bentley U. (SEIU)	✓		✓	✓		✓	✓	
Boston U. (SEIU)	✓	✓	✓	✓		✓	✓	
California State U. (CFA-AFT/AAUP/SEIU)	✓	✓	✓	✓	✓	✓		
Central New Mexico Community College (CNMEU)	✓	✓	✓			✓		
City U. of New York (PSC)	✓	✓	✓	✓			✓	
College of Saint Rose (SEIU)	✓	✓	✓	✓		✓	✓	
Community College of New Hampshire (SEIU)	✓	✓	✓	✓	✓	✓		
Dominican U. of California (SEIU)	✓	✓	✓	✓		✓		
Florida A&M (FEA-NEA/AFT/AFL-CIO)	✓	✓	✓	✓	✓	✓	✓	
George Washington U. (SEIU)	✓		✓	✓		✓	✓	
Georgetown U. (SEIU)	✓	✓	✓	✓	✓	✓	✓	
Hofstra U. (AAUP)	✓	✓	✓	✓		✓	✓	✓
Howard U. (SEIU)	✓	✓	✓	✓	✓	✓	✓	✓
Lesley U. (SEIU)	✓	✓	✓	✓		✓	✓	
Maine Community Colleges System (SEIU, AFL-CIO)	✓		✓	✓		✓	✓	
Maryland Institute College of Art (SEIU)	✓	✓		✓		✓	✓	

Institution								
Mills College, CA (SEIU)	✓	✓	✓	✓		✓	✓	✓
Montgomery Community College, MD (SEIU)	✓	✓	✓	✓		✓	✓	
New York U. (UAW)	✓	✓	✓	✓		✓	✓	
Northeastern U. (SEIU)	✓	✓	✓	✓		✓	✓	
Notre Dame de Namur U. (SEIU)	✓	✓	✓	✓	✓	✓	✓	✓
Pennsylvania State Colleges and U. (APSCUF)	✓	✓	✓	✓	✓	✓	✓	
Plymouth State U. (SEIU)	✓	✓	✓	✓	✓	✓	✓	
Rutgers U. (AAUP, AFT)	✓	✓	✓	✓		✓	✓	
Saint Mary's College, CA (SEIU)	✓	✓	✓	✓			✓	✓
Saint Michael's College, VT (SEIU)	✓	✓	✓	✓		✓	✓	
Seattle Community Colleges (AFT)	✓	✓	✓	✓	✓	✓	✓	
Tufts U. (SEIU)	✓	✓	✓	✓		✓	✓	
U. of Illinois, Urbana-Champaign (AFT/IFT/AAUP)	✓	✓	✓	✓		✓	✓	✓
U. of Oregon (AAUP, AFT, AFL-CIO)	✓	✓	✓	✓	✓	✓	✓	✓
U. of San Francisco (USFFA)	✓	✓	✓	✓		✓	✓	
Washington U. in St. Louis (SEIU, AFL-CIO)	✓	✓	✓	✓		✓	✓	
Whittier College (SEIU)	✓	✓	✓	✓				
TOTAL	**35 (100%)**	**31 (89%)**	**34 (97%)**	**33 (94%)**	**12 (34%)**	**29 (83%)**	**29 (83%)**	**8 (23%)**

Note: AAUP = American Association of University Professors, AFL–CIO = American Federation of Labor–Congress of Industrial Organizations, AFT = American Federation of Teachers, APSCUF = Association of Pennsylvania State College and University Faculties, CFA = California Faculty Association, CNMEU = Central New Mexico Community College Employees Union, FEA = Florida Education Association, IFT = Illinois Federation of Teachers, NEA = National Education Association, SEIU = Service Employees International Union, U. = university, UAW = United Auto Workers, USFFA = University of San Francisco Faculty Association.

APPENDIX TABLE 2.
Trends in Instructional Staff Employment Status, Including Graduate Student Instructors, 1989–2011

	Fall 1989		Fall 1995		Fall 2003		Fall 2007		Fall 2011	
	Number	%	Number	%	Number	%	Number	%	Number	%
Full-time tenured	272,661	28	284,870	25	282,429	19	290,581	17	308,103	17
Full-time tenure-track	112,593	11	110,311	10	128,602	9	134,826	8	128,199	7
Full-time non-tenure-track	139,173	14	155,641	14	219,388	15	251,361	15	290,749	16
Part-time	299,794	30	380,884	33	543,137	37	684,668	41	768,430	42
Graduate student	163,298	17	215,909	19	292,801	20	328,979	20	356,743	19
TOTAL	987,519	100	1,147,615	100	1,466,357	100	1,690,415	100	1,852,224	100
TOTAL contingent instructional staff	602,265	61	752,434	65	1,055,326	72	1,265,008	75	1,415,922	76

Source: John Curtis, *The Employment Status of Instructional Staff Members in Higher Education, Fall 2011* (Washington, DC: American Association of University Professors, 2014), table 1.
Note: Columns may not add up to 100 percent due to rounding.

A. J. ANGULO is a professor of education, history (faculty affiliate), and global studies (faculty affiliate) at the University of Massachusetts, Lowell. He conducts research in the history of higher education; education policy and politics; and global, comparative, and international education. His books include *Diploma Mills* (2016), *Miseducation* (2016), *Empire and Education* (2012), and *William Barton Rogers and the Idea of MIT* (2009). Since 2011, Angulo has served as the executive director and academic coordinator of international higher education grant programs. He received his doctorate from Harvard University in 2003.

TIMOTHY REESE CAIN is an associate professor at the University of Georgia's Institute of Higher Education. His work examines historical and modern issues involving academic freedom, student activism, and faculty and graduate student unionization, among other issues. In addition to authoring numerous journal articles and chapters, he has written *Establishing Academic Freedom: Politics, Principles, and the Development of Core Values* (2012), *Campus Unions: Organized Faculty and Graduate Students in US Higher Education* (2017), and, with colleagues at the National Institute for Learning Outcomes Assessment, *Using Evidence of Student Learning to Improve Higher Education* (2015). He is currently writing a book on the history of faculty unionization. His degrees are from the University of Michigan (PhD), Ohio State University (MA), and Duke University (AB).

ELIZABETH K. DAVENPORT is a professor of educational leadership at Florida A&M University. She is a graduate of Michigan State University's College of Education with a doctorate in teacher education, curriculum, and educational policy. She holds a bachelor of arts degree in education and a juris doctorate from the University of Michigan and an LLM from New York University School of Law. She also has master's degrees in telecommunications and in adult and lifelong learning from Michigan State University. She has published extensively on education, affirmative action, mentoring, and collective bargaining in Historically Black Colleges and Universities. Her research interests include educational law, policy, and curriculum. She currently serves as president of the United Faculty of Florida–FAMU.

MARIANNE DELAPORTE is a professor of religious studies at Notre Dame de Namur University. She received her PhD from Princeton Theological Seminary in medieval church history. Her dissertation focused on the vita of St. Denis by Hilduin of St. Denis. Recently she has been concentrating on mysticism and motherhood from the thirteenth century to the present and on religious communes in the United States. At NDNU, she is involved in faculty development and issues around teaching social justice in religious studies. In 2015–2016, Delaporte served on the organizing committee for NDNU Unites, which successfully unionized the university's adjunct and tenure-track faculty. In 2017 she was elected copresident of the NDNU faculty union.

TOM DEPAOLA is a provost's fellow in urban education policy in the Rossier School of Education at the University of Southern California. He is a first-year doctoral student and researcher with the Pullias Center for Higher Education and is advised by Adrianna Kezar. DePaola previously worked at Bronx Community College (CUNY) as an adjunct instructor in the first-year program and as a multifaceted administrator in the Division of Academic Affairs. He earned a double bachelor's degree in literature and philosophy from the State University of New York, Purchase. In 2013 he published an article on service learning and social justice in the peer-reviewed journal *New Directions for Community Colleges*. DePaola seeks to improve equity in higher education through research in contingent labor issues and organizing; university-driven urban development; postsecondary success and economic mobility for marginalized students; and critical pedagogy.

KRISTEN EDWARDS is a lecturer in history at Notre Dame de Namur University (NDNU) and at Stanford University Continuing Studies. She earned her PhD in history at Stanford in 1996 with a dissertation on the mass evacuation of the Soviet population during World War II. Edwards has been teaching Russian, Middle Eastern, and world history in the Bay Area since the 1990s. Currently, she is the faculty advisor for NDNU students involved in the Model Arab League program, and she and her students hosted the 2016 Model Arab League Conference of Northern California at NDNU. Edwards is also a contributor to *Seventeen Moments in Soviet History* (www.soviethistory.msu.edu), a multimedia website that provides access to thousands of Soviet texts, videos, songs, and images. Her interest in social justice in higher education was sparked in 2014, when she learned that a number of her colleagues at NDNU were living below the poverty line. She also works closely with LifeMoves, a Bay Area nonprofit organization that is committed to ending the cycle of homelessness. She served on NDNU's bargaining team in 2017.

LUKE ELLIOTT-NEGRI is a doctoral student at the Graduate Center of the City University of New York. He is the coauthor of a policy report on Connecticut's paid sick days law. His dissertation research analyzes three left-wing third parties (the Working Families Party, the Vermont Progressive Party, and the American Labor Party). He is currently working on a book chapter on social movement gains and losses leading to Seattle's $15/hour minimum wage legislation. Elliott-Negri came to graduate school at the CUNY Graduate Center with several years of labor and housing organizing experience and quickly became involved in CUNY's Professional Staff Congress (PSC). Initially, he worked as the labor relations coordinator of the Adjunct Project, an affiliate of the CUNY Graduate Center's Doctoral Students' Council. In this position, he helped to modify a PSC policy that had made graduate student–worker organizing difficult. He worked to reconstitute the defunct Graduate Center chapter of the union, and now serves as the chair of that body.

KIM GERON is the chair and a professor of political science at California State University, East Bay. He received his PhD in political science from the University of California, Riverside, in 1998. He has taught courses in American government, public policy, public administration, and race and ethnic politics. Since 2011, he has served as the CSUEB diversity and equity liaison officer and chairs the Faculty Diversity and Equity Committee of the academic senate. He has served as the California Faculty Association's vice president since 2009 and is active in the Campaign for the Future of Higher Education, the National Council for Higher Education (NEA), and Faculty Forward (SEIU). He is the author of numerous journal articles and the book *Latino Political Power* (2005), and coauthor, with Michael Liu and Tracy Lai, of *The Snake Dance of Asian American Activism: Community, Vision, and Power* (2008). His current research explores Asian American politics and the future of the American workforce.

LORENZO GIACHETTI is a full-time lecturer and language coordinator in the Department of French and Italian Studies at the University of Washington. Giachetti earned his PhD in French literature from Stanford University in 2015 with a dissertation challenging the exclusiveness of positive values in Albert Camus's otherwise "solar" humanism. His chapter "A Psychogeography of the Monstrous in *Le Premier Homme*" appears in *A Writer's Topography: Space and Place in the Life and Works of Albert Camus*, edited by Jason Herbeck and Vincent Grégoire (2015), and his current research focuses on teaching methods for both literature and film in the foreign language classroom. While still a graduate student, Giachetti worked as an adjunct at Notre Dame de Namur University between 2012 and 2015. In order to support himself during this difficult time living and commuting across one of the most expensive regions in the country, he also taught classes at an inner-city learning center in San José, worked evenings in a restaurant, and held various contract positions. Giachetti remains involved with the social and worker justice issues facing university faculty across the nation and is closely following efforts at his own institution to organize both adjunct and full-time faculty.

SHAWN GILMORE is a senior lecturer at the University of Illinois, Urbana-Champaign, and the president of the Non-Tenure Faculty Coalition, Local 6546 (AFT/IFT, AAUP), a union representing about 500 full-time non-tenure track faculty at UIUC. He earned his doctorate from UIUC in American literature and culture of the twentieth and twenty-first centuries and researches, teaches, and publishes on popular culture, comics and graphic narratives, modernisms and postmodernisms, media franchises, narratology, fiction across media, space, geography, maps, and architecture.

ADRIANNA KEZAR is a professor of higher education at the University of Southern California and co-director of the Pullias Center for Higher Education. She holds a PhD and MA in higher education administration from the University of Michigan. She is a national expert on change, governance, and leadership in higher education, and her research explores the change process in higher education institutions and the role of leadership in creating change. She is an international expert on the changing faculty, and she directs the Delphi Project on the Changing Faculty and Student Success (www.thechangingfaculty .org). Kezar has published 18 books/monographs, more than 100 journal articles, and more than 100 book chapters and reports. Her books include *How Colleges Change* (2013); *Enhancing Campus Capacity for Leadership* (2011), coauthored with Jaime Lester; *Understanding the New Majority of Non-Tenure-Track Faculty in Higher Education* (2010), coauthored with Cecile Sam; *Organizing for Collaboration* (2009); *Rethinking the "L" Word in Higher Education: The Revolution of Research on Leadership* (2006), coauthored with Rozana Carducci and Melissa Contreras-McGavin; and *Higher Education for the Public Good* (2005), coedited with Anthony C. Chambers and John C. Burkhardt.

JOSEPH A. MCCARTIN is a professor of history and the executive director of the Kalmanovitz Initiative for Labor and the Working Poor at Georgetown University. He received his PhD from the State University of New York, Binghamton, in 1990. He has published extensively in the field of labor history and is the author of *Labor's Great War: The Struggle for Industrial Democracy and the Origins of Modern American Labor Relations, 1912–21* (1997) and *Collision Course: Ronald Reagan, the Air Traffic Controllers, and the Strike That Changed America* (2011). He is coeditor, with Leon Fink and Joan Sangster, of the award-winning *Workers in Hard Times: Nineteenth-Century Panics to the Twenty-First-Century Great Recession in International Perspective* (2014), and coauthor, with Melvyn Dubofsky, of *Labor in America: A History*, 9th ed. (2017).

GRETCHEN M. REEVY is a lecturer in the Department of Psychology at California State University, East Bay, specializing in personality, stress and coping, psychological assessment, and history of psychology. She received her PhD in psychology from the University of California, Berkeley. Since 2006 she has served as a lecturer representative for the CSUEB chapter of the California Faculty Association and has also served several terms as a lecturer representative to the CSUEB academic senate. Since 2010 Reevy has served on or chaired the Faculty Affairs Committee's Subcommittee on Lecturers at CSUEB, which is devoted to creating and revising university policies that apply to or affect lecturers. Reevy conducts research on factors affecting the well-being of university faculty, with a particular emphasis on non-tenure-track faculty, and has published one peer-reviewed empirical article and several other articles on the topic.

GREGORY M. SALTZMAN is both a tenured faculty member (at Albion College, where he is a professor and chair of the Department of Economics and Management) and a contingent faculty member (at the University of Michigan, where he is an intermittent lecturer in the Department of Health Management and Policy). He has written articles in journals such as *Neurology, Industrial and Labor Relations Review*, and *Transportation Journal* and book chapters in *The NEA Almanac of Higher Education* and a National Bureau of Economic Research conference volume. His publications have addressed labor and employment law, labor relations in education, health-care cost effectiveness, health insurance, the impact of campaign contributions on congressional voting, and truck driver occupational safety and health. The Michigan Employment Relations Commission appointed him multiple times as a fact-finder or interest arbitrator in disputes between unions and local public employers. He received his PhD from the University of Wisconsin–Madison.

Kim Tolley is a historian of education and a professor at Notre Dame de Namur University. She received her doctorate from the University of California, Berkeley, in 1996. She is the author of *Heading South to Teach: The World of Susan Nye Hutchison, 1815–1845* (2015) and the award-winning *The Science Education of American Girls: A Historical Perspective* (2003). She is coeditor (with Nancy Beadie) of *Chartered Schools: Two Hundred Years of Independent Academies in the United States, 1727–1925* (2002) and editor of *Transformations in Schooling: Comparative and Historical Perspectives* (2007). Tolley has served as the education network representative for the Social Science History Association, on the editorial board of the *History of Education Quarterly,* and on the board of the History of Education Society. In 2016 she was elected vice president/president-elect of the History of Education Society. That year, she was also chair of the organizing committee for NDNU Unites, which successfully unionized the university's adjunct and tenure-track faculty.

Nicholas M. Wertsch is a graduate student at the Georgetown University Law Center. He is also the program coordinator of the Just Employment Project at the Kalmanovitz Initiative for Labor and the Working Poor. In that role, he has created an organizing fellowship and summer organizing internship to place students with community partners doing labor and community organizing. In 2011–2012, he was a Fulbright student researcher affiliated with Jawaharlal Nehru University, where he studied the role of democracy in India's efforts to meet its national energy demands. He has published news articles on democracy in India and is currently conducting research on fair and just employment practices on university campuses.